PROSE AND POETRY

OF THE

REVOLUTION

Philip Freneau

PROSE AND POETRY

OF THE

REVOLUTION

EDITED BY

FREDERICK C. PRESCOTT

AND

JOHN H. NELSON

The Establishment of the Nation
1765-1789

KENNIKAT PRESS, INC./PORT WASHINGTON, N. Y.

PROSE AND POETRY OF THE REVOLUTION

First published 1925
Reissued 1969 by Kennikat Press

Library of Congress Catalog Card No: 68-26293
Manufactured in the United States of America

INTRODUCTION

THE extracts which follow represent our literature from 1765 to 1789—from the outbreak of the Revolutionary agitation with the passing of the Stamp Act to the adoption of the Constitution and the establishing of a secure national government. The dates are thus not arbitrary, but both mark epochs in our political and likewise in our literary history. In the selection of the extracts, however, they have served as guides rather than as rigid limits. This volume slightly overlaps Vol. III of *Colonial Prose and Poetry,* edited by William P. Trent and B. W. Wells. Some writers there represented—like Franklin, who lived to see Washington inaugurated—might equally well have been treated as Revolutionary writers. For the sake of continuity this volume likewise includes a few extracts by date belonging to the national period. Some writers, like Freneau, passing through the Revolution as young men, fortunately lived to see its triumph, and continued to write. Their later writings, however, are usually influenced by their Revolutionary experience. Taken as a whole the literature here represented shows unusual unity of subject and spirit.

This is because nearly all the writings of the time take theme or color from the great events amid which they were produced. The Revolution, like war in general, was doubtless partly favorable, partly unfavorable, to our purely literary development. The lethargy into which the colonies had fallen in the first half of the eighteenth century now gave place to vigorous thought and high feeling. The result was a rapid—a surprisingly rapid—development to maturity in the kind of literature most directly affected—that is, in the political writing. On the other hand, men of the time were too much occupied with the political struggle—with the war of words or of arms—to pay much attention to "polite" literature. Indeed it is easy to see, in the "Yale poets" or in Freneau, how, at the Revolutionary outbreak, purely literary aims were checked or regretfully abandoned. In general the few writings ignoring the conflict are negligible; those most fully inspired by it are most permanent and valuable.

The Revolution had three large effects, primarily political in their nature and most important when viewed politically, but clearly traceable in our literature also, not only at the time, but even down to the present day.

The first is the most obvious. The Revolution secured our political independence, and this in turn favored independence in thought and literature. Though prepared by earlier events, our political independence was suddenly asserted and successfully maintained; our literary independence, on the other hand, has been the result of a very gradual growth, beginning at the first settlement and still unfinished at the present day. But during the period we are now considering the advance was, at least in appearance, rapid. Before the war the ruling and cultured classes were colonial; they fashioned not only their clothes and their houses, but their manners, their minds, and their writings after English models. After the peace, when the loyalists had been exiled, Americans, exulting in their triumph and resenting English influence, were too ready to claim and assert their literary independence. Accordingly our earliest national literature often has a chauvinistic tone.

The Revolution was no less important in securing our union. In 1760 Franklin saw little probability of a union of the colonies against England, "which 'tis well known they all love much more than they love one another." Boston and New York, the Quakers of Philadelphia and the planters of Charleston, were widely separated and distrustful, having in common little more than their British allegiance. Even after the war each colony regarded itself as an independent sovereign state; and "states' rights" and sectionalism long played their part in literature as well as in politics. But common action, in the French and Indian War and in the Revolution, in Congress and in the campaigns, brought the scattered Americans together, and showed them their common interest and destiny. After extreme local sovereignty had been tried and found wanting, the states at last truly united in 1789. A firm national government and gradual intellectual amalgamation for the first time made possible an American literature in the national sense.

The third effect of the Revolution is less obvious, but equally important to our literary development. The struggle for independence and union was also a movement toward democracy. Before the War the social organization, especially in the South, but also in New York and New England, was aristocratic. Even before the War, however,—as the reader of our colonial prose has seen—New Englanders like John Wise challenged the official and clerical leaders and asserted democratic principles. The contest between the "first families" and the people grew more pronounced as the Revolution approached. In the War, conservatives—holders of property, office, or social position—largely remained loyal; and, for better or worse, were lost to the country at their exile. Some American leaders, like Washington, were aristocratic; most, however, were young men, like John Adams and Alexander Hamilton, who had their way to make,—or, like Patrick Henry and Thomas Jefferson, who came down from the frontier counties to dispute the control with the planters of tide-water Virginia. It is not wrong to think of the Revolution as a radical movement, and of its soldiers as "embattled farmers." The most memorable, and only well remembered, phrases of the Declaration are those expressing democratic sentiments: "all men are created equal," and "governments derive their just powers from the consent of the governed." Thus Samuel Seabury, a Church of England clergyman, remained loyal; even moderate Americans like John Dickinson were soon left behind; and the writers perhaps most typical of the principles that survived were the democrats, Thomas Paine and Philip Freneau. After the War a new strife of partisans led finally to a new influx of democracy with the election of Jefferson over Adams in 1797. Thus began democratic tendencies which have been operative in our politics and our literature to the present day, traceable through Jackson and Lincoln, through Emerson and Whitman. To read our later literature intelligently, therefore, one must first read the writers in this volume; one must know their thought and share their feeling.

As is evident, the literature of the period lies especially close to its history, the two indeed becoming practically one. Most of the writers had a reputation as statesman or otherwise apart from literature, and there was still no profession of letters. The writings, however, may be divided into two classes: those primarily political or Revolutionary, and those non-political—poetry and general literature. The first class has the greater bulk and also the greater merit. As in the early periods we gave more thought to politics than to anything else except religion, and much more thought to politics than to literature, it is not strange that we should have come to maturity and independence first in the political field; and that we should have shown merit comparable to that of older countries first in our political writing. The second class—of pure literature—gives some idea of what might have been produced had there been no Revolution. Many books assignable to this class, however, refer to the War or are colored by it; even Dwight's biblical epic of Canaan contrives to include passages on the Revolution. Books of this class are less original; and indeed show with special clearness the difference between political and literary independence, and the difference between claiming the latter and genuinely possessing it. This of course introduces a subject, illustrated by our whole literary history, too large to be discussed here. Americans have had in the main to express fresh ideas in imported styles and forms. In the present period they were often torn between high notions of independence and loyalty to sound traditions. They often patriotically asserted their Americanism, but, as before 1776, continued to imitate English models; in Barlow's *Columbiad* or Tyler's *Contrast* the theme was independence, but the whole treatment betrayed an English debt. Americans still imitated Addison in prose and Pope in verse—as Englishmen were doing also of course, for the eighteenth century was not an original age—but our imitation had the peculiar brand of provincialism; we imitated more servilely and longer. In the notable political works indeed not merely the ideas but even the style and treatment are fresh. The Declaration of Independence is certainly not trite, and Paine is democratic in style as well as in substance. In Freneau our poetry also first becomes original. But for the most part our literature of this second class is still colonial and second-hand. Indeed the "Yale poets" exhibit our literary provincialism at its lowest depth; they furnish a warning example of the futility of imitation, and of the danger of putting even new wine into old bottles.

This volume opens with Crèvecoeur, whose idyllic descriptions of colonial country life represent the calm before the storm. *The Letters from an American Farmer* are mainly pre-Revolutionary. Even here, however, the contrast of free America with effete and oppressed Europe suggests separation; the air is overcharged; and in the last letter the storm breaks. The peaceful farmer is overwhelmed in "this unfortunate Revolution."

Naturally a large part of the volume is taken up with political prose. This includes first the State papers—statements, petitions, remonstrances, declarations of right. These papers are almost uniformly substantial in thought, dignified and elevated in tone, and excellent in style. "When your lordships look at the papers transmitted to us from America," said Chatham to the English Lords in 1775, "when you consider their decency, firmness, and wisdom, you cannot but respect their cause . . . For solidity of reasoning, force of sagacity, and wisdom of conclusion, no nation or body of men can stand in preference to the General Congress in Philadephia." It has become fashionable to represent the most shining example of this kind as somewhat tarnished by time, and, with Rufus Choate, to speak of the "glittering and sounding generalities" of the Declaration of Independence. But without its abstraction and rhetoric it would probably have lacked its signatures. Its influence on later thought is unquestionable, of which one example will suffice. "I have never had a feeling, politically," said Lincoln, "that did not spring from the sentiments embodied in the Declaration of Independence." If the reader catches the spirit of the time he will probably find this Declaration stirring; and he will at least find it an example of admirable prose.

The conflict of course called forth a flood of oratory. In the North James Otis, opposing the "writs of assistance" in 1761, "spoke the prologue" to the Revolutionary drama. In the South Patrick Henry, considered the greatest orator of the time, made a speech before the Virginia Convention in 1775, which is known to every American. This, like the speech of Otis, was preserved only in rough notes, and the familiar version from Wirt's biography (1817) doubtless owes something to other hands, and even to later oratorical ideals. If fictitious, like the speeches in Thucydides, its breathless periods may all the better represent the spirit of 1775.

Largest of all is the body of controversial writings— political letters, essays, and satires, appearing in pamphlets and newspapers—most of them ephemeral, many, however, permanently valuable to politics and even to literature. They were of every sort—by violent popular agitators, by adroit and well-informed party leaders, and by men of weighty thought and training in law or government. The controversy ran through three phases. Down to 1775 it was a temperate but increasingly vigorous debate between two parties—one for resistance, the other moderate or acquiescent. During the War it was carried on across the battle line between Americans and tories; these satires or invectives were most bitter, for the tories were more hated by the Revolutionists than the British enemy, and had good

reason to return the hate. And finally after 1783 similarly
opposed parties debated the nature of the new government.

New England led the way in this literary war.   James
Otis, in his *Rights of the British Colonies Asserted and
Proved,* 1764, declared that "no parts of his Majesty's
dominions can be taxed without their consent." The cause
of the colonies was supported by Samuel Adams and John
Adams in numerous letters, essays and pamphlets; that of
the King in a series of letters signed "Massachusettensis."
The repeal of the Stamp Act brought a lull in the conflict,
which, however, was renewed at the imposition of Townshend's new duties in 1767.   John Dickinson, a lawyer of
Pennsylvania, advocated peaceful resistance in able but
moderate *Letters from a Farmer in Pennsylvania to the Inhabitants of the British Colonies,* which were read throughout
America and in Europe.   In 1774 and 1775 the paper war
reached its height. Samuel Seabury, a conservative clergyman, in a series of outspoken pamphlets, written as by "A
Westchester Farmer," denounced the trade agreements and
the usurpations of Congress.   Among others Alexander
Hamilton, then an undergraduate in King's College, took
the opposite side. This interesting debate is represented by
our selections. Meanwhile Thomas Paine, after failing in
several undertakings in his native country, had come to
Philadelphia to do brilliantly successful work for the American cause. In a pamphlet, *Common Sense,* crude in its argument, but plain in style and full of skillful appeals to popular feeling, Paine first openly advocated independence. This
tract, originally published in January, 1776, and reprinted
in hundreds of thousands throughout the colonies, prepared
popular opinion for the momentous Declaration of July
Fourth; and indeed did such signal service to the cause that
it has been called an "event in history."

If with independence irrevocably declared and supported
by arms, the sword now became mightier than the pen, still,
as Francis Hopkinson remarked, "amongst the implements
of war the pen and the printing-press are not the most insig-

nificant." Hopkinson himself on the eve of independence had reviewed the issues in his allegorical *Pretty Story,* and he now wrote patriotic letters, using the weapon of good-natured but pointed irony. In a letter to the *New Jersey Gazette,* in 1778, he humorously proposed the appointment of a "liar general" to offset the British "lying-offices"—in other words, to counteract the "propaganda" issuing from the loyalist presses of Philadelphia and New York. William Rivington, printer of the New York *Royal Gazette,* was especially active in publishing on the British side, and is often the object of American satire. Meanwhile Paine kept up the spirit of Americans and urged them to support their army in a series of papers called *The Crisis* (1776-1783).

In the last number of *The Crisis,* of December, 1783, it is significant that the far-seeing Paine pled for a strong union; "that which includes and makes easy all our inferior concerns is the Union of the States." But men who had fought for an independent government now disagreed as to its proper nature. Henry, at first an advocate of a strong central government, finally spoke against it and opposed the adoption of the Constitution. The arguments which prevailed, and thus the principles which became fundamental in our government as finally established, are best stated in *The Federalist.* This series of papers—the ablest by Hamilton—addressed to the people of New York and well calculated to accomplish its immediate purpose of securing the adoption of the Constitution, was so sound in substance and so admirable in style, that it has remained a valuable treatise on the structure of government and a model for later legal writers.

The literary battles were carried on not only in prose but in verse. At the outbreak in 1775 Freneau wrote caustic satires on the tories in New York and the British in Boston. After his return from the West Indies in 1778 he renewed his attacks in *The British Prison Ship,* in stirring "naval lyrics," such as *The Memorable Victory of Paul Jones,* and in tirades, personally abusive rather than gen-

uinely satirical, like *The Fall of General Earl Cornwallis.*
John Trumbull, shortly to be mentioned again, produced the
most widely read and permanently interesting satire on the
tories in his *M'Fingal.* Loyalist satire is best represented
by Jonathan Odell, a Church of England clergyman of
New Jersey. His couplets, suggesting Pope's, which are
well represented in *The American Times,* 1780, quite match
Freneau's in bitterness and venom.

> "What pen can write, what human tongue can tell
> The endless murders of this man of hell."

So Freneau writes of Cornwallis; and Odell is equally unrestrained in addressing Washington:

> "Go, wretched author of thy country's grief,
> Patron of villainy, of villains chief."

Men who wrote thus hotly were not in the mood to produce
poetry, even satirical poetry, of value. After the War the
proper coolness and detachment are found again in the work
of the "Hartford Wits." In 1786 Trumbull and Barlow,
with Hopkins, Humphreys, and other Federalists of Hartford, composed, after the manner of the *Dunciad* and the
Rolliad, an *Anarchiad*—ingeniously described as an epic of
greater antiquity than Homer, recovered from the ruins of a
city of the New World. The satire was directed against
the democracy, faction, and political chaos of the period of
Shays's Rebellion, and was thus a plea for the Constitution.

The fugitive poetry of the period—hymns, songs, and
ballads, with burlesques and parodies—is abundant and interesting. It has not yet been properly collected and edited.
This too is from both sides. The loyalist verse, of which
less has been preserved, coming often from men of breeding
and education, is largely in the polite manner of the
eighteenth century; that on the American side is more crude,
popular, and home-spun. The best known ballad, *Yankee
Doodle,* though of doubtful origin evidently became the
prevailing song in New England about 1775. A true folk

ballad, it had many versions and "new verses," in which
one side parodied the other—some too coarse to be printed,
many certainly not preserved. To its prevailing tune the
War was fought; Burgoyne's Britishers, it is said, were
compelled to stack their arms to the tune of "Yankee
Doodle." The popular poetry is often idiomatic, pictur-
esque, and stirring; but wanting in high poetic merit. The
best ballad is the anonymous *Nathan Hale.* With the poems
assigned to this class in the selections belong others by authors
treated separately—Dwight's *Columbia,* Hopkinson's *Battle
of the Kegs,* and many lyrics by the patriotic Freneau and
the loyal Stansbury.

Most of the non-political poetry of the period, as of the
colonial time, is interesting now only to the student of our
literary development. It includes conventional "Songs to
Celia" and "Odes on Retirement," echoes of Milton, Pope,
and Gray, which suggest that our poetry, without the Revolution, would have continued jejune and second-hand. The
literary centre, which up to 1770 had stood definitely near
Boston and Harvard College, now shifts southward to Yale
and Princeton. During the period literary historians find
in Boston little to mention except a poetic prodigy in the
person of the negro girl, Phillis Wheatley, who could
mimic the style of Pope. But at New Haven three young
graduate students, John Trumbull, Timothy Dwight, and
Joel Barlow—who have come to be known as the "Yale
Poets"—for the first time in America had high aims in
poetry and pure literature. For the commencement of 1770,
at which he got his master's degree, Trumbull spoke on "the
Use and Advantages of the Fine Arts," protesting against
the puritan view of art and poetry. Between this time and
the outbreak of war these ambitious young men did what
they could to begin an American literature. They wrote
Addisonian essays. Trumbull satirized the prevailing notions of education in the *Progress of Dulness* (1772-1773).
Dwight began an epic, which he hoped to publish in London
with a similar production by Barlow. These high efforts

were interrupted by the War. Absorbed now in politics, Trumbull found in his reading of *Hudibras* the model for a satire on the tories. As chaplain in the army, Dwight preached and sang to the soldiers. After the war was over Dwight brought out his epic in *The Conquest of Canaan;* Barlow likewise his in *The Vision of Columbus*—which was later rewritten into the even more ambitious *Columbiad.* Though Trumbull and Dwight were now conservatives, while Barlow became a Jeffersonian Democrat with principles like those of Paine and Freneau, all these men had high notions of public service and patriotism which entitle them to great respect. They had likewise high aims in poetry—aims, however, which they had not genius to accomplish with success. They patriotically set about supplying the American literature which in a sense they themselves had founded with satires and epics which should rival those of Europe. The effort was heroic and in keeping with the spirit of the time; but it was doomed to failure. *The Columbiad,* to take one example, has a subject of epic proportions, it shows a certain intelligence in plan and workmanship, and it takes a high—even prophetic—view of our national destiny; but it is bombastic, imitative, and dull. The day of the epic in couplets was over. Our poetry was to be truly begun by men of greater talent writing under new influences in the next generation.

One writer of the period, however, showed a spark of true poetic genius, and anticipated our later poetical development. Freneau's youthful poems displayed a remarkable promise, which was not fulfilled. He had two "ruling passions," a love of poetry and a love of freedom. His purely poetic interest was crowded out by his interest in the struggle for human emancipation, which he followed with absorption as it went on first in America and then in France. Like Burns and Wordsworth he respected even humble human life; he could not tolerate tyranny, slavery, or cruelty. Like Burns he showed his love of animal life, and like (and before) Wordsworth, and with true poetic insight, he saw the life in what others called inanimate nature, and its sympathetic relation to our own. This, which for want of a better word may be called the humanitarian strain in Freneau, shows his kinship to currents in English thought which every reader of the "romantic" poetry will recognize; but it also shows him representative of the innermost feeling of the American Revolution. It is this trait which unifies and interprets his poetic work, extending over a long career, and including poems on many subjects and in many forms. In his Revolutionary poems Freneau is cogent, stirring, often bitter, and always true to his political ideals; but in general these poems have historical rather than purely poetic interest. A few poems, indicating what he might have accomplished in happier times, like *The House of Night, The Indian Burying Ground,* and *The Wild Honeysuckle,* show the poet's vision, his love of nature, his freshness of thought and feeling; and these have lasting value.

The period covered by this volume saw the first appearance of two literary forms, soon afterward to become of great importance, the drama and the novel, whose early history cannot be adequately treated here. The theatres which were flourishing at the beginning of the period, and for one of which Thomas Godfrey wrote our first American play—*The Prince of Parthia,* acted in Philadelphia in 1767—were closed during the Revolution. During the War a few insignificant plays were written for British or loyalist performances in the occupied cities; and the dramatic form was used for patriotic poems by Hugh Brackenridge and Mercy Warren. The former's *Battle of Bunkers-Hill* is represented in our selections. With the opening of the theatres after the War the writing of plays began in earnest. Royall Tyler, a lawyer of Massachusetts who visited New York in 1787 and saw English plays performed, attempted a play which should be American in its scenes and patriotic in its lesson. His prologue indicates his purpose:

"Exult each patriot heart!—this night is shown
A piece, which we may fairly call our own," etc.

The Contrast, written in three weeks and acted at the John Street Theatre in New York, in April 1787, is our first American comedy. The reader will find it still amusing and very characteristic of the confused social and literary currents of the time.

In America, somewhat as in England, the novel was anticipated by fiction in embryonic forms. The matter-of-fact Franklin was perhaps the creator of our first fictional characters. Poor Richard, Bridget, and Father Abraham were lifelike persons — and true Americans. During the War Francis Hopkinson in *A Pretty Story,* and later Jeremy Belknap in *The Foresters*—like Swift in *The Tale of a Tub*—used allegorical fiction for political purposes. As Brackenridge and Freneau had attempted a novel while they were still students at Princeton, the former was perhaps fulfilling a youthful ambition in writing his *Modern Chivalry* (begun in 1792), a novel which shrewdly observes and satirizes American life, on a plan after Cervantes, and in a style reminiscent of Swift, Fielding, and other English writers. Royall Tyler published in 1797 his picaresque and Smollett-like *Algerine Captive.* These works, however, and indeed the true development of drama and novel belong to the latter period.

In the extracts which follow, particularly in those making purely literary pretensions, the reader will probably find much of the crudeness and provinciality belonging to a new country, too greatly lacking in the culture it clearly sought and longed for. The poetic flowers are being cultivated in a stony and untilled soil. As in reading the colonial literature, he will feel that our time is not yet come. But he will feel also that even in pure literature the wilderness is at last beginning to be cultivated; and he will probably find some flowers that promise a later and better crop. When he turns from the general literature to the writings peculiarly the product of the Revolution and characteristic of that time of firm purpose and high hope, he will find much that is well worth reading. He will find these writings not second-hand, but rather starting new ideas, which have shaped later American thought, which soon crossed the Atlantic to mould the thought of Europe, and which it is well for us at the present frequently to recall. He will find them fresh and genuine, because they were composed by men of active minds under strong emotion. And if he catches the clear high tones that run through these writings—as if they came from men with hearts roused by the beating of drums and the blowing of bugles—his own heart will probably be stirred, and he will feel amply repaid for his reading in the prose and poetry of the Revolution.

TABLE OF CONTENTS

FAC-SIMILES OF TITLE-PAGES

J. HECTOR ST. JOHN DE CREVECŒUR

The author of *Letters from an American Farmer* was a Franco-American of good family and of refinement, born in 1735 at Caen in Normandy, and christened Michel-Guillaume Jean de Crèvecœur. He had some education at the Jesuit college at Caen. Leaving France when he was about eighteen, he lived a year in England, and came to Philadelphia in 1754. The next eight or nine years he spent chiefly in Pennsylvania, but he also made wide journeys, which gave him an unusually extensive knowledge of the colonies, from north to south. In 1765 he became a naturalized citizen of New York; and four years later he found a wife in Yonkers and settled as a farmer on one hundred and twenty acres in Orange County, between the present towns of Blooming Grove and Chester. Here his happy life was interrupted by the Revolution, toward which his attitude is uncertain; apparently he was suspected by both sides. Leaving his farm early in 1779, intending to return to France, he suffered poverty and imprisonment in New York, and was unable to sail until 1780. After the peace he served as French consul in New York for seven years, returning in 1790 again to France, where he died, at Sarcelles, in 1813.

The *Letters* were written in this country, "for the information of a friend in England," mainly before the Revolution; only the final letter shows the farmer discomfitted by dissension and war. Sold to an English bookseller by Crèvecœur, they were first published in London, 1782, as "by J. Hector St. John, a Farmer in Pennsylvania," an ascription probably chosen as sufficiently truthful—since he seems to have assumed this name in America and was quite familiar with Pennsylvania—and as best suited for English readers. The book, like its title-page, is partly fictitious, not exactly recording its author's individual experience, but

presenting rather an ideal conception which was then forma-
tive in America, and which indeed, Professor Tyler suspects,
also influenced the imaginations of Campbell and Byron,
Southey and Coleridge. It is valuable for its descriptions
of colonial tranquillity just before the Revolutionary up-
heaval—in the middle colonies, in Nantucket, and in
Charleston—and for its observations on nature, which suggest Thoreau. But, as Hazlitt remarks, it "gives not only
the objects, but the feelings of a new country." Its great
charm lies in its idyllic atmosphere, going back partly to the
author's own kindly and optimistic nature, partly to the
French philosophic conception of an ideal "state of nature,"
but chiefly perhaps to the hope and enthusiasm of the vigorous settler in a new and growing country. Its English is
graceful, natural, and pure.

The *Letters* were popular enough to be frequently reprinted—first in America by Matthew Carey, Philadelphia,
1793—and translated into several European languages. The
author himself turned them into French, with large addi-
tions; the new letters, however, are inferior, and the French
is full of Anglicisms. A later book also, *Voyage dans la
Haute Pennsylvanie et dans l' Etat de New York, par un
membre adoptif de la Nation Onéida* (1801), in three volumes, does not come up to the promise made by its title, and
by the *Letters*—on which Crèvecœur's position in our literature rests.

A SYSTEM OF FELICITY

[FROM "LETTERS FROM AN AMERICAN FARMER," II. 1782]

. . . I married; and this perfectly reconciled me to
my situation. My wife rendered my house all at once
cheerful and pleasing; it no longer appeared gloomy and
solitary as before. When I went to work in my fields, I
worked with more alacrity and sprightliness. I felt that
I did not work for myself alone, and this encouraged me
much. My wife would often come with her knitting in
her hand, and sit under the shady tree, praising the straight-
ness of my furrows and the docility of my horses. This
swelled my heart and made everything light and pleasant,

LETTERS

FROM AN

AMERICAN FARMER:

DESCRIBING

CERTAIN PROVINCIAL SITUATIONS,
MANNERS, AND CUSTOMS,

NOT GENERALLY KNOWN;

AND CONVEYING

SOME IDEA OF THE LATE AND PRESENT
INTERIOR CIRCUMSTANCES

OF THE

BRITISH COLONIES

IN

NORTH AMERICA.

WRITTEN, FOR THE INFORMATION OF A FRIEND
IN ENGLAND,

BY J. HECTOR ST. JOHN,

A FARMER IN PENNSYLVANIA.

A NEW EDITION, WITH AN ACCURATE INDEX.

LONDON:

PRINTED FOR THOMAS DAVIES, IN RUSSELL-STREET, COVENT-
GARDEN; AND LOCKYER DAVIS, IN HOLBORN.
M.DCC.LXXXIII.

and I regretted that I had not married before. I felt myself happy in my new situation, and where is that station which can confer a more substantial system of felicity than that of an American farmer, possessing freedom of action, freedom of thoughts, ruled by a mode of government which requires but little from us? I owe nothing but a peppercorn to my country, a small tribute to my king, with loyalty and due respect. I know no other landlord than the Lord of all land, to whom I owe the most sincere gratitude. . . . Often, when I plough my low ground, I place my little boy on a chair which screws to the beam of the plough. Its motion and that of the horses please him: he is perfectly happy, and begins to chat. As I lean over the handle, various are the thoughts which crowd into my mind. I am now doing for him, I say, what my father formerly did for me: may God enable him to live that he may perform the same operations for the same purposes when I am worn out and old! I relieve his mother of some trouble while I have him with me; the odoriferous furrow exhilarates his spirits, and seems to do the child a great deal of good, for he looks more blooming since I have adopted that practice. Can more pleasure, more dignity, be added to that primary occupation? The father, thus ploughing with his child, and to feed his family, is inferior only to the emperor of China ploughing as an example to his kingdom.

BEES AND BIRDS
[From the Same]

After I have done sowing, by way of recreation, I prepare for a week's jaunt in the woods, not to hunt either the deer or the bears, as my neighbors do, but to catch the more harmless bees. I cannot boast that this chase is so noble or so famous among men, but I find it less fatiguing, and full as profitable; and the last consideration is the only one that moves me. I take with me my dog, as a companion, for he is useless as to this game. My gun, for no man you know ought to enter the woods without one, my blanket, some provisions, some wax, vermilion, honey, and a small pocket-compass. With these implements I proceed to such woods as are at a considerable distance from any settlements. I carefully examine whether they abound with large trees; if so, I make a small fire, on some flat stones, in a convenient place. On the fire I put some wax: close by this fire, on another stone, I drop honey in distinct drops, which I surround with small quantities of vermilion, laid on the stone; and then I retire carefully to watch whether any bees appear. If there are any in that neighborhood, I rest assured that the smell of the burnt wax will unavoidably attract them. They will soon find out the honey, for they are fond of preying on that which is not their own; and, in their approach, they will necessarily tinge themselves with some particles of vermilion, which will adhere long to their bodies. I next fix my compass, to find out their course, which they keep invariably straight, when they are returning home loaded. By the assistance of my watch, I observe how long those are returning which are marked with vermilion. Thus, possessed of the course, and, in some measure, of the distance, which I can easily guess at, I follow the first, and seldom fail of coming to the tree where those republics are lodged. I then mark it; and thus, with patience, I have found out sometimes eleven swarms in a season; and it is inconceivable what a quantity of honey these trees will sometimes afford. It entirely depends on the size of the hollow, as the bees never rest nor swarm until it is all replenished; for, like men, it is only the want of room that induces them to quit the maternal hive. Next I proceed to some of the nearest settlements, where I procure proper assistance to cut down the trees, get all my prey secured, and then return home with my prize. The first bees I ever procured were thus found in the woods by mere accident; for, at that time, I had no kind of skill in this method of tracing them. The body of the tree being perfectly sound, they had lodged themselves in the hollow of one of its principal limbs, which I carefully sawed off, and, with a good deal of labor and industry, brought it home, where I fixed it up in the same position in which I found it growing. This was in April. I had five swarms that year, and they have been ever since very prosperous. This

business generally takes up a week of my time every fall, and
to me it is a week of solitary ease and refinement.   .   .   .

Some time ago, as I sat smoking a contemplative pipe in
my piazza, I saw, with amazement, a remarkable instance
of selfishness displayed in a very small bird, which I had
hitherto respected for its inoffensiveness.   Three nests were
placed almost contiguous to each other in my piazza.   That
of a swallow was affixed in the corner next to the house,
that of a phebe in the other; a wren possessed a little box,
which I had made on purpose, and hung between.   Be not
surprised at their tameness.   All my family had long been
taught to respect them as well as myself.   The wren had
shown before signs of dislike to the box which I had given
it, but I knew not on what account.   At last it resolved,
small as it was, to drive the swallow from its own habitation, and, to my very great surprise, it succeeded.   Im-
pudence often gets the better of modesty, and this exploit
was no sooner performed than it removed every material to
its own box with the most admirable dexterity.   The signs
of triumph appeared very visible; it fluttered its wings with
uncommon velocity; an universal joy was perceivable in all
its movements.   Where did this little bird learn that spirit
of injustice?   It was not endowed with what we term reason!   Here then is a proof that both those gifts border very
near on one another, for we see the perfection of the one
mixing with the errors of the other!   The peaceable swallow, like the passive Quaker, meekly sat at a small distance,
and never offered the least resistance.   But, no sooner was
the plunder carried away, than the injured bird went to
work with unabated ardor, and, in a few days, the depredations were repaired.   To prevent, however, a repetition of
the same violence, I removed the wren's box to another
part of the house.

WHAT IS AN AMERICAN?

[FROM THE SAME, III.]

I wish I could be acquainted with the feelings and
thoughts which must agitate the heart and present themselves to the mind of an enlightened Englishman, when he

first lands on this continent. He must greatly rejoice that
he lived at a time to see this fair country discovered and
settled. He must necessarily feel a share of national pride
when he views the chain of settlements which embellish these
extended shores. When he says to himself, this is the work
of my countrymen, who, when convulsed by factions, afflicted by a variety of miseries and wants, restless and impatient, took refuge here. They brought along with them
their national genius, to which they principally owe what
liberty they enjoy and what substance they possess. Here
he sees the industry of his native country displayed in a new
manner, and traces, in their works, the embryos of all the
arts, sciences, and ingenuity, which flourish in Europe. Here
he beholds fair cities, substantial villages, extensive fields,
an immense country filled with decent houses, good roads,
orchards, meadows, and bridges, where, a hundred years ago,
all was wild, wooded, and uncultivated! What a train of
pleasing ideas this fair spectacle must suggest! It is a prospect which must inspire a good citizen with the most heartfelt pleasure! The difficulty consists in the manner of viewing so extensive a scene. He is arrived on a new continent:
a modern society offers itself to his contemplation, different
from what he had hitherto seen. It is not composed, as in
Europe, of great lords who possess everything, and of a herd
of people who have nothing. Here are no aristocratical
families, no courts, no kings, no bishops, no ecclesiastical
dominion, no invisible power giving to a few a very visible
one, no great manufactures employing thousands, no great
refinements of luxury. The rich and the poor are not so far
removed from each other as they are in Europe. Some few
towns excepted, we are all tillers of the earth, from Nova
Scotia to West Florida. We are a people of cultivators,
scattered over an immense territory, communicating with
each other by means of good roads and navigable rivers,
united by the silken bands of mild government, all respecting the laws, without dreading their power, because they
are equitable. We are all animated with the spirit of an
industry which is unfettered and unrestrained, because each
person works for himself. If he travels through our rural
districts, he views not the hostile castle and the haughty

mansion contrasted with the clay-built hut and the miserable
cabin, where cattle and men help to keep each other warm,
and dwell in meanness, smoke, and indigence. A pleasing-
uniformity of decent competence appears throughout our
habitations. The meanest of our log-houses is a dry and
comfortable habitation. Lawyer or merchant are the fairest
titles our towns afford: that of a farmer is the only appella-
tion of the rural inhabitants of our country. It must take
some time ere he can reconcile himself to our dictionary,
which is but short in words of dignity and names of honor.
There, on a Sunday, he sees a congregation of respectable
farmers and their wives, all clad in neat homespun, well
mounted, or riding in their own humble waggons. There is
not among them an esquire, saving the unlettered magistrate.
There he sees a parson as simple as his flock, a farmer who
does not riot on the labor of others. We have no princes,
for whom we toil, starve, and bleed. We are the most perfect society now existing in the world. Here man is free as
he ought to be; nor is this pleasing equality so transitory as
many others are. Many ages will not see the shores of our
great lakes replenished with inland nations, nor the unknown
bounds of North America entirely peopled. Who can tell
how far it extends? Who can tell the millions of men whom
it will feed and contain? for no European foot has, as yet,
travelled half the extent of this mighty continent.

The next wish of this traveller will be, to know whence
came all these people? They are a mixture of English,
Scotch, Irish, French, Dutch, Germans, and Swedes. From
this promiscuous breed, that race, now called Americans,
have arisen. The Eastern provinces must indeed be excepted, as being the unmixed descendants of Englishmen. I
have heard many wish that they had been more intermixed
also: for my part, I am no wisher, and think it much better
as it has happened. They exhibit a most conspicuous figure
in this great and variegated picture. They too enter for a
great share in the pleasing perspective displayed in these
thirteen provinces. I know it is fashionable to reflect on
them, but I respect them for what they have done; for the
activity and wisdom with which they have settled their territory; for the decency of their manners; for their early love

of letters; their ancient college, the first in this hemisphere; for their industry, which to me, who am but a farmer, is the criterion of everything. There never was a people, situated as they are, who, with so ungrateful a soil, have done more in so short a time. Do you think that the monarchical ingredients, which are more prevalent in other governments, have purged them from all foul stains? Their histories assert the contrary.

In this great American asylum, the poor of Europe have by some means met together, and in consequence of various causes. To what purpose should they ask one another what countrymen they are? Alas, two-thirds of them had no country. Can a wretch, who wanders about, who works and starves, whose life is a continual scene of sore affliction or pinching penury; can that man call England or any other kingdom his country? A country that had no bread for him; whose fields procured him no harvest; who met with nothing but the frowns of the rich, the severity of the laws, with jails and punishments; who owned not a single foot of the extensive surface of this planet? No! Urged by a variety of motives here they came. Everything has tended to regenerate them. New laws, a new mode of living, a new social system. Here they are become men. In Europe they were as so many useless plants, wanting vegetative mould and refreshing showers. They withered, and were mowed down by want, hunger, and war; but now, by the power of transplantation, like all other plants, they have taken root and flourished! Formerly they were not numbered in any civil lists of their country, except in those of the poor: here they rank as citizens. By what invisible power has this surprising metamorphosis been performed? By that of the laws and that of their industry. The laws, the indulgent laws, protect them as they arrive, stamping on them the symbol of adoption: they receive ample rewards for their labors: these accumulated rewards procure them lands: those lands confer on them the title of freemen, and to that title every benefit is affixed which men can possibly require. This is the great operation daily performed by our laws. Whence proceed these laws? From our government. Whence that government? It is derived from the original genius and strong desire of the people ratified and confirmed by the crown. This is the great chain which links us all; this is the picture which every province exhibits, Nova Scotia excepted. There the crown has done all. Either there were no people who had genius, or it was not much attended to. The consequence is, that the province is very thinly inhabited indeed. The power of the crown, in conjunction with the mosquitoes, has prevented men from settling there. Yet some parts of it flourished once, and it contained a mild, harmless set of people. But, for the fault of a few leaders, the whole was banished. The greatest political error, the crown ever committed in America, was, to cut off men from a country which wanted nothing but men.

What attachment can a poor European emigrant have for a country where he had nothing? The knowledge of the language, the love of a few kindred as poor as himself, were the only cords that tied him. His country is now that which gives him his land, bread, protection, and consequence. *Ubi panis ibi patria* is the motto of all emigrants. What then is the American, this new man? He is neither an European, nor the descendant of an European: hence that strange mixture of blood, which you will find in no other country. I could point out to you a family, whose grandfather was an Englishman, whose wife was Dutch, whose son married a French woman, and whose present four sons have now four wives of different nations. He is an American, who, leaving behind him all his ancient prejudices and manners, receives new ones from the new mode of life he has embraced, the new government he obeys, and the new rank he holds. He becomes an American by being received in the broad lap of our great *alma mater*. Here individuals of all nations are melted into a new race of men, whose labors and posterity will one day cause great changes in the world. Americans are the western pilgrims, who are carrying along with them the great mass of arts, sciences, vigor, and industry, which began long since in the East. They will finish the great circle. The Americans were once scattered all over Europe. Here they are incorporated into one of the finest systems of population which has ever appeared, and which will hereafter become distinct by the power of the different climates they inhabit. The American ought therefore to love this country much better than that in which either he or his forefathers were born. Here the rewards of his industry follow, with equal steps, the progress of his labor. His labor is founded on the basis of nature, *self-interest:* can it want a stronger allurement? Wives and children, who before in vain demanded of him a morsel of bread, now, fat and frolicsome, gladly help their father to clear those fields whence exuberant crops are to raise, to feed and to clothe them all, without any part being claimed, either by a despotic prince, a rich abbot, or a mighty lord. Here religion demands but little of him; a small voluntary salary to the minister, and gratitude to God: can he refuse these? The American is a new man, who acts on new principles; he must therefore entertain new ideas and form new opinions. From involuntary idleness, servile dependence, penury, and useless labor, he has passed to toils of a very different nature, rewarded by ample subsistence.—This is an American.

HOW EUROPEANS BECOME AMERICANS

[FROM THE SAME]

There is no wonder that this country has so many charms, and presents to Europeans so many temptations to remain in it. A traveller in Europe becomes a stranger as soon as he quits his own kingdom; but it is otherwise here. We know, properly speaking, no strangers; this is every person's country; the variety of our soils, situations, climates, governments, and produce, hath something which must please everybody. No sooner does an European arrive, no matter of what condition, than his eyes are opened upon the fair prospect; he hears his language spoken, he retraces many of his own country manners, he perpetually hears the names of families and towns with which he is acquainted; he sees happiness and prosperity in all places disseminated; he meets with hospitality, kindness, and plenty, everywhere: he beholds hardly any poor, he seldom hears of punishments and executions; and he wonders at the elegance of our towns, those miracles of industry and freedom. He cannot admire enough our rural districts, our convenient roads, good taverns, and our many accommodations; he involuntarily loves a country where everything is so lovely. When in England, he was a mere Englishman; here he stands on a larger portion of the globe, not less than its fourth part, and may see the produc-tions of the North, in iron and naval stores; the provisions of Ireland, the grain of Egypt, the indigo, the rice, of China. He does not find, as in Europe, a crowded society, where every place is over-stocked; he does not feel that perpetual collision of parties, that difficulty of beginning, that conten-tion which oversets so many. There is room for everybody in America. Has he any particular talent or industry? he exerts it in order to procure a livelihood, and it succeeds. Is he a merchant? the avenues of trade are infinite. Is he eminent in any respect? he will be employed and respected. Does he love a country life? pleasant farms present them-selves; he may purchase what he wants, and thereby become an American farmer. Is he a laborer, sober and industrious? he need not go many miles, nor receive many informations before he will be hired, well fed at the table of his employer, and paid four or five times more than he can get in Europe. Does he want uncultivated lands? thousands of acres pre-sent themselves, which he may purchase cheap. Whatever be his talents or inclinations, if they are moderate, he may satisfy them. I do not mean that every one who comes will grow rich in a little time; no, but he may procure an easy decent maintenance by his industry. Instead of starving he will be fed; instead of being idle he will have employment; and these are riches enough for such men as come over here. The rich stay in Europe; it is only the middling and poor that emigrate. Would you wish to travel in independent idleness, from north to south, you will find easy access, and the most cheerful reception, at every house; society without ostentation, good cheer without pride, and every decent di-version which the country affords, with little expense. It is no wonder that the European, who has lived here a few years, is desirous to remain; Europe, with all its pomp, is not to be compared to this continent for men of middle sta-tions or laborers.

An European, when he first arrives, seems limited in his

intentions as well as in his views; but he very suddenly alters his scale; two hundred miles formerly appeared a very great distance, it is now but a trifle; he no sooner breathes our air than he forms schemes, and embarks in designs, he never would have thought of in his own country. There the plenitude of society confines many useful ideas, and often extinguishes the most laudable schemes which here ripen into maturity. Thus Europeans become Americans.

But how is this accomplished in that crowd of low, indigent people, who flock here every year from all parts of Europe? I will tell you; they no sooner arrive than they immediately feel the good effects of that plenty of provisions we possess: they fare on our best food, and are kindly entertained; their talents, character, and peculiar industry, are immediately inquired into; they find countrymen everywhere disseminated, let them come from whatever part of Europe. Let me select one as an epitome of the rest; he is hired, he goes to work, and works moderately; instead of being employed by a haughty person, he finds himself with his equal, placed at the substantial table of the farmer, or else at an inferior one as good; his wages are high, his bed is not like that bed of sorrow on which he used to lie: if he behaves with propriety, and is faithful, he is caressed, and becomes as it were a member of the family. He begins to feel the effects of a sort of resurrection; hitherto he had not lived, but simply vegetated; he now feels himself a man, because he is treated as such; the laws of his own country had overlooked him in his insignificancy; the laws of this cover him with their mantle. Judge what an alteration there must arise in the mind and the thoughts of this man; he begins to forget his former servitude and dependence, his heart involuntarily swells and glows; this first swell inspires him with those new thoughts which constitute an American. What love can he entertain for a country where his existence was a burden to him? If he is a generous good man, the love of this new adoptive parent will sink deep into his heart. He looks around, and sees many a prosperous person, who, but a few years before, was as poor as himself. This encourages him much; he begins to form some little scheme, the first, alas! he ever formed in his life. If he is wise, he thus spends two or three years, in which time he acquires knowledge, the use of tools, the modes of working the lands, felling trees, etc. This prepares the foundation of a good name, the most useful acquisition he can make. He is encouraged, he has gained friends; he is advised and directed, he feels bold, he purchases some land; he gives all the money he has brought over, as well as what he has earned, and trusts to the god of harvests for the discharge of the rest. His good name procures him credit; he is now possessed of the deed, conveying to him and his posterity the fee simple and absolute property of two hundred acres of land, situated on such a river. What an epoch in this man's life! He is become a freeholder, from perhaps a German boor; he is now an American, a Pennsylvanian, an English subject. He is naturalized, his name is enrolled with those of the other citizens of the province. Instead of being a vagrant, he has a place of residence; he is called the inhabitant of such a country, or of such a district, and, for the first time in his life, counts for something; for hitherto he had been a cipher. I only repeat what I have heard many say; and no wonder their hearts should glow, and be agitated with a multitude of feelings, not easy to describe. From nothing, to start into being; from a servant, to the rank of a master; from being the slave of some despotic prince, to become a free man, invested with lands, to which every municipal blessing is annexed! What a change indeed! It is in consequence of that change that he becomes an American. This great metamorphosis has a double effect; it extinguishes all his European prejudices, he forgets that mechanism of subordination, that servility of disposition, which poverty had taught him; and sometimes he is apt to forget it too much, often passing from one extreme to the other. If he is a good man, he forms schemes of future prosperity; he proposes to educate his children better than he has been educated himself; he thinks of future modes of conduct, feels an ardor to labor he never felt before. Pride steps in, and leads him to everything that the laws do not forbid: he respects them; with a heartfelt gratitude he looks toward the east, toward that insular government from whose wisdom all his new felicity is derived, and under whose wings and protection he now lives. These reflections constitute him the good man and the good subject. Ye poor Europeans, ye, who sweat, and work for the great; ye, who are obliged to give so many sheaves to the Church, so many to your lords, so many to your government, and have hardly any left for yourselves; ye, who are held in less estimation than favorite hunters or useless lapdogs; ye, who only breathe the air of nature, because it cannot be withholden from you; it is here that ye can conceive the possibility of those feelings I have been describing; it is here the laws of naturalization invite everyone to partake of our great labors and felicity, to till unrented, untaxed lands! Many, corrupted beyond the power of amendment, have brought with them all their vices, and, disregarding the advantages held to them, have gone on in their former career of iniquity, until they have been overtaken and punished by our laws. It is not every emigrant who succeeds; no, it is only the sober, the honest, and industrious: happy those to whom this transition has served as a powerful spur to labor, to prosperity, and to the good establishment of children, born in the days of their poverty! and who had no other portion to expect but the rags of their parents, had it not been for their happy emigration. Others, again, have been led astray by this enchanting scene; their new pride, instead of leading them to the fields, has kept them in idleness; the idea of possessing lands is all that satisfies them; though surrounded with fertility, they have mouldered away their time in inactivity, misinformed husbandry, and ineffectual endeavors. How much wiser, in general, the honest Germans than almost all other Europeans; they hire themselves to some of their wealthy landsmen, and, in that apprenticeship, learn everything that is necessary. They attentively consider the prosperous industry of others, which imprints in their minds a strong desire of possessing the same advantages. This forcible idea never quits them; they launch forth, and, by dint of sobriety, rigid parsimony, and the most persevering industry, they commonly succeed. Their astonishment at their first arrival from Germany is very great; it is to them a dream; the contrast must be very powerful indeed; they observe their countrymen flourishing in every place; they travel through whole counties where not a word of English is spoken; and, in the names and the language of the people, they retrace Germany. They have been an useful acquisition to this continent, and to Pennsylvania in particular; to them it owes some share of its prosperity: to their mechanical knowledge and patience it owes the finest mills in all America, the best teams of horses, and many other advantages. The recollection of their former poverty and slavery never quits them as long as they live.

ON SNAKES AND THE HUMMING-BIRD
[FROM THE SAME, X.]

One anecdote I must relate, the circumstances of which are as true as they are singular. One of my constant walks, when I am at leisure, is in my lowlands, where I have the pleasure of seeing my cattle, horses, and colts. Exuberant grass replenishes all my fields, the best representative of our wealth; in the middle of that track I have cut a ditch, eight feet wide, the banks of which nature adorns every spring with the wild salendine, and other flowering weeds, which on these luxuriant grounds shoot up to a great height. Over this ditch I have erected a bridge, capable of bearing a loaded waggon; on each side, I carefully sow every year some grains of hemp, which rise to the height of fifteen feet, so strong, and so full of limbs, as to resemble young trees; I once ascended one of them four feet above the ground. These produce natural arbors, rendered often still more compact by the assistance of an annual creeping plant, which we call a vine, that never fails to entwine itself among their branches, and always produces a very desirable shade. From this simple grove I have amused myself a hundred times in observing the great number of humming-birds with which our country abounds: the wild blossoms everywhere attract the attention of these birds, which, like bees, subsist by suction. From this retreat I distinctly watch them in all their various attitudes; but their flight is so rapid that you cannot distinguish the motion of their wings. On this little bird Nature has profusely lavished her most splendid colors; the most perfect azure, the most beautiful gold, the most dazzling red are forever in contrast, and help to embellish the plumes of his majestic head. The richest pallet of the most luxuriant painter could never invent anything to be compared to the variegated tints with which this insect-bird is arrayed. Its bill is as long and as sharp as a coarse sewing-needle; like the bee, Nature has taught it to find out the calix of flowers and blossoms, those mellifluous particles that serve it for sufficient food; and yet it seems to leave them untouched, undeprived of anything that our eyes can possibly distinguish. When it feeds it appears as if immovable, though continually on the wing; and, sometimes, from what motives I know not, it will tear and lacerate flowers into a hundred pieces; for, strange to tell, they are the most irascible of the feathered tribe. Where do passions find room in so diminutive a body? They often fight with the fury of lions, until one of the combatants falls a sacrifice and dies. When fatigued, it has often perched within a few feet of me, and, on such favorable opportunities, I have surveyed it with the most minute attention. Its little eyes appear like diamonds, reflecting light on every side: most elegantly finished in all parts, it is a miniature-work of our great Parent; who seems to have formed it the smallest, and, at the same time the most beautiful, of the winged species.

As I was one day sitting solitary and pensive in my primitive arbor, my attention was engaged by a strange sort of rustling noise at some paces distance. I looked all around without distinguishing anything, until I climbed one of my great hemp-stalks; when, to my astonishment, I beheld two snakes of considerable length, the one pursuing the other, with great celerity, through the hemp-stubble field. The aggressor was of the black kind, six feet long; the fugitive was a water-snake nearly of equal dimensions. They soon met, and, in the fury of their first encounter, they appeared in an instant firmly twisted together; and, whilst their united tails beat the ground, they mutually tried with open jaws to lacerate each other. What a fell aspect did they present! their heads were compressed to a very small size, their eyes flashed fire; and, after this conflict had lasted about five minutes, the second found means to disengage itself from the first, and hurried toward the ditch. Its antagonist instantly assumed a new posture; and, half creeping and half erect, with a majestic mien, overtook and attacked the other again; which placed itself in the same attitude and prepared to resist.   The scene was uncommon and beautiful; for, thus opposed, they fought with their jaws, biting each other with the utmost rage; but, notwithstanding this appearance of mutual courage and fury, the water-snake still seemed desirous of retreating toward the ditch, its natural element. This was no sooner perceived by the keen-eyed black one, than, twisting its tail twice round a stalk of hemp, and seizing its adversary by the throat, not by means of its jaws, but by twisting its own neck twice round that of the water-snake, pulled it back from the ditch. To prevent a defeat, the latter took hold likewise of a stalk on the bank, and, by the acquisition of that point of resistance, became a match for its fierce antagonist. Strange was this to behold; two great snakes strongly adhering to the ground, mutually fastened together, by means of the writhings, which lashed them to each other, and, stretched at their full length, they pulled, but pulled in vain; and, in the moments of greatest exertion, that part of their bodies which was entwined seemed extremely small, while the rest appeared inflated, and, now and then, convulsed with strong undulations rapidly following each other. Their eyes seemed on fire and ready to start out of their heads; at one time the conflict seemed decided; the water-snake bent itself into two great folds, and, by that operation, rendered the other more than commonly outstretched; the next minute, the new struggles of the black one gained an unexpected superiority; it acquired two great folds likewise, which necessarily extended the body of its adversary in proportion as it had contracted its own. These efforts were alternate; victory seemed doubtful; inclining sometimes to the one side and sometimes to the other; until, at last the stalk to which the black-snake fastened, suddenly gave way, and, in consequence of this accident, they both plunged into the ditch. The water did not extinguish their vindictive rage; for, by their agitations, I could trace, though not distinguish, their mutual attacks. They soon reappeared on the surface twisted together as in their first onset; but the black-snake seemed to retain its wonted superiority, for its head was exactly fixed above that of the other, which it incessantly pressed down under the water until it was stifled and sunk. The victor no sooner perceived its enemy incapable of farther resistance than, abandoning it to the current, it returned on shore and disappeared.

THIS UNFORTUNATE REVOLUTION

[FROM THE SAME, XII.]

. . . I am told that the great nation, of which we are a part, is just, wise, and free, beyond any other on earth, within its own insular boundaries, but not always so to its distant conquests. I shall not repeat all I have heard, because I cannot believe half of it. As a citizen of a smaller society, I find that any kind of opposition to its now prevailing sentiments, immediately begets hatred : how easily do men pass from loving, to hating and cursing one another! I am a lover of peace; what must I do? I am divided between the respect I feel for the ancient connection and the fear of innovations, with the consequence of which I am not well acquainted, as they are embraced by my own countrymen. I am conscious that I was happy before this unfortunate Revolution. I feel that I am no longer so; therefore I regret the change. This is the only mode of reasoning adapted to persons in my situation. . . .

Must I then bid farewell to Britain, to that renowned country? Must I renounce a name so ancient and so venerable? Alas! she herself, that once indulgent parent, forces me to take up arms against her. She herself first inspired the most unhappy citizens of our remote districts with the thoughts of shedding the blood of those whom they used to call by the name of friends and brethren. That great nation, which now convulses the world; which hardly knows the extent of her Indian kingdoms; which looks toward the universal monarchy of trade, of industry, of riches, of power: why must she strew our poor frontiers with the carcasses of her friends, with the wrecks of our insignificant villages, in which there is no gold? . . .

Restore peace and concord to our poor afflicted country;

assuage the fierce storm which has so long ravaged it! Permit, I beseech Thee, O Father of Nature, that our ancient virtues and our industry may not be totally lost: and that, as a reward for the great toils we have made on this new land, we may be restored to our ancient tranquillity, and enabled to fill it with successive generations, that will constantly thank Thee for the ample subsistence Thou hast given them!

JOHN DICKINSON

John Dickinson, member of an old family of Talbot County, Maryland, was born in 1732. He had good legal training, reading law first in Philadelphia and afterwards for three years in the Middle Temple, London. As a member of the Pennsylvania Assembly, of the Stamp Act Congress, 1765, and of the Continental Congress, 1774-1776, he took active part in the deliberations leading up to the Revolution. By writing for these bodies many admirably worded petitions, declarations, and other state papers he became known as "the Penman of the American Revolution." From the most notable of these, *The Declaration by the Representatives of the United Colonies* (1775), "setting forth the causes and necessity of their taking up arms," a brief extract is given below. The lull following the repeal of the Stamp Act was broken in 1767 by Townshend's acts laying port duties, creating resident customs commissioners, and suspending the legislature of New York. Against these measures Dickinson protested in his best known work, *Letters from a Farmer in Pennsylvania to the Inhabitants of the British Colonies* (a work often confused with Crèvecœur's book of similar title). These Letters, first published in the *Pennsylvania Chronicle* in 1767-1768, and reprinted in the newspapers and in book form throughout the colonies, as well as in England and France, gave the case of the colonies wide hearing. As Dickinson was a conservative and a lawyer, he carefully based his case on precedents from English constitutional history; he advocated loyalty coupled with firm resistance; he tried to convince the English government rather than to inflame the colonists; and more than any other writer of the time, he combined vigor of style with urbanity and moderation. In 1776, true to his principles, he disapproved of the Declaration of Independence; and as he thus lost favor with the prevailing party, he gave place as a Revolutionary apologist to Paine and Jefferson. But he fought loyally in the American army, and after the war had an honorable public career, ended by his death in 1808.

THE PENNSYLVANIA FARMER

[FROM "LETTERS FROM A FARMER IN PENNSYLVANIA," I.   1768]

My dear Countrymen,

I am a Farmer, settled, after a variety of fortunes, near the banks of the River Delaware, in the province of Pennsylvania.   I received a liberal education, and have been engaged in the busy scenes of life; but am now convinced, that a man may be as happy without bustle, as with it.   My farm is small; my servants are few, and good; I have a little money at interest; I wish for no more; my employment in my own affairs is easy; and with a contented grateful mind, (undisturbed by worldly hopes or fears, relating to myself,) I am completing the number of days allotted to me by the divine goodness.

Being generally master of my time, I spend a good deal of it in a library; which I think the most valuable part of my small estate; and being acquainted with two or three gentlemen of abilities and learning, who honor me with their friendship, I have acquired, I believe, a greater knowledge in history, and the laws and constitution of my country, than is generally attained by men of my class, many of them not being so fortunate as I have been in the opportunities of getting information.

From my infancy I was taught to love humanity and liberty.   Enquiry and experience have since confirmed my reverence for the lessons then given me, by convincing me more fully of their truth and excellence.   Benevolence towards mankind, excites wishes for their welfare, and such wishes endear the means of fulfilling them.   These can be found in liberty only, and therefore her sacred cause ought to be espoused by every man, on every occasion, to the utmost of his power.   As a charitable, but poor person does not withhold his mite, because he cannot relieve all the distresses of the miserable, so should not any honest man suppress his sentiments concerning freedom, however small their influence is likely to be. Perhaps he "may touch some wheel," that will have an effect greater than he could reasonably expect.

THE CAUSE OF LIBERTY

[FROM THE SAME, III.]

I will now tell the gentlemen what is "the meaning of these letters." The meaning of them is, to convince the people of these colonies, that they are at this moment exposed to the most imminent dangers; and to persuade them immediately, vigorously, and unanimously, to exert themselves, in the most firm, but the most peaceable manner, for obtaining relief.

The cause of liberty is a cause of too much dignity to be sullied by turbulence and tumult. It ought to be maintained in a manner suitable to her nature. Those who engage in it, should breathe a sedate, yet fervent spirit, animating them to actions of prudence, justice, modesty, bravery, humanity, and magnanimity. . . .

I hope, my dear countrymen, that you will, in every colony, be upon your guard against those, who may at any time endeavor to stir you up, under pretences of patriotism, to any measures disrespectful to our Sovereign and our mother country. Hot, rash, disorderly proceedings, injure the reputation of a people, as to wisdom, valor, and virtue, without procuring them the least benefit. I pray God, that he may be pleased to inspire you and your posterity, to the latest ages, with a spirit of which I have an idea, that I find a difficulty to express. To express it in the best manner I can, I mean a spirit, that shall so guide you, that it will be impossible to determine whether an American's character is most distinguishable, for his loyalty to his Sovereign, his duty to his mother country, his love of freedom, or his affection for his native soil.

Every government at some time or other falls into wrong measures. These may proceed from mistake or passion. But every such measure does not dissolve the obligation between the governors and the governed. The mistake may be corrected; the passion may subside. It is the duty of the governed to endeavor to rectify the mistake, and to appease the passion. They have not at first any other right, than to represent their grievances, and to pray for redress, unless an emergence is so pressing, as not to allow time for receiving an answer to their applications, which rarely happens. If their applications are disregarded, then that kind of opposition becomes justifiable, which can be made without breaking the laws, or disturbing the public peace.

This consists in the prevention of the oppressors reaping advantage from their oppressions, and not in their punishment. For experience may teach them, what reason did not; and harsh methods cannot be proper, till milder ones have failed.

If at length it becomes undoubted, that an inveterate resolution is formed to annihilate the liberties of the governed, the English history affords frequent examples of resistance by force. What particular circumstances will in any future case justify such resistance, can never be ascertained, till they happen. Perhaps it may be allowable to say generally, that it never can be justifiable, until the people are fully convinced, that any further submission will be destructive to their happiness.

When the appeal is made to the sword, highly probable is it, that the punishment will exceed the offence; and the calamities attending on war outweigh those preceding it. These considerations of justice and prudence, will always have great influence with good and wise men.

VIGILANCE THE PRICE OF LIBERTY

[From the Same, XI.]

My dear Countrymen,

I have several times, in the course of these letters, mentioned the late act of Parliament, as being the *foundation* of future measures injurious to these colonies; and the belief of this truth I wish to prevail, because I think it necessary to our safety.

A perpetual jealousy, respecting liberty, is absolutely requisite in all free states. The very texture of their constitution, in mixed governments, demands it. For the cautions with which power is distributed among the several orders, imply, that each has that share which is proper for the general welfare, and therefore that any further acquisition must be pernicious. Machiavel employs a whole chapter in his discourses, to prove that a state, to be long lived, must be frequently corrected, and reduced to its first principles. But of all states that have existed, there never was any, in which this jealousy could be more proper than in these colonies. For the government here is not only *mixed,* but *dependent,* which circumstance occasions a peculiarity in its form, of a very delicate nature.

Two reasons induce me to desire, that this spirit of apprehension may be always kept up among us, in its utmost vigilance. The first is this—that as the happiness of these provinces indubitably consists in their connection with Great Britain, any separation between them is less likely to be occasioned by civil discords, if every disgusting measure is opposed singly, and while it is new. For in this manner of proceeding, every such measure is most likely to be rectified. On the other hand, oppressions and dissatisfactions being permitted to accumulate—if ever the governed throw off the load, they will do more. A people does not reform with moderation. The rights of the subject therefore cannot be too often considered, explained, or asserted. And whoever attempts to do this, shows himself, whatever may be the rash and peevish reflections of pretended wisdom, and pretended duty, a friend to those who injudiciously exercise their power, as well as them over whom it is so exercised.

Had all the points of prerogative claimed by Charles the First, been separately contested and settled in preceding reigns, his fate would in all probability have been very different; and the people would have been content with that liberty which is compatible with regal authority. But he thought, it would be as dangerous for him to give up the powers which at any time had been by usurpation exercised by the crown, as those that were legally vested in it. This produced an equal excess on the part of the people. For when their passions were excited by multiplied grievances, they thought it would be as dangerous for them to allow the powers that were legally vested in the crown, as those which at any time had been by usurpation exercised by it. Acts, that might by themselves have been upon many considerations excused or extenuated, derived a contagious malignancy and odium from other acts, with which they were connected. They were not regarded according to the simple force of each, but as parts of a system of oppression. Every one therefore, however small in itself, became alarming, as an additional evidence of tyrannical designs. It was in vain for prudent and moderate men to insist, that there was no necessity to abolish royalty. Nothing less than the utter destruction of monarchy, could satisfy those who had suffered, and thought they had reason to believe, they always should suffer under it.

The consequences of these mutual distrusts are well known. But there is no other people mentioned in history, that I recollect, who have been so constantly watchful of their liberty, and so successful in their struggles for it, as the English. This consideration leads me to the second reason, why I "desire that the spirit of apprehension may be always kept up among us in its utmost vigilance."

The first principles of government are to be looked for in human nature. Some of the best writers have asserted, and it seems with good reason, that "government is founded on opinion."

Custom undoubtedly has a mighty force in producing opinion, and reigns in nothing more arbitrarily than in public affairs. It gradually reconciles us to objects even of dread and detestation; and I cannot but think these lines of Mr. Pope as applicable to vice in politics, as to vice in ethics—

> "Vice is a monster of so horrid mien,
> As to be hated, needs but to be seen;
> Yet seen too oft, familiar with her face,
> We first endure, then pity, then embrace."

When an act injurious to freedom has been once done, and the people bear it, the repetition of it is most likely to meet with submission. For as the mischief of the one was found to be tolerable, they will hope that of the second will prove so too; and they will not regard the infamy of the last, because they are stained with that of the first.

Indeed nations, in general, are not apt to think until they feel; and therefore nations in general have lost their liberty. For as violations of the rights of the governed, are commonly not only specious, but small in the beginning, they spread over the multitude in such a manner, as to touch individuals but slightly. Thus they are disregarded. The power or profit that arises from these violations, centering in a few persons, is to them considerable. For this reason the governors having in view their particular purposes, successively preserve an uniformity of conduct for attaining them. They regularly increase the first injuries, till at length the inattentive people are compelled to perceive the heaviness of their burdens. They begin to complain and inquire—but too late. They find their oppressors so strengthened by success, and themselves so entangled in examples of express authority on the part of their rulers, and tacit recognition on their own part, that they are quite confounded; for millions entertain no other idea of the legality of power, than that it is founded on the exercise of power. They voluntarily fasten their chains, by adopting a pusillanimous opinion, "that there will be too much danger in attempting a remedy,"—or another opinion no less fatal, "that the government has a right to treat them as it does." They then seek a wretched relief for their minds, by persuading themselves, that to yield their obedience, is to discharge their duty. The deplorable poverty of spirit, that prostrates all the dignity bestowed by Divine Providence on our nature—of course succeeds.

From these reflections I conclude, that every free state should incessantly watch, and instantly take alarm on any addition being made to the power exercised over them. . . .

THE LIBERTY SONG

To the Tune of "Hearts of Oak," etc.

[1768]

Come join hand in hand, brave Americans all,
And rouse your bold hearts at fair Liberty's call;
No tyrannous acts shall suppress your just claim,
Or stain with dishonor America's name.
  In freedom we're born, and in freedom we'll live,
    Our purses are ready,
    Steady, Friends, steady,
  Not as slaves, but as freemen our money we'll give.

Our worthy forefathers—let's give them a cheer—
To climates unknown did courageously steer;
Thro' oceans to deserts for freedom they came,
And dying bequeath'd us their freedom and fame.

Their generous bosoms all dangers despis'd
So highly, so wisely, their birthrights they priz'd;
We'll keep what they gave, we will piously keep,
Nor frustrate their toils on the land and the deep.

The tree their own hands had to liberty rear'd
They live to behold growing strong and rever'd;
With transport then cried, "Now our wishes we gain,
For our children shall gather the fruits of our pain."

Swarms of placemen and pensioners soon will appear
Like locusts deforming the charms of the year;
Suns vainly will rise, showers vainly descend,
If we are to drudge for what others shall spend.

Then join hand in hand, brave Americans all,
By uniting we stand, by dividing we fall;
In so righteous a cause let us hope to succeed,
For heaven approves of each generous deed.

All ages shall speak with amaze and applause,
Of the courage we'll show in support of our laws;
To die we can bear—but to serve we disdain,
For shame is to freemen more dreadful than pain.

This bumper I crown for our sovereign's health,
And this for Britannia's glory and wealth;
That wealth and that glory immortal may be,
If she is but just, and if we are but free.
  In freedom we're born, etc.

DECLARATION ON TAKING UP ARMS

[1775]

. . . In brief, a part of these colonies now feel, and
all of them are sure of feeling, as far as the vengeance of administration can inflict them, the complicated calamities of
fire, sword, and famine. We are reduced to the alternative
of choosing an unconditional submission to the tyranny of
irritated ministers, or resistance by force. The latter is our
choice. We have counted the cost of this contest, and find
nothing so dreadful as voluntary slavery! Honor, justice,
and humanity forbid us tamely to surrender that freedom
which we received from our gallant ancestors, and which
our innocent posterity have a right to receive from us. We
cannot endure the infamy and guilt of resigning succeeding
generations to that wretchedness which inevitably awaits
them, if we basely entail hereditary bondage upon them.

Our cause is just. Our union is perfect. Our internal
resources are great, and, if necessary, foreign assistance is
undoubtedly attainable. We gratefully acknowledge, as
signal instances of Divine favor towards us, that his providence would not permit us to be called into this severe controversy, until we were grown up to our present strength,
had been previously exercised in warlike operations, and
possessed the means of defending ourselves. With hearts
fortified by these animating reflections, we most solemnly,
before God and the world, DECLARE, that exerting the utmost
energy of those powers, which our beneficent Creator has

graciously bestowed upon us, the arms we have been compelled by our enemies to assume, we will, in defiance of every hazard, with unabating firmness and perseverance, employ for the preservation of our liberties; being with one mind resolved to die freemen rather than to live slaves.

SAMUEL SEABURY

Samuel Seabury, the most effective of the loyalist pamphleteers, was born in Groton, Connecticut, in 1729, and graduated at Yale. At the outbreak of the Revolution he was rector of a parish in Westchester, New York. Like many other Americans of education, social position, and Church of England connections, he took the conservative side. The no-trade agreement, adopted by the first Continental Congress in September, 1774, was immediately attacked in a well-written pamphlet, *Free Thoughts on the Proceedings of the Continental Congress,* by "a Westchester Farmer." The authorship, attributed to various loyalists, was then thought, and is now definitely known, to belong to Seabury. This, along with *The Congress Canvassed* and two other similar pamphlets written during the next two months, called forth many replies, the ablest, *A Full Vindication* and *The Farmer Refuted,* being from the youthful pen of Alexander Hamilton, then an undergraduate at King's College. For his toryism Seabury was a year later seized by a mob, which pillaged his rectory; he finally escaped within the British lines and was made chaplain of the King's American regiment. Unlike many loyalists he remained in this country after the war and outlived his unpopularity. He died in 1796, honored as the first bishop of the American Episcopal Church.

Though he had cultivated only his parish glebe, Seabury could convincingly assume the views and style of a farmer. He argued that farmers would suffer from the no-trade agreement; he denounced the Congress as an illegal and tyrannical body, and proposed loyalty with home rule as the best and safest solution. He showed narrowness in his suspicion of the other colonies—especially of "the mad schemes of our Eastern neighbors;" and shortsightedness in his prophecy that if the colonists should (quite improbably) win the impending war, they would "turn their arms on one another." But he wrote with great cogency, wit, and vigor in support of views which he held with honesty and courage. We who believe in independence and union cannot now find his arguments convincing; but we can respect an American who, like many others of his time, made great sacrifices for loyalty and freedom of speech.

THE DANGER TO THE FLAX-GROWERS

[FROM "FREE THOUGHTS ON THE PROCEEDINGS OF THE CONTINENTAL CONGRESS." 1774]

When a trading people carelessly neglect, or wilfully give up any branch of their trade, it is seldom in their power to recover it. Should the Irish turn their trade for flax-seed to Quebec; and the West Indians get their flour, horses, &c., from thence, or other places; the loss to the farmers of this province would be immense. . . .

You know, my Friends, that the sale of your seed not only pays your taxes, but furnishes you with many of the little conveniencies, and comforts of life; the loss of it for one year would be of more damage to you, than paying the three-penny duty on tea for twenty. Let us compare matters a little. It was inconvenient for me this year to sow more than one bushel of seed. I have threshed and cleaned up eleven bushels. The common price now is at least ten shillings; my seed then will fetch me five pounds, ten shillings. But I will throw in the ten shillings for expenses. There remain five pounds: in five pounds are four hundred three-pences; four hundred three pences currency, will pay the duty upon two hundred pounds of tea, even reckoning the exchange with London at 200 per cent., that is, reckoning 100 *l.* sterling, to be equal to 200 *l.* currency; whereas in fact it is only equal to 175 *l.* or 180 *l.* at the most. I use in my family about six pounds of tea: few farmers in my neighborhood use so much: but I hate to stint my wife and daughters, or my friendly neighbors when they come to see me. Besides, I like a dish of tea too, especially after a little more than ordinary fatigue in hot weather. Now 200 pounds of tea, at

FREE THOUGHTS,

ON

The PROCEEDINGS of

THE

CONTINENTAL CONGRESS,

Held at PHILADELPHIA, Sept. 5, 1774:

WHEREIN

Their ERRORS are exhibited,

THEIR

REASONINGS CONFUTED,

AND

The fatal Tendency of their NON-IMPORTATION, NON-EXPORTATION, and NON-CONSUMPTION MEASURES, are laid open to the plainest UNDERSTANDINGS;

AND

The ONLY MEANS pointed out

For Preserving and Securing

Our present HAPPY CONSTITUTION:

IN

A LETTER

TO

THE FARMERS,

AND OTHER INHABITANTS OF

NORTH AMERICA

In General

And to those of the Province of *New-York*

In Particular

By a FARMER.

Hear me, for I WILL speak!

PRINTED IN THE YEAR M.DCC.LXXIV.

six pounds a year, will last just 33 years, and eight months. So that in order to pay this monstrous duty upon tea, which has raised all this confounded combustion in the country, I have only to sell the produce of a bushel of flax-seed once in THIRTY-THREE years.   Ridiculous!

But, to leave jesting.   The loss of the sale of your seed only for one year, would be a considerable damage to you. And yet the Congress have been so inattentive to your interests, that they have laid you under, almost, an absolute necessity of losing it the next year.   They have decreed, and proclaimed a non-exportation, to commence in September next.   The Irish will be alarmed.   They will look out somewhere else.   Or should they determine to send their ships the earlier, we cannot, without the utmost inconvenience, get our seed to market by that time; especially, not from the remoter parts of the province.   The consequence will be, that we must sell our seed at the oil-mills in New York, just at the price the manufacturers shall please to give us.   .   .   .

TYRANNY OF THE CONGRESS

[FROM THE SAME]

Let us now attend a little to the Non-Consumption Agreement, which the Congress, in their Association, have imposed upon us.   After the first of March we are not to purchase or use any East India tea whatsoever; nor any goods, wares, or merchandise from Great Britain or Ireland, imported after the first day of December next: nor any molasses, syrups, &c., from the British plantations in the West Indies, or from Dominica; nor wines from Madeira, or the Western Islands; nor foreign indigo.

Will you submit to this slavish regulation?   You must. Our sovereign Lords and Masters, the High and Mighty Delegates, in Grand Continental Congress assembled, have ordered and directed it.   They have directed the committees in the respective colonies, to establish such further regulations as they may think proper, for carrying their association, of which this non-consumption agreement is a part, into execu-

tion. Mr.———— of New York, under the authority of
their High-Mightinesses, the Delegates, by, and with the
advice of his Privy Council, the Committee of New York,
hath issued his mandate, bearing date November 7, 1774,
recommending it to the freeholders and freemen of New
York, to assemble on the 18th of November, to choose eight
persons out of every ward, to be a committee, to carry the
Association of the Congress into execution. The business of
the committee so chosen is to be, to inspect the conduct of
the inhabitants, and see whether they violate the Association.
Among other things, whether they drink any tea or wine
in their familes, after the first of March; or wear any
British or Irish manufactures; or use any English molasses,
&c., imported after the first day of December next. If they
do, their names are to be published in the Gazette, that they
may be *publicly known,* and *universally contemned, as foes
to the Rights of British America,* and *enemies of American
Liberty.* And then *the parties of the said Association will
respectively break off all dealings with him or her.* In plain
English, they shall be considered as outlaws, unworthy of
the protection of civil society, and delivered over to the
vengeance of a lawless, outrageous mob, to be *tarred,
feathered, hanged, drawn, quartered, and burnt.* O rare
American Freedom!

Probably, as soon as this point is settled in New York,
the said Mr.———— in the plenitude of his power, by,
and with the advice of his Privy Council aforesaid, will
issue his mandate to the supervisors in the several counties,
as he did about the choice of delegates, and direct them to
have committees chosen in their respective districts, for the
same laudable purpose.

Will you be instrumental in bringing the most abject
slavery on yourselves? Will you choose such committees?
Will you submit to them, should they be chosen by the weak,
foolish, turbulent part of the country people? Do as you
please: but, by HIM that made me, I will not. No, if I
must be enslaved, let it be by a KING at least, and not by a
parcel of upstart, lawless committee-men. If I must be devoured, let me be devoured by the jaws of a lion, and not
gnawed to death by rats and vermin.

Did you choose your supervisors for the purpose of enslaving you? What right have they to fix up advertisements to call you together, for a very different purpose from that for which they were elected? Are our supervisors our masters? And should half a dozen foolish people meet together again, in consequence of their advertisement, and choose themselves to be a committee, as they did in many districts, in the affair of choosing delegates, are we obliged to submit to such a committee? You ought, my friends, to assert your own freedom. Should such another attempt be made upon you, assemble yourselves together: tell your supervisor, that he has exceeded his commission; that you will have no such committees; that you are Englishmen, and will maintain your rights and privileges, and will eat, and drink, and wear, whatever the public laws of your country permit, without asking leave of any illegal, tyrannical congress or committee on earth.

But however, as I said before, do as you please. If you like it better, choose your committee, or suffer it to be chosen by half a dozen fools in your neighborhood,—open your doors to them,—let them examine your tea-cannisters, and molasses-jugs, and your wives' and daughters' petticoats,—bow, and cringe, and tremble, and quake,—fall down and worship our sovereign Lord the Mob. But I repeat it, By H——n, I will not. No, my house is my castle: as such I will consider it, as such I will defend it, while I have breath. No *king's* officer shall enter it without my permission, unless supported by a warrant from a magistrate. And shall my house be entered, and my mode of living enquired into, by a domineering committee-man? Before *I* submit, I will die: live *you,* and be slaves.

Do, I say, as you please: but should any pragmatical committee-gentleman come to my house, and give himself airs, I shall show him the door, and if he does not soon take himself away, a good hickory cudgel shall teach him better manners.

LIBERTY AND THE BOSTON POOR
[FROM "THE CONGRESS CANVASSED." 1774]

In God's name, are not the people of Boston able to relieve their *own* poor? Must they go begging from Dan to Beersheba; *levying* contributions, and *exacting* fines, from Nova Scotia to Georgia, to support a few poor people whom their perverseness and ill-conduct have thrown into distress? If they are *really* under such violent concern for their poor, why don't they *pay* for the tea which they destroyed, and thereby qualify themselves to have their port opened? This would effectually answer the purpose, and is only an act of bare justice which they ought to have done long ago. They have made a great parade about employing their poor, in paving their streets, and repairing their wharves and docks; —are they unable to pay them for their labor? Can't they *spare* some small portion of that wealth, which is now pouring in upon them from the army and navy, for so good a purpose? Or will not the labor of the poor support them now, as well as formerly? Must they command the wealth of the continent, to ornament their town, and render it more commodious? Do they expect a *literal* completion of the promise, that the *Saints shall inherit the earth?* In my conscience, I believe they do. Nor can I, on this occasion, help recollecting the observation of a queer fellow some time ago. Discoursing with him on this very subject, he said, that the conduct of the Boston people seemed to him to indicate an opinion "that God had made Boston for himself, and all of the rest of the world for Boston."

For Heaven's sake, gentlemen, have you no poor of your own to relieve? Are you sure that your non-importation, non-exportation, non-consumption schemes, will not draw the resentment of the British Parliament on *you,* as well as on *Boston?*

BRITISH RULE BOTH DESIRABLE AND LEGAL

[FROM "A VIEW OF THE CONTROVERSY BETWEEN GREAT BRITAIN AND HER COLONIES." 1775]

I wish you had explicitly declared to the public your ideas of the *natural rights of mankind.* Man in a state of nature may be considered as perfectly free from all restraints of law and government: and then the *weak* must submit to the *strong.* From such a state, I confess, I have a violent aversion. I think the form of government we lately enjoyed a much more eligible state to live in, and cannot help regretting our having lost it, by the *equity, wisdom,* and *authority* of the Congress, who have introduced in the room of it, confusion and violence; where all must submit to the power of a mob.

You have taken some pains to prove what would readily have been granted you—that *liberty* is a very *good* thing, and *slavery* a very *bad* thing. But then I must think that liberty under a King, Lords, and Commons is as good as liberty under a republican Congress, and that slavery under a republican Congress is as bad, at least, as slavery under a King, Lords, and Commons; and upon the whole, that *liberty* under the supreme authority and protection of Great Britain, is infinitely preferable to *slavery* under an American Congress. I will also agree with you, "that Americans are entitled to freedom." I will go further: I will own and acknowledge that not only *Americans,* but *Africans, Europeans, Asiatics,* all men, of all countries and degrees, of all sizes and complexions, have a right to as much freedom as is consistent with the security of civil society; and I hope you will not think me an "enemy to the *natural* rights of mankind" because I cannot wish them more. We must however remember, that more liberty may, without inconvenience, be allowed to individuals in a small government, than can be admitted of in a large empire. . . .

Now the dependence of the colonies on the mother-country has ever been acknowledged. It is an impropriety of speech to talk of an independent colony. The words *independence* and *colony,* convey contradictory ideas: much like *killing* and *sparing*. As soon as a colony becomes independent of its parent state, it ceases to be any longer a colony, just as when you *kill* a sheep, you cease to *spare* him. The British colonies make a part of the British empire. As parts of the body they must be subject to the general laws of the body. To talk of a colony independent of the mother-country, is no better sense than to talk of a limb independent of the body to which it belongs.

In every government there must be a supreme, absolute authority lodged somewhere. In arbitrary governments this power is in the monarch; in aristocratical governments, in the nobles; in democratical, in the people, or the deputies of their electing. Our own government being a mixture of all these kinds, the supreme authority is vested in the King, Nobles, and People, *i.e.,* the King, House of Lords, and House of Commons elected by the people. This supreme authority extends as far as the British dominions extend. To suppose a part of the British dominions which is not subject to the power of the British legislature, is no better sense than to suppose a country, at one and the same time, to be and not to be a part of the British dominions. If therefore the colony of New York be a part of the British dominions, the colony of New York is subject, and dependent on the supreme legislative authority of Great Britain.

ALEXANDER HAMILTON

Alexander Hamilton, the son of a Scottish merchant in the West Indies, was born in 1757 on the island of Nevis. He early showed unusual promise, and in 1772 friends sent him to New York to be educated. Landing during the period of bitterest controversy between colonists and crown, he was not long in taking sides; a visit to Boston and the hospitality of new friends decided him to throw in his lot with the American party. In 1774-5, as a seventeen-year-old student in King's College (now Columbia University), he showed his sympathies by opposing Samuel Seabury, ablest of the tory pamphleteers and better known as the "Westchester Farmer." Hamilton's contributions to the controversy, *A Full Vindication* and *The Farmer Refuted,* hardly equalled his opponent's in satirical force or clever invective, but they showed a logical, astute mind, clear in its analysis, and sure in detecting real issues.

During the Revolution Hamilton served on Washington's staff with distinction, although somewhat dissatisfied with his dependent position. In 1780, before hostilities ceased, he married Elizabeth Schuyler, member of an influential New York family; and in a short time he became highly successful in the practice of law. As early as 1779, he had begun the political activities which deservedly brought him fame. Clearly perceiving the weaknesses of the Confederacy, he was among the first to point them out, and among the first, too, to advocate the change which came later with the adoption of the Constitution. In the words of Chancellor Kent, "he surpassed all his contemporaries in his exertions to create, recommend, adopt, and defend the Constitution of the United States." As a delegate to the Constitutional Convention, he entered the ranks of the strong-government party; and after the work of the Convention was completed, he went home to New York to defend it.

This he did so ably in *The Federalist,* a series of essays written jointly with John Jay and James Madison, that this work still remains a classic commentary on American law and governmental principles.

As the first secretary of the treasury, Hamilton placed the nation on a safe financial basis, thus generating confidence in the new government. He became Washington's most influential adviser, and in the early days of the republic was able largely to formulate the political creed of the Federalist Party, of which he remained to the end perhaps the strongest, if not the most popular, leader. In 1804 he was killed in a duel with Aaron Burr, long his political rival.

As a writer, Hamilton was clear, logical, forcible, rather than witty or graceful. His legal mind showed to greatest advantage in expository writing—notably in *The Federalist.* His works have been best edited by H. C. Lodge (twelve volumes, 1904). A commendable biography of him is that by W. G. Sumner. Interesting, also, and accurate historically, is Gertrude Atherton's romance of Hamilton, *The Conqueror* (1902).

THE RIGHT TO FREEDOM

[FROM "A FULL VINDICATION OF THE MEASURES OF THE CONGRESS." 1774]

A little consideration will convince us, that the Congress, instead of having "ignorantly misunderstood, carelessly neglected, or basely betrayed the interests of the colonies," have, on the contrary, devised and recommended the only effectual means to secure the freedom, and establish the future prosperity of America upon a solid basis. If we are nòt free and happy hereafter, it must proceed from the want of integrity and resolution, in executing what they have concerted; not from the temerity or impolicy of their determinations.

Before I proceed to confirm this assertion by the most obvious arguments, I will premise a few brief remarks. The only distinction between freedom and slavery consists in this: in the former state, a man is governed by the laws to which he has given his consent, either in person, or by his representative; in the latter he is governed by the will of another. In the one case his life and property are his own; in the other, they depend upon the pleasure of a master. It is easy to discern which of these two states is preferable. No man in his senses can hesitate in choosing to be free, rather than a slave.

That Americans are entitled to freedom, is incontestible upon every rational principle. All men have one common original: they participate in one common nature, and consequently have one common right. No reason can be assigned why one man should exercise any power or preëminence over his fellow creatures more than another, unless they have voluntarily vested him with it. Since, then, Americans have not by any act of theirs empowered the British Parliament to make laws for them, it follows they can have no just authority to do it.

COMMERCIAL INDEPENDENCE

[FROM THE SAME]

.   .   .   The colonies contain above three millions of people. Commerce flourishes with the most rapid progress throughout them. This commerce Great Britain has hitherto regulated to her own advantage. Can we think the annihilation of so exuberant a source of wealth, a matter of trifling import. On the contrary, must it not be productive of the most disastrous effects? It is evident it must. It is equally evident, that the conquest of so numerous a people, armed in the animating cause of liberty, could not be accomplished without an inconceivable expense of blood and treasure.

We cannot therefore suspect Great Britain to be capable of such frantic extravagance as to hazard these dreadful consequences. . . .

But should we admit a possibility of [another] course, as our pamphleteer supposes, that is, the endeavoring to bring us to a compliance by putting a stop to our whole trade— even this would not be so terrible as he pretends. We can live without trade of any kind. Food and clothing we have within ourselves. Our climate produces cotton, wool, flax, and hemp, which, with proper cultivation, would furnish us with summer apparel in abundance. The article of cotton indeed would do more; it would contribute to defend us from the inclemency of winter. We have sheep, which, with due care in improving and increasing them, would soon yield a sufficiency of wool. The large quantity of skins, we have among us, would never let us want a warm and comfortable suit. It would be no unbecoming employment for our daughters to provide silks of their own country. The silk-worm answers as well here as in any part of the world. Those hands, which may be deprived of business by the cessation of commerce, may be occupied in various kinds of manufactures and other internal improvements. If by the necessity of the thing, manufactures should once be established and take root among us, they will pave the way, still more, to the future grandeur and glory of America, and by lessening its need of external commerce, will render it still securer against the encroachments of tyranny. . . .

Upon the whole, it appears, that the supplies of flax-seed, which Ireland might draw elsewhere, could be trifling in comparison with those received from us, and not at all equivalent to her wants. But if this were not the case, if she might procure a sufficiency without our help, yet could she not do without us. She should want purchasers for her linens after they were manufactured; and where could she find any so numerous and wealthy as we are? I must refer it to the profound sagacity of Mr. A. W. Farmer, to explore them; it is too arduous a task for me.

AMERICA FACED BY A SOBERING RESPONSIBILITY

[FROM "THE FEDERALIST," No. I.]

After full experience of the insufficiency of the existing Federal Government, you are invited to deliberate upon a new Constitution for the United States of America.

The subject speaks of its own importance; comprehending in its consequences, nothing less than the existence of the UNION—the safety and welfare of the parts of which it is composed—the fate of an empire, in many respects, the most interesting in the world. It has been frequently remarked, that, it seems to have been reserved to the people of this country, to decide by their conduct and example, the important question, whether societies of men are really capable or not, of establishing good government from reflection and choice, or whether they are forever destined to depend, for their political constitutions, on accident and force. If there be any truth in the remark, the crisis, at which we are arrived, may with propriety be regarded as the period when that decision is to be made; and a wrong election of the part we shall act, may, in this view, deserve to be considered as the general misfortune of mankind.

THE NEED OF A CHANGE IN GOVERNMENT

[FROM "THE FEDERALIST," No. XV.]

In pursuance of the plan, which I have laid down for the discussion of the subject, the point next in order to be examined, is the "insufficiency of the present confederation to the preservation of the union." . . .

We may indeed, with propriety, be said to have reached almost the last stage of national humiliation. There is scarcely anything that can wound the pride, or degrade the character, of an independent people, which we do not experience. Are there engagements, to the performance of which we are held by every tie respectable among men? These are the subjects of constant and unblushing violation. Do we owe debts to foreigners, and to our own citizens, contracted in a time of imminent peril, for the preservation of our political existence? These remain without any proper or satisfactory provision for their discharge. Have we valuable territories and important posts in the possession of a foreign power, which, by express stipulations, ought long since to have been surrendered? These are still retained, to the prejudice of our interest not less than of our rights. Are we in a condition to resent, or to repel the aggression? We have neither troops, nor treasury, nor government.[1] Are we even in a condition to remonstrate with dignity? The just imputations on our own faith, in respect to the same treaty,

---

[1] I mean for the union.

ought first to be removed. Are we entitled, by nature and compact, to a free participation in the navigation of the Mississippi? Spain excludes us from it. Is public credit an indispensable resource in time of public danger? We seem to have abandoned its cause as desperate and irretrievable. Is commerce of importance to national wealth? Ours is at the lowest point of declension. Is respectability in the eyes of foreign powers, a safeguard against foreign encroachments? The imbecility of our government even forbids them to treat with us: our ambassadors abroad are the mere pageants of mimic sovereignty. Is a violent and unnatural decrease in the value of land, a symptom of national distress? The price of improved land, in most parts of the country, is much lower than can be accounted for by the quantity of waste land at market, and can only be fully explained by that want of private and public confidence, which are so alarmingly prevalent among all ranks, and which have a direct tendency to depreciate property of every kind. Is private credit the friend and patron of industry? That most useful kind which relates to borrowing and lending, is reduced within the narrowest limits, and this still more from an opinion of insecurity than from a scarcity of money. To shorten an enumeration of particulars which can afford neither pleasure nor instruction, it may in general be demanded, what indication is there of national disorder, poverty, and insignificance, that could befall a community so peculiarly blessed with natural advantages as we are, which does not form a part of the dark catalogue of our public misfortunes?

This is the melancholy situation to which we have been brought by those very maxims and counsels, which would now deter us from adopting the proposed constitution; and which, not content with having conducted us to the brink of a precipice, seem resolved to plunge us into the abyss that awaits us below. Here, my countrymen, impelled by every motive that ought to influence an enlightened people, let us make a firm stand for our safety, our tranquillity, our dignity, our reputation. Let us at last break the fatal charm which has too long seduced us from the paths of felicity and prosperity.

ON TAXATION

[FROM "THE FEDERALIST," NO. XXX.]

Money is with propriety considered as the vital principle of the body politic; as that which sustains its life and motion, and enables it to perform its most essential functions. A complete power, therefore, to procure a regular and adequate supply of revenue, as far as the resources of the community will permit, may be regarded as an indispensable ingredient in every constitution. From a deficiency in this particular, one of two evils must ensue: either the people must be subjected to continual plunder, as a substitute for a more eligible mode of supplying the public wants, or the government must sink into a fatal atrophy, and in a short course of time perish.

In the Ottoman or Turkish empire, the sovereign, though in other respects absolute master of the lives and fortunes of his subjects, has no right to impose a new tax. The consequence is, that he permits the bashaws or governors of provinces to pillage the people at discretion; and, in turn, squeezes out of them the sums of which he stands in need, to satisfy his own exigencies, and those of the state. In America, from a like cause, the government of the union has gradually dwindled into a state of decay, approaching nearly to annihilation. Who can doubt, that the happiness of the people in both countries would be promoted by competent authorities in the proper hands, to provide the revenues which the necessities of the public might require?

The present confederation, feeble as it is, intended to repose in the United States, an unlimited power of providing for the pecuniary wants of the union. But proceeding upon an erroneous principle, it has been done in such a manner, as entirely to have frustrated the intention. Congress, by the articles which compose that compact (as has been already stated), are authorized to ascertain and call for any sums of money necessary, in their judgment, to the service of the United States; and their requisitions, if conformable to the rule of apportionment, are, in every constitutional sense, obligatory upon the states. These have no right to question the propriety of the demand: no discretion beyond that of devising the ways and means of furnishing the sums demanded. But though this be strictly and truly the case; though the assumption of such a right would be an infringement of the articles of union; though it may seldom or never have been avowedly claimed: yet in practice it has been constantly exercised, and would continue to be so, as long as the revenues of the confederacy should remain dependent on the intermediate agency of its members. What the consequences of the system have been, is within the knowledge of every man, the least conversant in our public affairs, and has been abundantly unfolded in different parts of these inquiries. It is this which has chiefly contributed to reduce us to a situation, that affords ample cause of mortification to ourselves, and of triumph to our enemies.

What remedy can there be for this situation, but in a change of the system, which has produced it? in a change of the fallacious and delusive system of quotas and requisitions? What substitute can there be imagined for this *ignis fatuus* in finance, but that of permitting the national government to raise its own revenues by the ordinary methods òf taxation, authorized in every well ordered constitution of civil government? Ingenious men may declaim with plausibility on any subject; but no human ingenuity can point out any other expedient to rescue us from the inconveniences and embarrassments, naturally resulting from defective supplies of the public treasury.

THE INDEPENDENCE OF THE FEDERAL JUDGES

[FROM "THE FEDERALIST," No. LXXIX.]

Next to permanency in office, nothing can contribute more to the independence of the judges, than a fixed provision for their support. The remark made in relation to the president, is equally applicable here. In the general course of human nature, *a power over a man's subsistence amounts to a power over his will.* And we can never hope to see realized in practice the complete separation of the judicial from the legislative power, in any system, which leaves the former dependent for pecuniary resource on the occasional grants of the latter. The enlightened friends to good government, in every state, have seen cause to lament the want of precise and explicit precautions in the state constitutions on this head. Some of these indeed have declared that *permanent* salaries should be established for the judges; but the experiment has in some instances shown, that such expressions are not sufficiently definite to preclude legislative evasions. Something still more positive and unequivocal has been evinced to be requisite. The plan of the convention accordingly has provided, that the judges of the United States "shall at *stated times* receive for their services a compensation, which shall not be *diminished* during their continuance in office."

This, all circumstances considered, is the most eligible provision that could have been devised. It will readily be understood, that the fluctuations in the value of money, and in the state of society, rendered a fixed rate of compensation in the constitution inadmissible. What might be extravagant to-day, might in half a century become penurious and inadequate. It was therefore necessary to leave it to the discretion of the legislature to vary its provisions in conformity to the variations in circumstances; yet under such restrictions as to put it out of the power of that body to change the condition of the individual for the worse. A man may then be sure of the ground upon which he stands, and can never be deterred from his duty by the apprehension of being placed in a less eligible situation. . . .

THE SUPREME LAW OF THE LAND
[FROM "THE FEDERALIST," No. XXXIII.]

But it is said, that the laws of the union are to be the *supreme law* of the land. What inference can be drawn from this, or what would they amount to, if they were not to be supreme? It is evident they would amount to nothing. A *law,* by the very meaning of the term, includes supremacy. It is a rule, which those to whom it is prescribed are bound to observe. This results from every political association. If individuals enter into a state of society, the laws of that society must be the supreme regulator of their conduct. If a number of political societies enter into a larger political society, the laws which the latter may enact, pursuant to the powers intrusted to it by its constitution, must necessarily be supreme over these societies, and the individuals of whom they are composed. It would otherwise be a mere treaty, dependent on the good faith of the parties, and not a government; which is only another word for *political power and supremacy*. But it will not follow from this doctrine, that acts of the larger society which are *not pursuant* to its constitutional powers, but which are invasions of the residuary authorities of the smaller societies, will become the supreme law of the land. These will be merely acts of usurpation, and will deserve to be treated as such. Hence we perceive, that the clause which declares the supremacy of the laws of the union, like the one which we have just before considered, only declares a truth, which flows immediately and necessarily from the institution of a federal government. It will not, I presume, have escaped observation, that it *expressly* confines this supremacy to laws made *pursuant to the constitution;* which I mention merely as an instance of caution in the convention; since that limitation would have been to be understood, though it had not been expressed.

THOMAS JEFFERSON

Although Thomas Jefferson was first of all a statesman, and as such is best known, incidentally he was a prolific man of letters. Born in 1743 in the frontier county of Albemarle, Virginia, Jefferson was brought up among a hardy and sensible American country folk who gave him a lasting confidence in democratic principles. After graduating from the College of William and Mary, he successfully practiced law, but like many another ambitious young lawyer, he was soon involved in the political crisis in the colonies. He entered the Virginia House of Burgesses, where, as in the larger political arena later, his energy, his clear thinking, and his ready pen won him early and almost consistent success. Some instructions he wrote for the Virginia delegates to the First Continental Congress were printed in England and brought him "the honor," as he himself said, "of having my name inserted in a long list of proscriptions." Two years later the Congressional committee selected him to write the Declaration of Independence. During and after the Revolution he became successively member of Congress, governor of Virginia, American minister to France, secretary of state under Washington, Vice-President, and finally President. He persistently and ably opposed Alexander Hamilton in his centralizing policies, and more than any other man was instrumental in founding the Republican Party. In 1808, after completing two terms as President, he retired to his country mansion, Monticello, to rest from his labors, to read the books he had been able to enjoy only in spare moments, and to entertain lavishly the many friends who flocked thither in such numbers as to impoverish their host. His last years were spent in founding and organizing the University of Virginia, a pleasant task of which he had long dreamed. When he died on July 4, 1826, just fifty years after the adoption of his famous Declaration, he was widely revered for his versatility, wisdom, and achievements in politics, science, and literature.

Jefferson's writings consist chiefly of letters (of which hundreds are extant), a few pamphlets, many documents written when he was cabinet member or President, various notes and opinions jotted down in spare moments, a poem or two, the Declaration of Independence, an autobiography, and his *Notes on Virginia.* Except the Declaration, his writings are not consistently good: although they contain purple patches, the intervening portions are likely to be dull, perfunctory, or hurriedly written. The *Notes on Virginia,* for instance, is delightful in parts, but contains too much statistical tabulation, too much dry detailing of facts, to take high rank as a whole, and can be read most profitably in selections. Jefferson's style is clear, systematic, sometimes animated; he had a remarkable talent for marshalling facts in argument, and a genius for stating generalities happily. His principal faults are those of the age—a diction too pompous and a formality which to-day seems labored. His works have been edited several times, perhaps best by P. L. Ford (N. Y., 1892-9). A commendable biography is by James Schouler (N. Y., 1893), and a good essay on him is to be found in Professor Trent's *Southern Statesmen of the Old Regime* (N. Y., 1897).

AN ADMONITION TO THE KING

[FROM "A SUMMARY VIEW OF THE RIGHTS OF BRITISH AMERICA." 1774]

. . . These are our grievances which we have thus laid before his majesty, with that freedom of language and sentiment which becomes a free people claiming their rights, as derived from the laws of nature, and not as the gift of their chief magistrate. Let those flatter who fear, it is not an American art. To give praise which is not due might be well from the venal, but would ill beseem those who are asserting the rights of human nature. They know, and will therefore say, that kings are the servants, not the proprietors of the people. Open your breast, sire, to liberal and ex-

panded thought. Let not the name of George the Third be
a blot in the page of history. You are surrounded by English counsellors, but remember that they are parties. You
have no minister for American affairs, because you have none
taken up from among us, nor amenable to the laws on which
they are to give you advice. It behooves you, therefore, to
think and to act for yourself and your people. The great
principles of right and wrong are legible to every reader; to
pursue them requires not the aid of many counsellors. The
whole art of government consists in the art of being honest.
Only aim to do your duty, and mankind will give you credit
where you fail. No longer persevere in sacrificing the rights
of one part of the empire to the inordinate desires of another; but deal out to all equal and impartial right. Let no
act be passed by any one legislature which may infringe on
the rights and liberties of another. This is the important
post in which fortune has placed you, holding the balance of
a great, if a well poised empire. This, sire, is the advice of
your great American council, on the observance of which
may perhaps depend your felicity and future fame, and the
preservation of that harmony which alone can continue both
in Great Britain and America the reciprocal advantages of
their connection. It is neither our wish nor our interest to
separate from her. We are willing, on our part, to sacrifice
everything which reason can ask to the restoration of that
tranquillity for which all must wish. On their part, let them
be ready to establish union on a generous plan. Let them
name their terms, but let them be just. Accept of every
commercial preference it is in our power to give for such
things as we can raise for their use, or they make for ours.
But let them not think to exclude us from going to other
markets to dispose of those commodities which they cannot
use, or to supply those wants which they cannot supply.
Still less let it be proposed that our properties within our
own territories shall be taxed or regulated by any power on
earth but our own. The God who gave us life gave us
liberty at the same time; the hand of force may destroy, but
cannot disjoin them. This, sire, is our last, our determined
resolution; and that you will be pleased to interpose with
that efficacy which your earnest endeavors may ensure to

procure redress of these our great grievances to quiet the minds of your subjects in British America, against any apprehensions of future encroachment, to establish fraternal love and harmony through the whole empire, and that these may continue to the latest ages of time, is the fervent prayer of all British America.

THE DECLARATION OF INDEPENDENCE
[1776]

When in the course of human events, it becomes necessary for one people to dissolve the political bands which have connected them with another, and to assume among the powers of the earth the separate and equal station to which the laws of nature and of nature's God entitle them, a decent respect to the opinions of mankind requires that they should declare the causes which impel them to the separation.

We hold these truths to be self-evident, that all men are created equal, that they are endowed by their Creator with certain inalienable rights, that among these are life, liberty, and the pursuit of happiness. That to secure these rights, governments are instituted among men, deriving their just powers from the consent of the governed. That whenever any form of government becomes destructive of these ends, it is the right of the people to alter or to abolish it, and to institute new government, laying its foundation on such principles, and organizing its powers in such form, as to them shall seem most likely to effect their safety and happiness. Prudence, indeed, will dictate that governments long established should not be changed for light and transient causes; and accordingly all experience hath shown, that mankind are more disposed to suffer, while evils are sufferable, than to right themselves by abolishing the forms to which they are accustomed. But when a long train of abuses and usurpations pursuing invariably the same object, evinces a design to reduce them under absolute despotism, it is their right, it is their duty, to throw off such government, and to provide new guards for their future security. Such has been the patient sufferance of these Colonies; and such is now the necessity which constrains them to alter their former systems of government. The history of the present King of Great Britain is a history of repeated injuries and usurpations, all having in direct object the establishment of an absolute tyranny over these States. To prove this let facts be submitted to a candid world. . . .

[Here follows an enumeration of grievances.]

We, therefore, the Representatives of the United States of America, in General Congress assembled, appealing to the Supreme Judge of the World for the rectitude of our intentions, do, in the name, and by authority of the good People of these Colonies, solemnly publish and declare, that these United Colonies are, and of right ought to be, Free and Independent States; that they are absolved from all allegiance to the British Crown, and that all political connection between them and the State of Great Britain, is and ought to be totally dissolved; and that as free and independent states, they have full power to levy war, conclude peace, contract alliances, establish commerce, and to do all other acts and things which independent states may of right do. And for the support of this declaration, with a firm reliance on the protection of Divine Providence, we mutually pledge to each other our lives, our fortunes, and our sacred honor.

THE PASSAGE OF THE POTOMAC

[FROM THE "NOTES ON VIRGINIA." 1784]

. . . The passage of the Potomac through the Blue Ridge is perhaps one of the most stupendous scenes in nature. You stand on a very high point of land. On your right comes up the Shenandoah, having ranged along the foot of the mountain an hundred miles to seek a vent. On your left approaches the Potomac, in quest of a passage also. In the moment of their junction, they rush together against the mountain, rend it asunder, and pass off to the sea. The first glance of this scene hurries our senses into the opinion that this earth has been created in time, that the mountains were formed first, that the rivers began to flow afterwards, that in this place particularly they have been dammed up by the Blue Ridge of mountains, and have formed an ocean which filled the whole valley; that continuing to rise they have at length broken over at this spot, and have torn the mountain down from its summit to its base. The piles of rock on each hand, but particularly on the Shenandoah, the evident marks of their disrupture and avulsion from their beds by the most powerful agents of nature, corroborate the impression. But the distant finishing which nature has given to the picture, is of a very different character. It is a true contrast to the foreground. It is as placid and delightful as that is wild and tremendous. For the mountain being cloven asunder, she presents to your eye, through the cleft, a small catch of smooth blue horizon, at an infinite distance in the plain country, inviting you, as it were, from the riot and tumult roaring around, to pass through the breach and participate of the calm below. Here the eye ultimately composes itself; and that way too the road happens actually to lead. You cross the Potomac above the junction, pass along its side through the base of the mountain for three miles, its terrible precipices hanging in fragments over you, and within about twenty miles reach Fredericktown and the fine country around that. This scene is worth a voyage across the Atlantic. Yet here, as in the neighborhood of the Natural Bridge, are people who have passed their lives within half a dozen miles, and have never been to survey these monuments of a war between rivers and mountains which must have shaken the earth itself to its centre.

ON THE AMERICAN INDIANS

[FROM THE SAME]

Before we condemn the Indians of this continent as wanting genius, we must consider that letters have not yet been introduced among them. Were we to compare them in their present state with the Europeans north of the Alps, when the Roman arms and arts first crossed those mountains, the comparison would be unequal, because, at that time, those parts of Europe were swarming with numbers; because numbers produce emulation and multiply the chances of improvement, and one improvement begets another.   Yet I may safely ask, how many good poets, how many able mathematicians, how many great inventors in arts and sciences, had Europe, north of the Alps, then produced? And it was sixteen centuries after this before a Newton could be formed. I do not mean to deny that there are varieties in the race of man, distinguished by their powers both of body and mind. I believe there are, as I see to be the case in the races of other animals.   I only mean to suggest a doubt, whether the bulk and faculties of animals depend on the side of the Atlantic on which their food happens to grow, or which furnishes the elements of which they are compounded? Whether nature has enlisted herself as a Cis- or Trans-Atlantic partisan?   I am induced to suspect there has been more eloquence than sound reasoning displayed in support of this theory.   .   .   .

Great question has arisen from whence came those aboriginals of America?   Discoveries, long ago made, were sufficient to show that the passage from Europe to America was always practicable, even to the imperfect navigation of ancient times.   In going from Norway to Iceland, from Iceland to Greenland, from Greenland to Labrador, the first traject is the widest; and this having been practised from the earliest times of which we have any account of that part of the earth, it is not difficult to suppose that the subsequent trajects may have been sometimes passed.   Again, the late discoveries of Captain Cook, coasting from Kamschatka to California, have proved that if the two continents of Asia and America be separated at all, it is only by a narrow strait.   So that from this side also, inhabitants may have passed into America; and the resemblance between the Indians of America and the eastern inhabitants of Asia, would induce us to conjecture, that the former are the descendants of the latter, or the latter of the former; excepting indeed the Esquimaux, who, from the same circumstance of resemblance, and from identity of language must be derived from the Greenlanders, and these probably from some of the northern parts of the old continent.   A knowledge of their several languages would be the most certain evidence of their

derivation which could be produced. In fact, it is the best
proof of the affinity of nations which ever can be referred to.
How many ages have elapsed since the English, the Dutch,
the Germans, the Swiss, the Norwegians, Danes and Swedes
have separated from their common stock? Yet how many
more must elapse before the proofs of their common origin,
which exist in their several languages, will disappear? It is
to be lamented, then, very much to be lamented, that we
have suffered so many of the Indian tribes already to extinguish, without our having previously collected and deposited
in the records of literature, the general rudiments at least
of the languages they spoke. Were vocabularies formed of
all the languages spoken in North and South America, preserving their appellations of the most common objects in
nature, of those which must be present to every nation barbarous or civilized, with the inflections of their nouns and
verbs, their principles of regimen and concord, and these deposited in all the public libraries, it would furnish opportunities to those skilled in the languages of the old world to
compare them with these, now, or at any future time, and
hence to construct the best evidence of the derivation of this
part of the human race.

AN UNHAPPY INFLUENCE OF SLAVERY

[FROM THE SAME]

There must doubtless be an unhappy influence on the
manners of our people produced by the existence of slavery
among us. The whole commerce between master and slave
is a perpetual exercise of the most boisterous passions, the
most unremitting despotism, on the one part, and degrading
submissions on the other. Our children see this, and learn
to imitate it; for man is an imitative animal. This quality
is the germ of all education in him. From his cradle to his
grave he is learning to do what he sees others do. If a
parent could find no motive either in his philanthropy or his
self-love, for restraining the intemperance of passion towards
his slave, it should always be a sufficient one that his child
is present. But generally it is not sufficient. The parent

storms, the child looks on, catches the lineaments of wrath, puts on the same airs in the circle of smaller slaves, gives a loose to the worst of passions, and thus nursed, educated, and daily exercised in tyranny, cannot but be stamped by it with odious peculiarities. The man must be a prodigy who can retain his manners and morals undepraved by such circumstances.

THE RULE OF THE PEOPLE
[FROM THE SAME]

Every government degenerates when trusted to the rulers of the people alone. The people themselves therefore are its only safe depositories. And to render even them safe, their minds must be improved to a certain degree. This indeed is not all that is necessary, though it be essentially necessary. An amendment of our constitution must here come in aid of the public education. The influence over government must be shared among all the people. If every individual which composes their mass participates of the ultimate authority, the government will be safe; because the corrupting the whole mass will exceed any private resources of wealth; and public ones cannot be provided but by levies on the people. In this case every man would have to pay his own price.

ARCHITECTURE IN VIRGINIA
[FROM THE SAME]

The private buildings are very rarely constructed of stone or brick, much the greater proportion being of scantling and boards, plastered with lime. It is impossible to devise things more ugly, uncomfortable, and happily more perishable. There are two or three plans, on one of which, according to its size, most of the houses in the State are built. The poorest people build huts of logs, laid horizontally in pens, stopping the interstices with mud. These are warmer in winter, and cooler in summer, than the more expensive constructions of scantling and plank. . . The only public buildings worthy of mention are the Capitol, the Palace, the

College, and the Hospital for Lunatics, all of them in Williamsburg, heretofore the seat of our government. The Capitol is a light and airy structure, with a portico in front of two orders, the lower of which, being Doric, is tolerably just in its proportions and ornaments, save only that the intercolonations are too large. The upper is Ionic, much too small for that on which it is mounted, its ornaments not proper to the order, nor proportioned within themselves. It is crowned with a pediment, which is too high for its span. Yet, on the whole, it is the most pleasing piece of architecture we have. The Palace is not handsome without, but it is spacious and commodious within, is prettily situated, and with the grounds annexed to it, is capable of being made an elegant seat. The College and Hospital are rude, mis-shapen piles, which, but that they have roofs, would be taken for brick-kilns. There are no other public buildings but churches and courthouses, in which no attempts are made at elegance. Indeed, it would not be easy to execute such an attempt, as a workman could scarcely be found here capable of drawing an order. The genius of architecture seems to have shed its maledictions over this land. Buildings are often erected, by individuals, of considerable expense. To give these symmetry and taste, would not increase their cost. It would only change the arrangement of the materials, the form and combination of the members. This would often cost less than the burthen of barbarous ornaments with which these buildings are sometimes charged. But the first principles of the art are unknown, and there exists scarcely a model among us sufficiently chaste to give an idea of them. Architecture being one of the fine arts, and as such within the department of a professor of the college, according to the new arrangement, perhaps a spark may fall on some young subjects of natural taste, kindle up their genius, and produce a reformation in this elegant and useful art.

ON RELIGIOUS TOLERATION

[FROM THE SAME]

.   .   .   Our rulers can have no authority over such natural rights, only as we have submitted to them. The rights of conscience we never submitted, we could not submit. We are answerable for them to our God. The legitimate powers of government extend to such acts only as are injurious to others. But it does me no injury for my neighbor to say there are twenty gods, or no god. It neither picks my pocket nor breaks my leg. If it be said his testimony in a court of justice cannot be relied on, reject it then, and be the stigma on him. Constraint may make him worse by making him a hypocrite, but it will never make him a truer man. It may fix him obstinately in his errors, but will not cure them. Reason and free inquiry are the only effectual agents against error. Give a loose to them, they will support the true religion by bringing every false one to their tribunal, to the test of their investigation. They are the natural enemies of error, and of error only. Had not the Roman government permitted free inquiry, Christianity could never have been introduced. Had not free inquiry been indulged at the era of the Reformation, the corruptions of Christianity could not have been purged away. If it be restrained now, the present corruptions will be protected, and new ones encouraged. Was the government to prescribe to us our medicine and diet, our bodies would be in such keeping as our souls are now. Thus in France the emetic was once forbidden as a medicine, and the potato as an article of food. Government is just as infallible, too, when it fixes systems in physics. Galileo was sent to the Inquisition for affirming that the earth was a sphere; the government had declared it to be as flat as a trencher, and Galileo was obliged to abjure his error. This error, however, at length prevailed, the earth became a globe, and Descartes declared it was whirled round its axis by a vortex. The government in which he lived was wise enough to see that this was no question of civil jurisdiction, or we should all have been involved by authority in vortices.

In fact the vortices have been exploded, and the Newtonian principle of gravitation is now more firmly established, on the basis of reason, than it would be were the government to step in and to make it an article of necessary faith. Reason and experiment have been indulged, and error has fled before them. It is error alone which needs the support of government. Truth can stand by itself. Subject opinion to coercion: whom will you make your inquisitors? Fallible men; men governed by bad passions, by private as well as public reasons. And why subject it to coercion? To produce uniformity. But is uniformity of opinion desirable? No more than of face and stature. Introduce the bed of Procrustes then, and as there is danger that the large men may beat the small, make us all of a size, by lopping the former and stretching the latter. Difference of opinion is advantageous in religion. The several sects perform the office of a *censor morum* over each other. Is uniformity attainable? Millions of innocent men, women, and children, since the introduction of Christianity, have been burnt, tortured, fined, imprisoned; yet we have not advanced one inch towards uniformity. What has been the effect of coercion? To make one half the world fools, and the other half hypocrites. To support roguery and error all over the earth. Let us reflect that it is inhabited by a thousand millions of people. That these profess probably a thousand different systems of religion. That ours is but one of that thousand. That if there be but one right, and ours that one, we should wish to see the nine hundred and ninety-nine wandering sects gathered into the fold of truth. But against such a majority we cannot effect this by force. Reason and persuasion are the only practicable instruments. To make way for these, free inquiry must be indulged; and how can we wish others to indulge it while we refuse it ourselves.

PATRICK HENRY

Patrick Henry, traditionally accepted as the greatest of Revolutionary orators, was born in Studley, Virginia, in 1736. With a limited education and after a few weeks' reading of law he was admitted to the bar, on condition that he should continue his legal studies. He was soon recognized as an orator and popular leader. Elected to the House of Burgesses in the year of the Stamp Act, 1765, he led the "up-country" radical party against the more moderate counsels of "tide-water" Virginia. Introducing plain-spoken resolutions claiming for the colonial assembly the "sole right to lay taxes," he won over the house in a speech of which we have only the celebrated climax: "Caesar had his Brutus; Charles the First, his Cromwell; and George the Third [shouts of "treason"]—and George the Third may profit by their example. If this be treason, make the most of it." These resolutions raised the spirit of the other colonies; "the Virginia action," Frothingham says, "roused the patriots like an alarum." In the Continental Congress, in which he took a prominent part in 1775-1776, Henry rose above provincial lines; "I am not a Virginian," he declared, "I am an American." After the dissolution of the Virginia Assembly by the governor in 1774, he sat in the revolutionary convention which met in Richmond in 1775. Here on the resolution, "That this colony be put in a posture of defense," he delivered the speech for which he is famous. Even in print the peroration shows the passion of the born orator which catches fire from occasion and audience; "voice, countenance, and gestures gave an irresistible force to his words." This speech is preserved only in a version given by Wirt in his *Life of Henry*, 1817, which may be more or less apocryphal. Yet the most competent judge, Professor Tyler (in his *Patrick Henry*), thinks it "probably far more accurate and authentic than are most of the famous speeches attributed to public characters before reporters' galleries were opened." After the Revolution Henry was several times governor of Virginia; he declined appointments as secretary of state and chief justice of the United States. Until 1786 he advocated a strong central government; but changing his views he declined to sit in the Constitutional Convention of 1787, and opposed the adoption of the Constitution. In 1795 he retired with ample means to his estate at Red Hill, Charlotte County, where he died in 1799.

LIBERTY OR DEATH

[A SPEECH IN THE VIRGINIA CONVENTION, 1775, AS REPORTED IN WIRT'S "LIFE OF PATRICK HENRY." 1817]

No man thinks more highly than I do of the patriotism, as well as abilities, of the very worthy gentlemen who have just addressed the house. But different men often see the same subjects in different lights; and, therefore, I hope it will not be thought disrespectful to those gentlemen, if, entertaining as I do, opinions of a character very opposite to theirs, I shall speak forth *my* sentiments freely, and without reserve. This is no time for ceremony. The question before the house is one of awful moment to this country. For my own part, I consider it as nothing less than a question of freedom or slavery. And in proportion to the magnitude of the subject, ought to be the freedom of the debate. It is only in this way that we can hope to arrive at truth, and fulfil the great responsibility which we hold to God and our country. Should I keep back my opinions at such a time, through fear of giving offense, I should consider myself as guilty of treason towards my country, and of an act of disloyalty toward the majesty of Heaven, which I revere above all earthly kings.

Mr. President, it is natural to man to indulge in the illusions of hope. We are apt to shut our eyes against a painful truth—and listen to the song of that siren, till she transforms us into beasts. Is this the part of wise men, engaged in a great and arduous struggle for liberty? Are we disposed to be of the number of those, who having eyes, see not, and having ears, hear not, the things which so nearly concern their temporal salvation? For my part, whatever anguish of spirit it may cost, I am willing to know the whole truth; to know the worst, and to provide for it.

I have but one lamp by which my feet are guided; and that is the lamp of experience. I know of no way of judging of the future but by the past. And judging by the past, I wish to know what there has been in the conduct of the British ministry for the last ten years, to justify those hopes with which gentlemen have been pleased to solace themselves and the house? Is it that insidious smile with which our petition has been lately received? Trust it not, sir; it will prove a snare to your feet. Suffer not yourselves to be betrayed with a kiss. Ask yourselves how this gracious reception of our petition comports with those warlike preparations which cover our waters and darken our land. Are fleets and armies necessary to a work of love and reconciliation? Have we shown ourselves so unwilling to be reconciled, that force must be called in to win back our love? Let us not deceive ourselves, sir. These are the implements of war and subjugation—the last arguments to which kings resort. I ask gentlemen, sir, what means this martial array, if its purpose be not to force us to submission? Can gentlemen assign any other possible motive for it? Has Great Britain any enemy in this quarter of the world, to call for all this accumulation of navies and armies? No, sir, she has none. They are meant for us: they can be meant for no other. They are sent over to bind and rivet upon us those chains, which the British ministry have been so long forging. And what have we to oppose to them? Shall we try argument? Sir, we have been trying that for the last ten years. Have we anything new to offer upon the subject? Nothing. We have held the subject up in every light of which it is capable; but it has been all in vain. Shall we resort to entreaty and humble supplication? What terms shall we find, which have not been already exhausted? Let us not, I beseech you, sir, deceive ourselves longer. Sir, we have done everything that could be done, to avert the storm which is now coming on. We have petitioned—we have remonstrated—we have supplicated—we have prostrated ourselves before the throne, and have implored its interposition to arrest the tyrannical hands of the ministry and Parliament. Our petitions have been slighted; our remonstrances have produced additional violence and insult, our supplications have been disregarded; and we have been spurned, with contempt, from the foot of the throne. In vain, after these things, may we indulge the fond hope of peace and reconciliation. *There is no longer any room for hope.* If we wish to be free—if we mean to preserve inviolate those inestimable privileges for which we have been so long contending—if we mean not basely to abandon the noble struggle in which we have been so long engaged, and which we have pledged ourselves never to abandon, until the glorious object of our contest shall be obtained—we must fight!—I repeat it, sir, we must fight!! An appeal to arms and to the God of Hosts, is all that is left us!

They tell us, sir, that we are weak—unable to cope with so formidable an adversary. But when shall we be stronger? Will it be the next week or the next year? Will it be when we are totally disarmed, and when a British guard shall be stationed in every house? Shall we gather strength by irresolution and inaction? Shall we acquire the means of effectual resistance by lying supinely on our backs, and hugging the delusive phantom of hope, until our enemies shall have bound us hand and foot? Sir, we are not weak, if we make a proper use of those means which the God of nature hath placed in our power. Three millions of people, armed in the holy cause of liberty, and in such a country as that which we possess, are invincible by any force which our enemy can send against us. Besides, sir, we shall not fight our battles alone. There is a just God who presides over the destinies of nations; and who will raise up friends to fight our battles for us. The battle, sir, is not to the strong alone; it is to the vigilant, the active, the brave. Besides, sir, we have no election. If we were base enough to desire it, it is now too late to retire from the contest. There is no retreat but in submission and slavery! Our chains are forged. Their clanking may be heard on the plains of Boston! The war is inevitable—and let it come!! I repeat it, sir, let it come!!!

It is vain, sir, to extenuate the matter. Gentlemen may cry, peace, peace—but there is no peace. The war is actually begun! The next gale that sweeps from the north will bring to our ears the clash of resounding arms! Our brethren are already in the field! Why stand we here idle? What is it that gentlemen wish? What would they have? Is life so dear, or peace so sweet, as to be purchased at the price of chains and slavery? Forbid it, Almighty God! I know not what course others may take; but as for me, give me liberty, or give me death!

THOMAS PAINE

Thomas Paine, an invaluable and, on the whole, ill-repaid servant of the Revolutionary cause, was an Englishman of humble birth and little education, who after a not very successful or creditable career at home, decided, at the age of thirty-eight, to transfer his fortunes to America. With a letter of recommendation from Franklin—whom he met in London, and who perhaps divined his usefulness—he appeared in Philadelphia in November, 1774. From being a disaffected Englishman he became, as it were overnight, an active, well-informed, and useful American. Though he says he had never "published a syllable," he had in some way acquired a prose style, he was a born journalist and propagandist, and he soon caught the revolutionary spirit. "It was the cause of America," he afterward said, "that made me an author." During 1775 he edited the newly established *Pennsylvania Magazine,* and for the *Pennsylvania Journal* he wrote against slavery, and (in "A Serious Thought") probably made the first open mention of independence. This led to his famous pamphlet, published in January, 1776, *Common Sense,* which was reprinted in colony after colony, to the number (Paine says) of 120,000 in three months, and which did more than any other writing to bring about the Declaration in July. He then served in the army, taking his full part throughout in the labors and privations of the war. He shared in the series of disasters ending in Washington's escape across the Delaware. During this retreat, "writing," he says, "at every place we stopped at," he composed No. I of *The Crisis*—a fitly named pamphlet, beginning, "These are the times that try men's souls." This appeared in December, 1776. Employing the same title he continued to rally and encourage the Americans at each crisis of the war—until in No. XIII, published in December, 1783, he could say, "The times that tried men's souls are over." Returning in 1787 to England he published in answer to Burke's *Reflections on the Revolution in France* his *Rights of Man,* to spread the doctrines learned in America,—which he declared "were to liberty what grammar is to language." To escape arrest he fled to France, took part in the French Revolution, and while in prison wrote in defence of deism his *Age of Reason.* Coming back in 1802 to end his international career in the United States, he was ostracized for an unjustified attack on Washington, for his opposition to slavery, and for his radicalism and infidelity. He died in poverty in New York in 1809, and was buried in New Rochelle.

Paine knew little of law or government, and at best could attack great problems only with "common sense." He was intemperate,—often coarse and abusive. But he could write with unequalled effectiveness for the people; and in the main he supported great causes,—those of abolition, independence, and union. The style, like the ideas, of his pamphlets marks a revolution; it throws off the dignity and formality of the eighteenth century and becomes democratic, —simple, vigorous, colloquial and direct. And his theory of style, like his chief theories of American government, is found to be correct; "To fit the powers of thinking and the turn of language to the subject, so as to bring out a clear conclusion that shall hit the point in question, is the true criterion of writing."

A SERIOUS THOUGHT

[FROM THE "PENNSYLVANIA JOURNAL," OCTOBER 18, 1775]

When I reflect on the horrid cruelties exercised by Britain in the East Indies, how thousands perished by artificial famine; how religion and every manly principle of honor and honesty were sacrificed to luxury and pride; when I read of the wretched natives being blown away, for no other crime than because, sickened with the miserable scene, they refused to fight;—when I reflect on these and a thousand instances of similar barbarity, I firmly believe that the Almighty, in compassion to mankind, will curtail the power of Britain.

And when I reflect on the use she hath made of the

discovery of this new world,; that the little paltry dignity of earthly kings hath been set up in preference to the great cause of the King of kings; that instead of Christian examples to the Indians, she hath basely tampered with their passions, imposed on their ignorance, and made them tools of treachery and murder; and when to these and many other malancholy reflections I add this sad remark, that ever since the discovery of America she hath employed herself in the most horrid of all traffics, that of human flesh, unknown to the most savage nations, hath yearly (without provocation and in cold blood) ravaged the hapless shores of Africa, robbing it of its unoffending inhabitants to cultivate her stolen dominions in the West;—when I reflect on these, I hesitate for not a moment to believe that the Almighty will finally separate America from Britain. Call it Independence or what you will, if it is the cause of God and humanity it will go on.

And when the Almighty shall have blessed us, and made us a people *dependent only upon Him,* then may our first gratitude be shown by an act of continental legislation, which shall put a stop to the importation of negroes for sale, soften the hard fate of those already here, and in time procure their freedom.

Humanus.

THOUGHTS ON THE PRESENT STATE OF AMERICAN AFFAIRS

[FROM "COMMON SENSE." 1776]

In the following pages I offer nothing more than simple facts, plain arguments, and common sense: and have no other preliminaries to settle with the reader, than that he will divest himself of prejudice and prepossession, and suffer his reason and his feelings to determine for themselves: that he will put on, or rather that he will not put off, the true character of a man, and generously enlarge his views beyond the present day.

Volumes have been written on the subject of the struggle between England and America. Men of all ranks have embarked in the controversy, from different motives, and with various designs; but all have been ineffectual, and the period of debate is closed. Arms as the last resource decide the contest; the appeal was the choice of the King, and the Continent has accepted the challenge. . . .

But Britain is the parent country, say some. Then the more shame upon her conduct. Even brutes do not devour their young, nor savages make war upon their families. Wherefore, the assertion, if true, turns to her reproach; but it happens not to be true, or only partly so, and the phrase *parent* or *mother country* hath been jesuitically adopted by the King and his parisites, with the low papistical design of gaining an unfair bias on the credulous weakness of our minds. Europe, and not England, is the parent country of America. This new World hath been the asylum for the persecuted lovers of civil and religious liberty from *every part* of Europe. Hither have they fled, not from the tender embraces of the mother, but from the cruelty of the monster; and it is so far true of England, that the same tyranny which drove the first emigrants from home, pursues their descendents still.

In this extensive quarter of the globe, we forget the narrow limits of three hundred and sixty miles (the extent of England) and carry our friendship on a larger scale; we claim brotherhood with every European Christian, and triumph in the generosity of the sentiment. . . .

I challenge the warmest advocate for reconciliation to show a single advantage that this continent can reap by being connected with Great Britain. I repeat the challenge; not a single advantage is derived. Our corn will fetch its price in any market in Europe, and our imported goods must be paid for, buy them where we will.

But the injuries and disadvantages which we sustain by that connection, are without number; and our duty to mankind at large, as well as to ourselves, instruct us to renounce the alliance: because, any submission to, or dependence on, Great Britain, tends directly to involve this Continent in European wars and quarrels, and set us at variance with nations who would otherwise seek our friendship, and against whom we have neither anger nor complaint. As Europe is our market for trade, we ought to form no partial connection with any part of it. It is the true interest of America to steer clear of European contentions, which she can never do, while, by her dependence on Britain, she is made the make-weight in the scale of British politics.

Europe is too thickly planted with kingdoms to be long at peace, and whenever a war breaks out between England and any foreign power, the trade of America goes to ruin, *because of her connection with Britain*. The next war may not turn out like the last, and should it not, the advocates of reconciliation now will be wishing for separation then, because neutrality in that case would be a safer convoy than a man of war. Everything that is right or reasonable pleads for separation. The blood of the slain, the weeping voice of nature cries, 'TIS TIME TO PART. Even the distance at which the Almighty hath placed England and America is a strong and natural proof that the authority of the one over the other, was never the design of Heaven. The time likewise at which the Continent was discovered, adds weight to the argument, and the manner in which it was peopled, increases the force of it. The Reformation was preceded by the discovery of America: as if the Almighty graciously meant to open a sanctuary to the persecuted in future years, when home should afford neither friendship nor safety.

The authority of Great Britain over this continent, is a form of government, which sooner or later must have an end: and a serious mind can draw no true pleasure by looking forward, under the painful and positive conviction that what he calls "the present constitution" is merely temporary. As parents, we can have no joy, knowing that this government is not sufficiently lasting to ensure anything which we may bequeath to posterity: and by a plain method of argument, as we are running the next generation into debt, we ought to do the work of it, otherwise we use them meanly and pitifully. In order to discover the line of our duty rightly, we should take our children in our hand, and fix our station a few years farther in life; that eminence will present a prospect which a few present fears and prejudices conceal from our sight.

Though I would carefully avoid giving unnecessary offence, yet I am inclined to believe, that all those who espouse the doctrine of reconciliation, may be included within the following descriptions.

Interested men, who are not to be trusted, weak men who *cannot* see, prejudiced men who will not see, and a certain set of moderate men who think better of the European world than it deserves; and this last class, by an ill-judged deliberation, will be the cause of more calamities to this continent than all the other three.

It is the good fortune of many to live distant from the scene of present sorrow; the evil is not sufficiently brought to their doors to make them feel the precariousness with which all American property is possessed. But let our imaginations transport us a few moments to Boston; that seat of wretchedness will teach us wisdom, and instruct us forever to renounce a power in whom we can have no trust. The inhabitants of that unfortunate city who but a few months ago were in ease and affluence, have now no other alternative than to stay and starve, or turn out to beg. Endangered by the fire of their friends if they continue within the city, and plundered by the soldiery if they leave it, in their present situation they are prisoners without the hope of redemption, and in a general attack for their relief they would be exposed to the fury of both armies.

Men of passive tempers look somewhat lightly over the offences of Great Britain, and, still hoping for the best, are apt to call out, *Come, come, we shall be friends again for all this*. But examine the passions and feelings of mankind; bring the doctrine of reconciliation to the touchstone of nature, and then tell me whether you can hereafter love, honor, and faithfully serve the power that hath carried fire and sword into your land? If you cannot do all these, then are you only deceiving yourselves, and by your delay bringing ruin upon posterity. Your future connection with Britain, whom you can neither love nor honor, will be forced and unnatural, and being formed only on the plan of present convenience, will in a little time fall into a relapse more wretched than the first. But if you say, you can still pass the violations over, then I ask, hath your house been burnt? Hath your property been destroyed before your face? Are your wife and children destitute of a bed to lie on, or bread to live on? Have you lost a parent or a child by their hands, and yourself the ruined and wretched survivor? If you have not, then you are not a judge of those who have. But if you have, and can still shake hands with the murderers, then are you unworthy of the name of husband, father, friend, or lover, and whatever may be your rank or title in life, you have the heart of a coward, and the spirit of a sycophant.

This is not inflaming or exaggerating matters, but trying them by those feelings and affections which nature justifies, and without which we should be incapable of discharging the social duties of life, or enjoying the felicities of it. I mean not to exhibit horror for the purpose of provoking revenge, but to awaken us from fatal and unmanly slumbers, that we may pursue determinedly some fixed object. 'Tis not in the power of Britain or of Europe to conquer America, if she doth not conquer herself by delay and timidity. The present winter is worth an age if rightly employed, but if lost or neglected the whole continent will partake of the misfortune; and there is no punishment which that man doth not deserve, be he who or what, or where he will, that may be the means of sacrificing a season so precious and useful.

'Tis repugnant to reason, to the universal order of things, to all the examples of former ages, to suppose that this Continent can long remain subject to any external power. The most sanguine in Britain doth not think so. The utmost stretch of human wisdom cannot, at this time, compass a plan, short of separation, which can promise the continent even a year's security. Reconciliation is *now* a fallacious dream. Nature hath deserted the connection, and art cannot supply her place. For, as Milton wisely expresses, "never can true reconcilement grow where wounds of deadly hate have pierced so deep."

Every quiet method for peace hath proved ineffectual. Our prayers have been rejected with disdain; and only tended to convince us that nothing flatters vanity or confirms obstinacy in Kings more than repeated petitioning—and nothing hath contributed more than that very measure to

make the Kings of Europe absolute. Witness Denmark and
Sweden.   Wherefore, since nothing but blows will do, for
God's sake let us come to a final separation, and not leave the
next generation to be cutting throats under the violated
unmeaning names of parent and child.

THE TIMES THAT TRY MEN'S SOULS

[FROM "THE CRISIS," I. 1776]

These are the times that try men's souls. The summer
soldier and the sunshine patriot will, in this crisis, shrink
from the service of their country; but he that stands it *now,*
deserves the love and thanks of man and woman. Tyranny,
like hell, is not easily conquered; yet we have this consolation
with us, that the harder the conflict, the more glorious the
triumph. What we obtain too cheap, we esteem too lightly:
it is dearness only that gives everything its value. Heaven
knows how to put a proper price upon its goods; and it
would be strange indeed if so celestial an article as FREEDOM
should not be highly rated. Britain, with an army to
enforce her tyranny, has declared that she has a right (*not
only to* TAX) but "to BIND US IN ALL CASES WHATSOEVER,"
and it being *bound in that manner* is not slavery, then is
there not such a thing as slavery upon earth. Even the
expression is impious; for so unlimited a power can belong
only to God.

Whether the independence of the continent was declared
too soon, or delayed too long, I will not now enter into as
an argument; my own simple opinion is, that had it been
eight months earlier, it would have been much better. We
did not make a proper use of last winter, neither could we,
while we were in a dependent state. However, the fault, if
it were one, was all our own; we have none to blame but
ourselves. But no great deal is lost yet. All that Howe has
been doing for this month past, is rather a ravage than a
conquest, which the spirit of the Jerseys, a year ago, would
have quickly repulsed, and which time and a little resolution
will soon recover.

I have as little superstition in me as any man living, but

my secret opinion has ever been, and still is, that God Almighty will not give up a people to military destruction, or leave them unsupportedly to perish, who have so earnestly and so repeatedly sought to avoid the calamities of war, by every decent method which wisdom could invent. Neither have I so much of the infidel in me, as to suppose that He has relinquished the government of the world, and given us up to the care of devils; and as I do not, I cannot see on what grounds the king of Britain can look up to heaven for help against us: a common murderer, a highwayman, or a house-breaker, has as good a pretence as he.

TO THOSE WHO HAVE STOOD
[FROM THE SAME]

Quitting this class of men, I turn with the warm ardor of a friend to those who have nobly stood, and are yet determined to stand the matter out: I call not upon a few, but upon all: not on *this* state or *that* state, but on *every* state: up and help us; lay your shoulders to the wheel; better have too much force than too little, when so great an object is at stake. Let it be told to the future world, that in the depth of winter, when nothing but hope and virtue could survive, the city and the country, alarmed at one common danger, came forth to meet and to repulse it. Say not that thousands are gone, turn out your tens of thousands; throw not the burden of the day upon Providence, but *"show your faith by your works,"* that God may bless you. It matters not where you live, or what rank of life you hold, the evil or the blessing will reach you all. The far and the near, the home counties and the back, the rich and the poor, will suffer or rejoice alike. The heart that feels not now, is dead: the blood of his children will curse his cowardice, who shrinks back at a time when a little might have saved the whole, and made *them* happy. I love the man that can smile in trouble, that can gather strength from distress, and grow brave by reflection. 'Tis the business of little minds to shrink; but he whose heart is firm, and whose conscience approves his conduct, will pursue his principles unto death.

My own line of reasoning is to myself as straight and clear as a ray of light.

TO LORD HOWE [1]

[FROM "THE CRISIS," II.]

As a military man your lordship may hold out the sword of war, and call it the *"ultima ratio regum": the last reason of kings;* we in return can show you the sword of justice, and call it, "the best scourge of tyrants." The first of these two may threaten, or even frighten for a while, and cast a sickly languor over an insulted people, but reason will soon recover the debauch, and restore them to tranquil fortitude. Your lordship, I find, has now commenced author, and published a Proclamation; I have published a Crisis: as they stand, they are the antipodes of each other; both cannot rise at once, and one of them must descend; and so quick is the revolution of things, that your lordship's performance, I see, has already fallen many degress from its first place, and is now just visible on the edge of the political horizon.

It is surprising to what a pitch of infatuation, blind folly and obstinacy will carry mankind, and your lordship's drowsy proclamation is a proof that it does not even quit them in their sleep. Perhaps you thought America too was taking a nap, and therefore chose, like Satan to Eve, to whisper the delusion softly, lest you should awaken her. This continent, sir, is too extensive to sleep all at once, and too watchful, even in its slumbers, not to startle at the unhallowed foot of an invader. You may issue your proclamations, and welcome, for we have learned to "reverence ourselves," and scorn the insulting ruffian that employs you. America, for your deceased brother's sake, would gladly have shown you respect, and it is a new aggravation to her feelings, that Howe should be forgetful, and raise his sword against those, who at their own charge raised a monument to his brother.[2]   But your

---

[1] [Viscount Howe had been sent to negotiate with Congress.]

[2] [George Augustus Howe fell at Ticonderoga, 1758. The General Court of Massachusetts appropriated £250 for a monument in Westminster Abbey.]

master has commanded, and you have not enough nature left to refuse. Surely there must be something strangely degenerating in the love of monarchy, that can so completely wear a man down to an ingrate, and make him proud to lick the dust that kings have trod upon. A few more years, should you survive them, will bestow on you the title of an "old man": and in some hour of future reflection you may probably find the fitness of Wolsey's despairing penitence—"had I served my God as faithfully as I served my king, he would not thus have forsaken me in my old age."

The character you appear to us in, is truly ridiculous. Your friends, the tories, announced your coming, with high descriptions of your unlimited powers; but your proclamation has given them the lie, by showing you to be a commissioner without authority. Had your powers been ever so great they were nothing to us, further than we pleased; because we had the same right which other nations had, to do what we thought was best. *"The* UNITED STATES OF AMERICA," will sound as pompously in the world or in history, as "the kingdom of Great Britain;" the character of *General Washington* will fill a page with as much lustre as that of *Lord Howe*: and the *congress* have as much right to command the *king and parliament* in London to desist from legislation, as *they* or *you* have to command the congress. Only suppose how laughable such an edict would appear from us, and then, in that merry mood, do but turn the tables upon yourself, and you will see how your proclamation is received here. Having thus placed you in a proper position in which you may have a full view of your folly, and learn to despise it, I hold up to you, for that purpose, the following quotation from your own lunarian proclamation.—"And we (Lord Howe and General Howe) do command (and in his Majesty's name forsooth) all such persons as are assembled together, under the name of general or provincial congresses, committees, conventions or other associations, by whatever name or names known and distinguished, to desist and cease from all such treasonable actings and doings."

You introduce your proclamation by referring to your declarations of the 14th of July and 19th of September. **In**

the last of these you sunk yourself below the character of a
private gentleman. That I may not seem to accuse you
unjustly, I shall state the circumstance: by a verbal invita-
tion of yours, communicated to congress by General Sullivan,
then a prisoner on his parole, you signified your desire of
conferring with some members of that body as private gentlemen. It was beneath the dignity of the American congress
to pay any regard to a message that at best was but a genteel
affront, and had too much of the ministerial complexion of
tampering with private persons; and which might probably
have been the case, had the gentlemen who were deputed on
the business possessed that kind of easy virtue which an
English courtier is so truly distinguished by. Your request,
however, was complied with, for honest men are naturally
more tender of their civil than their political fame. The
interview ended as every sensible man thought it would; for
your lordship knows, as well as the writer of the Crisis, that
it is impossible for the king of England to promise the
repeal, or even the revisal of any acts of parliament; wherefore, on your part, you had nothing to say, more than to
request, in the room of demanding, the entire surrender of
the continent; and then, if that was complied with, to
promise that the inhabitants should escape with their lives.
This was the upshot of the conference. You informed the
conferees that you were two months in soliciting these
powers. We ask, what powers? for as commissioner you
have none. If you mean the power of pardoning, it is an
oblique proof that your master was determined to sacrifice all
before him, and that you were two months in dissuading
him from his purpose. Another evidence of his savage obstinacy! From your own account of the matter we may
justly draw these two conclusions: 1st, That you serve a
monster; and 2nd, That never was a messenger sent on a
more foolish errand than yourself. This plain language may
perhaps sound uncouthly to an ear vitiated by courtly refinements, but words were made for use, and the fault lies in
deserving them, or the abuse in applying them unfairly.

Soon after your return to New York, you published a
very illiberal and unmanly handbill against the congress; for
it was certainly stepping out of the line of common civility,

first to screen your national pride by soliciting an interview with them as private gentlemen, and in the conclusion to endeavor to deceive the multitude by making a handbill attack on the whole body of the congress; you got them together under one name, and abused them under another. But the king you serve, and the cause you support, afford you so few instances of acting the gentleman, that out of pity to your situation the congress pardoned the insult by taking no notice of it.

You say in that handbill, "that they, the congress, disavowed every purpose for reconciliation not consonant with their extravagant and inadmissable claim of independence." Why, God bless me! what have you to do with our independence? We ask no leave of yours to set it up; we ask no money of yours to support it; we can do better without your fleets and armies than with them; you may soon have enough to do to protect yourselves without being burdened with us. We are very willing to be at peace with you, to buy of you and sell to you, and, like young beginners in the world, to work for our living; therefore, why do you put yourselves out of cash, when we know you cannot spare it, and we do not desire you to run into debt? I am willing, sir, that you should see your folly in every point of view I can place it in, and for that reason descend sometimes to tell you in jest what I wish you to see in earnest. But to be more serious with you, why do you say, "their independence?" To set you right, sir, we tell you, that the independency is ours, not theirs. The congress were authorized by every state on the continent to publish it to all the world, and in so doing are not to be considered as the inventors, but only as the heralds that proclaimed it, or the office from which the sense of the people received a legal form; and it was as much as any or all their heads were worth, to have treated with you on the subject of submission under any name whatever. But we know the men in whom we have trusted; can England say the same of her parliament?

PEACE AND UNION

[From "The Crisis," XIII.]

"The times that tried men's souls," are over—and the greatest and completest revolution the world ever knew, gloriously and happily accomplished.

But to pass from the extremes of danger to safety—from the tumult of war to the tranquillity of peace, though sweet in contemplation, requires a gradual composure of the senses to receive it. Even calmness has the power of stunning, when it opens too instantly upon us. The long and raging hurricane that should cease in a moment, would leave us in a state rather of wonder than enjoyment; and some moments of recollection must pass, before we could be capable of tasting the felicity of repose. There are but few instances, in which the mind is fitted for sudden transitions: it takes in its pleasures by reflection and comparison and those must have time to act, before the relish for new scenes is complete.

In the present case, the mighty magnitude of the object, the various uncertainties of fate it has undergone, the numerous and complicated dangers we have suffered or escaped, the eminence we now stand on, and the vast prospect before us, must all conspire to impress us with contemplation.

To see it in our power to make a world happy, to teach mankind the art of being so, to exhibit, on the theatre of the universe, a character hitherto unknown, and to have, as it were, a new creation intrusted to our hands, are honors that command reflection, and can neither be too highly estimated, nor too gratefully received.

In this pause then of recollection, while the storm is ceasing, and the long agitated mind vibrating to a rest, let us look back on the scenes we have passed, and learn from experience what is yet to be done. . . .

With the blessings of peace, independence, and an universal commerce, the states, individually and collectively, will have leisure and opportunity to regulate and establish their domestic concerns, and to put it beyond the power of calumny to throw the least reflection on their honor. Character is much easier kept than recovered, and that man, if any such there be, who, from sinister views, or littleness of soul, lends unseen his hand to injure it, contrives a wound it will never be in his power to heal.

As we have established an inheritance for posterity, let that inheritance descend, with every mark of an honorable conveyance. The little it will cost, compared with the worth of the states, the greatness of the object, and the value of the national character, will be a profitable exchange.

But that which must more forcibly strike a thoughtful, penetrating mind, and which includes and renders easy all inferior concerns, is the UNION OF THE STATES. On this our great national character depends. It is this which must give us importance abroad and security at home. It is through this only that we are, or can be, nationally known in the world; it is the flag of the United States which renders our ships and commerce safe on the seas, or in a foreign port. Our Mediterranean passes must be obtained under the same style. All our treaties, whether of alliance, peace, or commerce, are formed under the sovereignty of the United States, and Europe knows us under no other name or title.

The division of the empire into states is for our own convenience, but abroad this distinction ceases. The affairs of each state are local. They can go no further than to itself. And were the whole worth of even the richest of them expended in revenue, it would not be sufficient to support sovereignty against foreign attack. In short, we have no other national sovereignty than as United States. It would even be fatal for us if we had—too expensive to be maintained, and impossible to be supported. Individuals, or individual states, may call themselves what they please; but the world, and especially the world of enemies, is not to be held in awe by the whistling of a name. Sovereignty must have power to protect all the parts that compose and constitute it: and as UNITED STATES we are equal to the importance of the title, but otherwise we are not. Our union, well and wisely regulated and cemented, is the cheapest way of being great— the easiest way of being powerful, and the happiest invention in government which the circumstances of America can admit of. Because it collects from each state, that which, by being inadequate, can be of no use to it, and forms an aggregate that serves for all.

The states of Holland are an unfortunate instance of the effects of individual sovereignty. Their disjointed condition exposes them to numerous intrigues, losses, calamities, and enemies; and the almost impossibility of bringing their measures to a decision, and that decision into execution, is to them, and would be to us, a source of endless misfortune.

It is with confederated states as with individuals in society; something must be yielded up to make the whole secure. In this view of things we gain by what we give, and draw an annual interest greater than the capital. I ever feel myself hurt when I hear the union, that great palladium of our liberty and safety, the least irreverently spoken of. It is the most sacred thing in the constitution of America, and that which every man should be most proud and tender of. Our citizenship in the United States is our national character. Our citizenship in any particular state is only our local distinction. By the latter we are known at home, by the former to the world. Our great title is AMERICANS; our inferior one varies with the place.

REVOLUTIONARY SONGS AND BALLADS

Perhaps nowhere, not even in the pamphlet literature, is "the complexion of the times" better shown than in the popular verse of the Revolution. In songs, ballads, satires, epigrams, and patriotic hymns, the colonists proclaimed their opposition to tyranny and royal aggression; while in the same manner, but frequently with more dignity, the loyalists upheld their side. But apart from the historical significance of these compositions, a few have real merit as literature. Most of them were printed (in colonial newspapers or broadsides) almost as soon as they were composed; but frequently the author's name was withheld, and is unknown to the present day. Practically all appear to have been the work of single authors; with the exception of "Yankee Doodle" there is no important folk ballad of the period—a lack which is to be regretted. Unquestionably much of the contemporary verse now extant could have been improved by the rigorous course of popular transmission—by being subjected to some such "popular editing" as that which contributed so much to the greatness of Spanish and English ballads; but even without this "editing" a number are surprisingly effective. Some, indeed, might have been mutilated by the impatient crowd, and are thus all the better for having come direct from the hands of able individual poets. Whatever excellencies any of them has, however, must be ascribed largely to the deep and ennobling passions which inspired them, and to the worthiness of the British models upon which many of them, especially the songs, were directly fashioned. Considering the conditions under which it was written—the newness of the national life on the continent, the divided opinions existing among the colonists, the brief period of time over which it was composed—Americans have little reason to be ashamed of their Revolutionary verse.

Of the several types—narrative, drinking song, hymn,

prayer, invocation to partisans—the narratives are most numerous and best deserve attention. In their artistry they range from the popular and now famous "Yankee Doodle" to the stirring and melodious "Nathan Hale;" as subjects they treat, in varying degrees of dignity and power, of our best loved military heroes and of our best remembered exploits. There must be a permanent place in our literature, too, for a few compositions of other kinds—such, for instance, as those dignified but eloquently simple poems, "The American Patriot's Prayer" and "The American Soldier's Hymn." The balladry of the chief Revolutionary poets is not included in this section. Freneau and Hopkinson (for the patriots), Odell and Stansbury (for the loyalists) are discussed elsewhere; but it should be kept in mind that much of their work belongs to the poetical genre here illustrated. Whenever known, names of the authors have been given, and likewise the dates of first appearance. The selections have been gathered from various sources, but mostly from Frank Moore's excellent anthology, "Songs and Ballads of the American Revolution."

THE AMERICAN HERO

[By Nathaniel Niles. 1775]

Why should vain mortals tremble at the sight of
Death and destruction in the field of battle,
Where blood and carnage clothe the field in crimson,
      Sounding with death-groans?

Death will invade us by the means appointed;
And we must all bow to the king of terrors;
Nor am I anxious, if I am preparèd,
      What shape he comes in.

Infinite Wisdom teacheth us submission;
Bids us be quiet under all His dealings;
Never repining, but forever praising
      God our Creator.

Well may we praise Him: all His ways are perfect,
Though a resplendence infinitely glowing,
Much hides the glory from the sight of mortals,
      Struck blind by lustre.

Good is Jehovah in bestowing sunshine;
Nor less His goodness in the storm and thunder:
Mercies and judgment both proceed from kindness—
      Infinite kindness!

O then exult that God forever reigneth!
Clouds that around Him hinder our perception,
Bind us the stronger to exalt His name, and
      Shout louder praises!

Then to the goodness of my Lord and Master,
I will commit all that I have or wish for:
Sweetly as babes sleep, will I give my life up
      When called to yield it.

Now, War, I dare thee, clad in smoky pillars,
Bursting from bomb-shells, roaring from the cannon
Rattling in grape-shot, like a storm of hailstones,
      Torturing ether!

To the bleak heavens let the spreading flame rise,
Breaking like Ætna through the smoky columns,
Lowering like Egypt o'er the burning city—
      Wantonly ruined.[1]

While all their hearts quick palpitate for havoc,
Let slip your blood-hounds, named the British lions,
Dauntless as death-stares, nimble as the whirl-wind,
      Dreadful as demons!

Let ocean waft on all your floating castles,
Fraught with combustion, horrible to nature;
Then, with your sails filled by a storm of vengeance,
      Bear down to battle.

[1] Charlestown, near Boston.

From the dire caverns made by ghostly miners,
Let the explosion, dreadful as volcanoes,
Heave the broad town, with all its wealth and people,
    Quick to destruction.

Still shall the banner of the King of Heaven
Never advance where I'm afraid to follow:
While that precedes me, with an open bosom,
    Mars, I defy thee!

Fame and dear Freedom lure me on to battle;
While a fell despot, grimmer than a death's-head,
Stings me with serpents fiercer than Medusa's,
    To the encounter.

Life for my country and the cause of freedom,
Is but a cheap price for a worm to part with:
And if preservèd in so great a contest,
    Life is redoubled.

THE YANKEE'S RETURN FROM CAMP

[ABOUT 1775]

Father and I went down to camp,
  Along with Captain Gooding,
And there we see the men and boys,
  As thick as hasty pudding.
    Chorus—Yankee Doodle, keep it up,
        Yankee Doodle, dandy,
        Mind the music and the step,
        And with the girls be handy.

And there we see a thousand men,
  As rich as 'Squire David;
And what they wasted every day,
  I wish it could be saved.

The 'lasses they eat every day,
  Would keep an house a winter;
They have as much that, I'll be bound,
  They eat it when they're a mind to.

And there we see a swamping gun,
  Large as a log of maple,
Upon a deuced little cart,
  A load for father's cattle.

And every time they shoot it off,
  It takes a horn of powder,
And makes a noise like father's gun,
  Only a nation louder.

I went as nigh to one myself,
  As Siah's underpinning;
And father went as nigh again,
  I thought the deuce was in him.

Cousin Simon grew so bold,
  I thought he would have cock'd it;
It scar'd me so, I shrink'd it off,
  And hung by father's pocket.

And Captain Davis had a gun,
  He kind of clapt his hand on't,
And stuck a crooked stabbing iron
  Upon the little end on't.

And there I see a pumpkin shell
  As big as mother's bason;
And every time they touch'd it off,
  They scamper'd like the nation.

I see a little barrel too,
  The heads were made of leather,
They knock'd upon't with little clubs,
  And call'd the folks together.

And there was Captain Washington,
   And gentlefolks about him,
They say he's grown so tarnal proud,
   He will not ride without 'em.

He got him on his meeting clothes,
   Upon a slapping stallion,
He set the world along in rows,
   In hundreds and in millions.

The flaming ribbons in his hat,
   They look'd so taring fine ah,
I wanted pockily to get,
   To give to my Jemimah.

I see another snarl of men
   A digging graves, they told me,
So tarnal long, so tarnal deep,
   They 'tended they should hold me.

It scar'd me so, I hook'd it off,
   Nor stop'd, as I remember,
Nor turn'd about, 'till I got home,
   Lock'd up in mother's chamber.

YANKEE DOODLE'S SIMPLICITY

Yankee Doodle took a saw,
   With a patriot's devotion,
To trim the tree of liberty
   According to his notion.

He set himself upon a limb,
   Just like some other noodle,
He cut between the tree and him,
   And down came Yankee Doodle.

Yankee Doodle broke his neck,
   And every bone about him,
And then the tree of liberty
   Did very well without him.

THE AMERICAN SOLDIER'S HYMN

'Tis God that girds our armor on
And all our just designs fulfills;
Through Him our feet can swiftly run,
And nimbly climb the steepest hills.

Lessons of war from Him we take,
And manly weapons learn to wield;
Strong bows of steel with ease we break,
Forced by our stronger arms to yield.

'Tis God that still supports our right,
His just revenge our foes pursues;
'Tis He that with resistless might,
Fierce nations to His power subdues.

Our universal safeguard He!
From Whom our lasting honors flow;
He made us great, and set us free
From our remorseless bloody foe.

Therefore to celebrate His fame,
Our grateful voice to Heaven we'll raise;
And nations, strangers to His name,
Shall thus be taught to sing His praise.

THE AMERICAN PATRIOT'S PRAYER

[1776]

Parent of all, omnipotent
In heaven, and earth below,
Through all creation's bounds unspent,
Whose streams of goodness flow,

Teach me to know from whence I rose,
And unto what designed;
No private aims let me propose,
Since link'd with human kind.

But chief to hear my country's voice,
  May all my thoughts incline;
'Tis reason's law, 'tis virtue's choice,
  'Tis nature's call and Thine.

Me from fair Freedom's sacred cause,
  Let nothing e'er divide;
Grandeur, nor gold, nor vain applause,
  Nor friendship false, misguide.

Let me not faction's partial hate
  Pursue to this land's woe;
Nor grasp the thunder of the state
  To wound a private foe.

If, for the right to wish the wrong
  My country shall combine,
Single to serve th' erroneous throng,
  Spite of themselves, be mine.

THE CONGRESS

A SONG

[1776]

Ye Tories all rejoice and sing
Success to George our gracious king;
The faithful subjects tribute bring
    And execrate the Congress.

These hardy knaves and stupid fools;
Some apish and pragmatic mules;
Some servile acquiescing tools;
    These, these compose the Congress.

When Jove resolv'd to send a curse,
And all the woes of life rehearse;
Not plague, not famine, but much worse;
    He curs'd us with a Congress.

Then peace forsook this helpless shore;
Then cannons blaz'd with horrid roar;
We hear of blood, death, wounds and gore;
 The offspring of the Congress.

  * * * * *

With freemen's rights they wanton play;
At their command, we fast and pray;
With worthless paper they us pay;
 A fine device of Congress.

  * * * * *

Our mushroom champions they dragoon;
We cry out hero, not poltroon;
The next campaign we'll storm the moon,
 And there proclaim the Congress.

  * * * * *

O goddess, hear our hearty prayers;
Confound the villains by the ears;
Disperse the plebeians—try the peers;
 And execute the Congress.

See, see, our hope begins to dawn;
Bold Carleton scours the northern lawn;
The sons of faction sigh forlorn;
 Dejected is the Congress.

Clinton, Burgoyne, and gallant Howe,
Will soon reward our conduct true,
And to each traitor give his due;
 Perdition waits the Congress.

See noble Dunmore keeps his post;
Marauds and ravages the coast;
Despises Lee and all his host,
 That hair-brain tool of Congress.

There's Washington and all his men—
Where Howe had one, the goose had ten—
March'd up the hill, and down again;
 And sent returns to Congress.

Prepare, prepare, my friends prepare,
For scenes of blood, the field of war;
To royal standards we'll repair,
    And curse the haughty Congress.

Huzza! Huzza! we thrice huzza!
Return peace, harmony, and law!
Restore such times as once we saw,
    And bid adieu to Congress.

BATTLE OF TRENTON

On Christmas day in seventy-six,
Our ragged troops with bayonets fix'd,
    For Trenton marched away.
The Delaware see! the boats below!
The light obscured by hail and snow!
    But no signs of dismay.

Our object was the Hessian band,
That dared invade fair freedom's land,
    And quarter in that place.
Great Washington he led us on,
Whose streaming flag, in storm or sun,
    Had never known disgrace.

In silent march we pass'd the night,
Each soldier panting for the fight,
    Though quite benumb'd with frost.
Greene, on the left, at six began,
The right was led by Sullivan,
    Who ne'er a moment lost.

Their pickets stormed, the alarm was spread,
That rebels risen from the dead
    Were marching into town.
Some scamper'd here, some scamper'd there,
And some for action did prepare;
    But soon their arms laid down.

Twelve hundred servile miscreants,
With all their colors, guns, and tents,
　　Were trophies of the day.
The frolic o'er, the bright canteen,
In centre, front, and rear was seen
　　Driving fatigue away.

Now, brothers of the patriot bands,
Let's sing deliverance from the hands
　　Of arbitrary sway.
And as our life is but a span,
Let's touch the tankard while we can,
　　In memory of that day.

NATHAN HALE

The breezes went steadily thro' the tall pines,
　　A saying "oh! hu-ush!" a saying "oh! hu-ush!"
As stilly stole by a bold legion of horse,
　　For Hale in the bush; for Hale in the bush.

"Keep still!" said the thrush as she nestled her young,
　　In a nest by the road; in a nest by the road.
"For the tyrants are near, and with them appear,
　　What bodes us no good; what bodes us no good."

The brave captain heard it, and thought of his home,
　　In a cot by the brook; in a cot by the brook.
With mother and sister and memories dear,
　　He so gaily forsook; he so gaily forsook.

Cooling shades of the night were coming apace,
　　The tattoo had beat; the tattoo had beat.
The noble one sprang from his dark lurking place,
　　To make his retreat; to make his retreat.

He warily trod on the dry rustling leaves,
　　As he pass'd thro' the wood; as he pass'd thro' the wood;
And silently gain'd his rude launch on the shore,
　　As she play'd with the flood; as she play'd with the flood.

The guards of the camp, on that dark, dreary night,
　　Had a murderous will; had a murderous will.
They took him and bore him afar from the shore,
　　To a hut on the hill; to a hut on the hill.

No mother was there, nor a friend who could cheer,
　　In that little stone cell; in that little stone cell.
But he trusted in love, from his Father above.
　　In his heart, all was well; in his heart, all was well.

An ominous owl with his solemn bass voice,
　　Sat moaning hard by; sat moaning hard by.
"The tyrant's proud minions most gladly rejoice,
　　For he must soon die; for he must soon die."

The brave fellow told them, no thing he restrain'd,
　　The cruel gen'ral; the cruel gen'ral.
His errand from camp, of the ends to be gain'd,
　　And said that was all; and said that was all.

They took him and bound him and bore him away,
　　Down the hill's grassy side; down the hill's grassy side.
'Twas there the base hirelings, in royal array,
　　His cause did deride; his cause did deride.

Five minutes were given, short moments, no more,
　　For him to repent; for him to repent;
He pray'd for his mother, he ask'd not another,
　　To Heaven he went; to Heaven he went.

The faith of a martyr, the tragedy show'd,
　　As he trod the last stage; as he trod the last stage.
And Britons will shudder at gallant Hale's blood,
　　As his words do presage, as his words do presage.

"Thou pale king of terrors, thou life's gloomy foe,
　　Go frighten the slave, go frighten the slave;
Tell tyrants, to you, their allegiance they owe.
　　No fears for the brave; no fears for the brave."

THE FATE OF JOHN BURGOYNE
[1777]

When Jack, the King's commander,
  Was going to his duty,
Through all the crowd he smil'd and bow'd,
  To every blooming beauty.

The city rung with feats he'd done,
  In Portugal and Flanders,
And all the town thought he'd be crown'd
  The first of Alexanders.

To Hampton Court he first repairs,
  To kiss great George's hand, sirs,
Then to harangue on state affairs,
  Before he left the land, sirs.

The "lower house" sat mute as mouse,
  To hear his grand oration;
And "all the peers" with loudest cheers,
  Proclaim'd him to the nation.

Then off he went to Canada,
  Next to Ticonderoga,
And quitting those, away he goes,
  Straightway to Saratoga.

With great parade his march he made,
  To gain his wished for station,
When far and wide his minions hied,
  To spread his "Proclamation."

To such as staid he offers made,
  Of "pardon on submission;
But savage bands should waste the lands
  Of all in opposition."

But ah, the cruel fate of war!
  This boasted son of Britain,
When mounting his triumphal car,
  With sudden fear was smitten.

The sons of freedom gathered round,
  His hostile bands confounded,
And when they'd fain have turn'd their backs,
  They found themselves surrounded!

In vain they fought, in vain they fled,
  Their chief, humane and tender,
To save the rest, soon thought it best
  His forces to surrender.

Brave St. Clair when he first retired,
  Knew what the fates portended;
And Arnold and heroic Gates,
  His conduct have defended.

Thus may America's brave sons
  With honor be rewarded,
And be the fate of all her foes,
  The same as here recorded.

BOLD HAWTHORNE

The twenty-second of August,
  Before the close of day,
All hands on board our privateer,
  We got her under weigh;
We kept the eastern shore along,
  For forty leagues or more,
Then our departure took for sea,
  From the isle Mauhegan shore.

Bold Hawthorne was commander,
  A man of real worth,
Old England's cruel tyranny
  Induced him to go forth;

She, with relentless fury,
  Was plundering all our coast,
And thought, because her strength was great,
  Our glorious cause was lost.

*   *   *   *   *   *

We cruised to the eastward,
  Near the coast of Portingale;
In longitude of twenty-seven
  We saw a lofty sail;
We gave her chase, and soon we saw
  She was a British scow
Standing for fair America,
  With troops for General Howe.

Our captain did inspect her
  With glasses, and he said—
"My boys, she means to fight us,
  But be you not afraid;
All hands now beat to quarters,
  See every thing is clear,
We'll give her a broadside, my boys,
  As soon as she comes near."

She was prepared with nettings,
  And had her men secured,
And bore directly for us,
  And put us close on board;
When cannon roar'd like thunder,
  And muskets fired amain,
But soon we were alongside,
  And grappled to her chain.

And now the scene it alter'd,
  The cannon ceased to roar,
We fought with swords and boarding-pikes
  One glass or something more,
Till British pride and glory
  No longer dared to stay,
But cut the Yankee grapplings,
  And quickly bore away.

Our case was not so desperate
  As plainly might appear;
Yet sudden death did enter
  On board our privateer.
Mahoney, Crew, and Clemmons,
  The valiant and the brave,
Fell glorious in the contest,
  And met a watery grave.

Ten other men were wounded
  Among our warlike crew,
With them our noble captain,
  To whom all praise is due;
To him and all our officers,
  Let's give a hearty cheer:
Success to fair America
  And our good privateer!

THE VOLUNTEER BOYS

[BY HENRY ARCHER (?). 1780]

Hence with the lover who sighs o'er his wine,
  Chloes and Phillises toasting,
Hence with the slave who will whimper and whine,
  Of ardor and constancy boasting.
    Hence with love's joys,
    Follies and noise,
The toast that I give is the Volunteer Boys.

Nobles and beauties and such common toasts,
  Those who admire may drink, sir;
Fill up the glass to the volunteer hosts,
  Who never from danger will shrink, sir.
    Let mirth appear,
    Every heart cheer,
The toast that I give is the brave volunteer.

Here's to the squire who goes to parade,
　Here's to the citizen soldier;
Here's to the merchant who fights for his trade,
　Whom danger increasing makes bolder.
　　Let mirth appear,
　　Union is here,
The toast that I give is the brave volunteer.

Here's to the lawyer, who, leaving the bar,
　Hastens where honor doth lead, sir,
Changing the gown for the ensigns of war,
　The cause of his country to plead, sir.
　　Freedom appears,
　　Every heart cheers,
And calls for the health of the law volunteers.

Here's to the soldier, though batter'd in wars,
　And safe to his farm-house retir'd;
When called by his country, ne'er thinks of his scars,
　With ardor to join us inspir'd.
　　Bright fame appears,
　　Trophies uprear,
To veteran chiefs who became volunteers.

Here's to the farmer who dares to advance
　To harvest of honor with pleasure;
Who with a slave the most skilful in France,
　A sword for his country would measure.
　　Hence with cold fear,
　　Heroes rise here;
The ploughman is chang'd to the stout volunteer.

Here's to the peer, first in senate and field,
　Whose actions to titles and grace, sir;
Whose spirit undaunted would never yet yield
　To a foe, to a pension or place, sir.
　　Gratitude here,
　　Toasts to the peer,
Who adds to his titles, "the brave volunteer."

Thus the bold bands for old Jersey's defence,
   The muse hath with rapture review'd, sir;
With our volunteer boys, as our verses commence,
   With our volunteer boys they conclude, sir.
     Discord or noise,
     Ne'er damp our joys,
But health and success to the volunteer boys.

THE DANCE

[1781]

Cornwallis led a country dance,
   The like was never seen, sir,
Much retrograde and much advance,
   And all with General Greene, sir.

They rambled up and rambled down,
   Join'd hands, then off they run, sir,
Our General Greene to Charlestown,
   The earl to Wilmington, sir

Greene, in the South, then danc'd a set,
   And got a mighty name, sir,
Cornwallis jigg'd with young Fayette,
   But suffer'd in his fame, sir.

Then down he figur'd to the shore,
   Most like a lordly dancer,
And on his courtly honor swore,
   He would no more advance, sir.

Quoth he, my guards are weary grown
   With footing country dances,
They never at St. James's shone,
   At capers, kicks or prances.

Though men so gallant ne'er were seen,
   While sauntering on parade, sir,
Or wriggling o'er the park's smooth green,
   Or at a masquerade, sir.

Yet are red heels and long-lac'd skirts,
   For stumps and briars meet, sir?
Or stand they chance with hunting-shirts,
   Or hardy veteran feet, sir?

Now hous'd in York he challeng'd all,
   At minuet or all 'amande,
And lessons for a courtly ball,
   His guards by day and night conn'd.

This challenge known, full soon there came,
   A set who had the bon ton,
De Grasse and Rochambeau, whose fame
   Fut brillant pour un long tems.

And Washington, Columbia's son,
   Whom easy nature taught, sir,
That grace which can't by pains be won,
   Or Plutus' gold be bought, sir.

Now hand in hand they circle round,
   This ever-dancing peer, sir;
Their gentle movements, soon confound
   The earl, as they draw near, sir.

His music soon forgets to play—
   His feet can no more move, sir,
And all his bands now curse the day,
   They jiggèd to our shore, sir.

Now Tories all, what can ye say?
   Come—is not this a griper,
That while your hopes are danc'd away,
   'Tis you must pay the piper.

JOSEPH STANSBURY AND JONATHAN ODELL

The two outstanding Revolutionary poets on the side of the tories were Joseph Stansbury and Jonathan Odell; and for the sake of convenience they will be treated together here.

Stansbury was preëminently the song writer for his party. Born in London in 1740, he emigrated to Philadelphia in 1767, and settled as a merchant. His ability in business, his wit, and his pleasing manners speedily established him in the good graces of the best families of the city. In the dispute with the Crown, he seems at first to have sided with the colonies; but as the struggle progressed, he more and more opposed the resort to arms. He believed the British ministers stubborn and foolish, but not more so than the colonists in resisting them by force. During most of the War, he resided behind the British lines in Philadelphia and New York, from which safe retreat he sent forth many popular songs to cheer the loyal soldiery and colonists. Despite his tory sympathies, however, he more than once protested against the apathy and inefficiency of certain British leaders. Stansbury was naturally of a suave and conciliatory disposition, and after hostilities ceased, he hoped to settle down again to the life of a Philadelphia merchant. This he was not allowed to do; it was only after several years of persecution, and a temporary sojourn in Nova Scotia, that he was able to make a home in New York, where he spent his last years in prosperity and happiness. In his writing Stansbury was usually light, genial, and frequently mirthful; he was at his best in gay lines for the drinking bout. He was also a satirist, but his satire is tempered and mild, never thorough-going and bitter.

Of a sterner temper was Jonathan Odell, who was a more bitter and vindictive partisan, and on the whole, the ablest and most influential of the tory writers. He was born at Newark, New Jersey, in 1737, and was for some years a surgeon in the British army. Withdrawing from this profession, he went to England to prepare for the ministry, and in 1767 was ordained to the priesthood in the Church of England. Soon afterward he was put in charge of the parish of Burlington, New Jersey. Though in the Revolutionary struggle he was from the first on the King's side, for a time he kept his sentiments to himself. His loyalty was doubted, however, and in 1776 he was paroled in his own parish. When later in the same year he was recognized as a tory, he was driven from the city, and took refuge behind the British lines. Here his services brought him into high favor with the British leaders in New York. He acted both as chaplain and physician to the British troops, and employed his talent as a writer for his party. By nature a satirist, he angrily ridiculed the pretensions of the colonists. His songs and satires were widely read; his indictments of the colonists and his stout assertions of England's right to subdue the rebels undoubtedly strengthened the loyalist cause. Odell believed firmly and persistently in the ultimate triumph of the British, and in all his long life never outgrew his hostility toward the American revolutionists. When the war was over, he could not reconcile himself to the new state of affairs, and took refuge in Nova Scotia, where he rose to civic importance, and where in extreme old age he died.

WHEN GOOD QUEEN ELIZABETH GOVERNED THE REALM [1]

A SONG

[BY JOSEPH STANSBURY. PROBABLY 1774]

When good Queen Elizabeth govern'd the Realm,
And Burleigh's sage counsels directed the helm,
In vain Spain and France our conquests oppos'd;
For Valor conducted what Wisdom propos'd.

[1] [Written, apparently, for a banquet of the American "Sons of St. George."]

Beef and beer was their food;
Love and truth arm'd their band;
Their courage was ready—
Steady, boys, steady—
To fight and to conquer by sea and by land.

But since tea and coffee, so much to our grief,
Have taken the place of strong beer and roast beef,
Our laurels have wither'd, our trophies been torn;
And the lions of England French triumphs adorn.
Tea and slops are their food;
They unnerve every hand—
Their courage unsteady
And not always ready—
They often are conquer'd by sea and by land.

St. George views with transport our generous flame:
"My sons, rise to glory, and rival my fame.
Ancient manners again in my sons I behold
And this age must eclipse all the ages of gold."
Beef and beer are our food;
Love and truth arm our band;
Our courage is steady
And always is ready
To fight and to conquer by sea and by land.

While thus we regale as our fathers of old,
Our manners as simple, our courage as bold,
May vigor and prudence our freedom secure
Long as rivers, or ocean, or stars shall endure.

Beef and beer are our food;
Love and truth arm our band;
Our courage is steady
And always is ready
To fight and to conquer by sea and by land.

SONG

FOR A FISHING PARTY NEAR BURLINGTON, ON THE
DELAWARE, IN 1776.

[BY JONATHAN ODELL]

How sweet is the season, the sky how serene;
On Delaware's banks how delightful the scene;
The Prince of the Rivers, his waves all asleep,
In silence majestic glides on to the deep.

Away from the noise of the fife and the drum,
And all the rude din of Bellona we come;
And a plentiful store of good humor we bring
To season our feast in the shade of Cold Spring.

A truce then to all whig and tory debate;
True lovers of freedom, contention we hate:
For the demon of discord in vain tries his art
To possess or inflame a true *Protestant* heart.

True Protestant friends to fair Liberty's cause,
To decorum, good order, religion and laws,
From avarice, jealousy, perfidy, free;
We wish all the world were as happy as we.

We have wants, we confess, but are free from the care
Of those that abound, yet have nothing to spare:
Serene as the sky, as the river serene,
We are happy to want envy, malice, and spleen.

While thousands around us, misled by a few,
The phantoms of pride and ambition pursue,
With pity their fatal delusion we see;
And wish all the world were as happy as we!

A BIRTHDAY SONG

For the King's Birthday, June 4, 1777

[By Jonathan Odell]

Time was when America hallow'd the morn
On which the lov'd monarch of Britain was born,
Hallow'd the day, and joyfully chanted
   God save the King!
Then flourish'd the blessings of freedom and peace,
And plenty flow'd in with a yearly increase.
Proud of our lot we chanted merrily
   Glory and joy crown the King!

With envy beheld by the nations around,
We rapidly grew, nor was anything found
Able to check our growth while we chanted
   God save the King!
O bless'd beyond measure, had honor and truth
Still nurs'd in our hearts what they planted in youth!
Loyalty still had chanted merrily
   Glory and joy crown the King!

But see! how rebellion has lifted her head!
How honor and truth are with loyalty fled!
Few are there now who join us in chanting
   God save the King!
And see! how deluded the multitude fly
To arm in a cause that is built on a lie!
Yet are we proud to chant thus merrily
   Glory and joy crown the King!

Though faction by falsehood awhile may prevail,
And loyalty suffers a captive in jail,
Britain is rous'd, rebellion is falling:
   God save the King!
The captive shall soon be releas'd from his chain;
And conquest restore us to Britain again,
Ever to join in chanting merrily
   Glory and joy crown the King!

JOY TO GREAT CONGRESS

[FROM "THE CONGRATULATION," BY JONATHAN ODELL. 1779]

Joy to great Congress, joy an hundred fold:
The grand cajolers are themselves cajol'd!
In vain has [Franklin's] artifice been tried,
And Louis swell'd with treachery and pride;
Who reigns supreme in heav'n deception spurns,
And on the author's head the mischief turns.
What pains were taken to procure D'Estaing!
His fleet's dispersed, and Congress may go hang.

Joy to great Congress, joy an hundred fold:
The grand cajolers are themselves cajol'd!
Heav'n's King sends forth the hurricane and strips
Of all their glory the perfidious ships.
His Ministers of Wrath the storm direct;
Nor can the Prince of Air his French protect.
Saint George, Saint David show'd themselves true hearts;
Saint Andrew and Saint Patrick topp'd their parts.
With right Eolian puffs the wind they blew;
Crack went the masts; the sails to shivers flew.
Such honest saints shall never be forgot;
Saint Dennis, and Saint Tammany, go rot.

MOLLY ODELL ON HER BIRTHDAY

[BY HER FATHER]

Amidst the rage of civil strife,
The orphan's cries, the widow's tears,
This day my rising dawn of life
Has measured five revolving years.

Unconscious of the howling storm,
No signs of shipwreck'd peace I see;
For what, with all its bustling swarm,
What is the noisy world to me?

My needle and my book employ
The busy moments of my day;
And, for the rest, with harmless joy,
I pass them in a round of play!

And if, ere long, my vacant heart
Is to be fill'd with care and pain,
Still I shall bravely bear my part
While truth and innocence remain.

THE LORDS OF THE MAIN [1]

[BY JOSEPH STANSBURY.   1780]

When Faction, in league with the treacherous Gaul,
    Began to look big and paraded in state;
A meeting was held at *Credulity Hall,*
    And Echo proclaim'd their ally *good and great!*
            By sea and by land
            Such wonders are plann'd;
No less than the bold British Lion to chain!
            Well hove! says Jack Lanyard,
            French, Congo, and Spaniard,
Have at you—remember we're Lords of the Main!
    Lords of the Main—aye, Lords of the Main;
The tars of Old England are Lords of the Main.

Though party-contention awhile may perplex,
    And lenity hold us in doubtful suspense;
If perfidy rouse, or ingratitude vex,
    In defiance of Hell we'll chastise the offense.
            When danger alarms,
            'Tis then that in arms
United we rush on the foe with disdain:
            And when the storm rages
            It only presages

[1] [Written for the British seamen engaged in fighting the French
and Spanish, at that time allies of the Americans. The Congress
is referred to under the name of "Congo," a favorite derisive term
of the Tories.]

Fresh triumphs to Britons, as Lords of the Main.
  Lords of the Main—aye, Lords of the Main—
Let *Thunder* proclaim it, we're Lords of the Main.

Then, Britons, *strike home*—make sure of your blow:
  The chase is in view; never mind a lee-shore.
With vengeance o'ertake the confederate foe:
  'Tis now we may rival our heroes of yore!
        Brave Anson and Drake,
        Hawke, Russell, and Blake,
With ardor like yours we defy France and Spain!
        Combining with Treason,
        They're deaf to all reason:
Once more let them *feel* we are Lords of the Main.
  Lords of the Main—aye, Lords of the Main—
The first-born of Neptune are Lords of the Main.

Nor are we alone in the noble career;
  The soldier partakes of the generous flame:
To glory he marches, to glory we steer;
  Between us we share the rich harvest of fame.
        Recorded on high,
        Their names never die,
Of heroes by sea and by land what a train!
        To the King, then, God bless him!
        The world shall confess him
"The Lord of those men who are Lords of the Main."
  Lords of the Main—aye, Lords of the Main—
The tars of Old England are Lords of the Main.

A PASQUINADE [1]

STUCK UP AT NEW YORK ON THE 25TH OF AUGUST, 1780

[BY JOSEPH STANSBURY]

Has the Marquis la Fayette
Taken off all our hay yet?
Says Clinton to the wise heads around him:
Yes, faith, great Sir Harry,
Each stack he did carry,
And likewise the cattle—confound him!

Besides he now goes
Just *under your* nose,
To burn all the houses to cinder.
If that be his project,
It is not an object
Worth a great man's attempting to hinder.

For forage and house
I care not a louse;
For revenge let the Loyalists bellow.
I swear I'll not *do* more
To keep them in humor,
Than play on my violoncello.

Since Charles Town is taken,
'Twill sure save my bacon:
I can live a whole year on that same, sir.
Ride about all the day;
At night, concert or play;
So a fig for those men that dare blame, sir.

If growlers complain
I inactive remain,
Will do nothing, nor let any others;
'Tis sure no new thing
To serve thus our King;
Witness Burgoyne and two famous Brothers!

[1] [Written to protest against the delinquency of Sir Henry Clinton, who in 1780 allowed the Americans in the vicinity of New York to commit many outrages.]

AN INDICTMENT OF WASHINGTON

[FROM "THE AMERICAN TIMES," BY JONATHAN ODELL. 1780]

Hear thy indictment, Washington, at large;
Attend and listen to the solemn charge:
Thou hast supported an atrocious cause
Against thy King, thy Country, and the laws;
Committed perjury, encourag'd lies,
Forced conscience, broken the most sacred ties;
Myriads of wives and fathers at thy hand
Their slaughter'd husbands, slaughter'd sons demand;
That pastures hear no more the lowing kine,—
That towns are desolate, all—all is thine;
The frequent sacrilege that pain'd my sight:
The blasphemies my pen abhors to write;
Innumerable crimes on thee must fall—
For thou maintainest, thou defendest all.

*　　*　　*　　*　　*　　*

What could, when half-way up the hill of fame,
Induce thee to go back, and link with shame?
Was it ambition, vanity, or spite,
That prompted thee with Congress to unite;
Or did all three within thy bosom roll,
"Thou heart of hero with a traitor's soul"?
Go, wretched author of thy country's grief,
Patron of villainy, of villains chief;
Seek with thy cursed crew the eternal gloom,
Ere Truth's avenging sword begin thy doom;
Or sudden vengeance of celestial dart
Precipitate thee with augmented smart.

LET US BE HAPPY AS LONG AS WE CAN

[BY JOSEPH STANSBURY. PROBABLY 1782]

I've heard in old times that a sage us'd to say
The seasons were nothing—December or May—
The heat or the cold never enter'd his plan;
That all should be happy whenever they can.

No matter what power directed the state,
He look'd upon such things as order'd by Fate.
Whether govern'd by many, or rul'd by one man,
His rule was—be happy whenever you can.

He happen'd to enter this world the same day
With the supple, complying, fam'd Vicar of Bray.
Thro' both of their lives the same principle ran:
My boys, we'll be happy as long as we can.

Time-serving I hate, yet I see no good reason
A leaf from their book should be thought out of season.
When kick'd like a foot-ball from Sheba to Dan,
Egad, let's be happy as long as we can.

Since no one can tell what to-morrow may bring,
Or which side shall triumph, the Congress or King;
Since Fate must o'errule us and carry her plan,
Why, let us be happy as long as we can.

To-night let's enjoy this good wine and a song,
And relish the hour which we cannot prolong.
If evil will come, we'll adhere to our plan,
And baffle misfortune as long as we can.

THE UNITED STATES

[BY JOSEPH STANSBURY. 1783]

Now this War at length is o'er;
Let us think of it no more.
Every party lie or name,
Cancel as our mutual shame.
Bid each wound of faction close,
Blushing we were ever foes.

Now restor'd to peace again,
Active commerce ploughs the main;
All the arts of civil life
Swift succeed to martial strife;
Britain now allows their claim,
Rising empire, wealth, and fame.

TO PEACE

[FROM THE MANUSCRIPT OF JOSEPH STANSBURY]

O come, light borne on eastern gales,
And bid our sorrows cease:
With flow'rets crown our smiling vales,
Thou gentle cherub Peace!
Efface the horrid marks of war;
Each private grudge remove;
With plenty load the rustic's car,
And fill the land with love.

FRANCIS HOPKINSON

Francis Hopkinson deserves a place among Revolutionary writers both for his literary accomplishments and for his services to the American cause. He was born in 1737 in Philadelphia, where his father was a lawyer,—the associate of Franklin in the "Junto," and in electrical experiment. He was the first student to enter the College of Philadelphia (now the University of Pennsylvania), from which he got both the bachelor's and the master's degrees. Like his father, he became a distinguished lawyer, a judge of the admiralty, and an active and esteemed citizen of Philadelphia. He was a member of the Continental Congress and a signer of the Declaration of Independence. Along with his legal and public labors, however, he found time for lighter interests. He was described in a letter by John Adams as "one of your pretty, little, ingenious men,"—"genteel, well-bred, and very social," with a taste for "painting, sculpture, architecture, and music." He had indeed a culture and versatility unusual in his time, as is shown also by the *Miscellaneous Essays and Occasional Writings* published from his manuscripts shortly after his death in 1791. These include two volumes of orations and addresses, essays in the manner of Addison, revolutionary and social satires, and scientific papers; and a third volume curiously divided between "Judgments in the Admiralty of Pennsylvania" and "Poems on Various Subjects." Lacking in high merit or interest, these "miscellanies" still give a pleasing impression of their author as a man of wide intelligence, cultivated taste, good sense, and good nature. By the last named quality in particular Hopkinson is distinguished from other satirists of the Revolution; the subjects which Paine and Freneau treat with harshness or bitterness, he looks upon no less seriously but with unfailing good humor. Even compared with Trumbull he is more genial. But he lacks the energy of Paine and

Freneau's touch of genius; and the final impression he leaves is one of amateurish ingenuity. He is now chiefly remembered for *A Pretty Story,* in which, after reading Swift's *Tale of a Tub* and Arbuthnot's *History of John Bull,* he treats under the safe guise of allegory the dispute between the colonies and the mother country down to the time of writing—1774. In spite of its debt to English satirists this is fresher than his new versions of *L'Allegro* and *Il Penseroso.* The *Pretty Story* is perhaps our first example of American prose fiction,—of fiction, however, used like Swift's for political instruction rather than for amusement. *The Battle of the Kegs,* written to ridicule the inertness of the British troops occupying Philadelphia, was one of the most popular ballads of the Revolution. The letter printed in the extracts under the title "Lying Offices" is typical of Hopkinson's Revolutionary satire, and his use of humorous irony.

A PRETTY STORY

[1774]

[The title-page reads: "A Pretty Story. Written in the Year of our Lord 1774, by Peter Grievous, Esq., A. B. C. D. E. Veluti in Speculo. Philadelphia. Printed and sold by John Dunlap. MDCCLXXIV."

The story is of the "Old Farm" and the "New Farm"— England and America. The "nobleman," his "wife," and the "steward" are the king, parliament, and ministry; the "sons" are the colonies, and their "wives" the colonial legislatures. Hopkinson's own footnotes explain other allusions.

Chapters II-IV, omitted here, tell in allegory of the settlement and growth of the colonies, of the trade acts, and of the passing and repeal of the Stamp Act.]

CHAPTER I.

Once upon a time, a great while ago, there lived a certain nobleman, who had long possessed a very valuable farm, and had a great number of children and grandchildren.

Besides the annual profits of his farm, which were very

considerable, he kept a large shop of goods; and being very successful in trade, he became, in process of time, exceeding rich and powerful, insomuch that all his neighbors feared and respected him.

He had examined all the known systems of economy, and selected from them, for the government of his own family, all such parts as appeared to be equitable and beneficial, and omitted those which experience had shown to be inconvenient or prejudicial: or rather, by blending their several constitutions together, he had so ingeniously counterbalanced the evils of one by the benefits of another, that the advantages were fully enjoyed, and the inconveniences scarcely felt.

He never exercised any undue authority over his children or servants; neither indeed could he greatly oppress them, if he was ever so disposed; for it was particularly covenanted in his marriage articles, that he should never impose any task or hardships upon his children without the consent of his wife.

Now the custom in his family was this:—that at the end of every seven years his marriage became null and void, at which time his children and grandchildren met together and chose another wife for him, whom the old gentleman was obliged to marry under the same articles and restrictions as before. By this means the children had always a great interest in their mother-in-law, and through her a reasonable check upon their father's temper. For, besides that he could do nothing material respecting them without her approbation, she was sole mistress of the purse-strings, and gave him from time to time such sums as *she* thought necessary for the expenses of his family.

Being one day in a very extraordinary good humor, he gave his children a writing under hand and seal, by which he released them from many badges of dependence, and confirmed to them several very important privileges. The chief of these were, that none of his children should be punished for any offence, or supposed offence, until twelve of his brethren had examined the facts, and declared him subject to such punishment; and, secondly, he renewed his assurances that no tasks or hardships should be imposed upon them without the consent of their mother-in-law.

This writing, on account of its singular importance, was called *the great paper*.   .   .   .

CHAP. V.

In the meantime the new settlers increased exceedingly, their dealings at their father's shop became proportionately enlarged, and their partiality for their brethren of the old farm was sincere and manifest. They suffered, indeed, some inconveniences from the *protectors* which had been stationed amongst them, who became very troublesome in their houses. They introduced riot and intemperance into their families, debauched their daughters, and derided the orders they had made for their own good government. Moreover, the old nobleman had, at different times, sent over to them a great number of thieves, murderers, and robbers, who did much mischief by practising those crimes for which they had been banished from the old farm. But they bore those evils with as much patience as could be expected; not choosing to trouble their old father with complaints, unless in cases of important necessity.

Now the steward began to hate the new settlers with exceeding great hatred, and determined to renew his attack upon their peace and happiness. He artfully insinuated to the nobleman and his foolish wife, that it was very mean, and unbecoming their greatness, to receive the contributions of the people of the new farm through the consent of their respective wives: that upon this footing they might some time or other refuse to comply with his requisitions, if they should take into their heads to think them oppressive and unreasonable; and that it was high time they should be compelled to acknowledge his unlimited power and his wife's *omnipotence,* which, if not enforced now, they would soon be able to resist, as they were daily increasing in numbers and strength.

Another decree was, therefore, prepared and published, directing that the people of the new farm should pay a certain stipend upon particular goods,[1] which they were not

[1] Painter's colors, glass, &c.

allowed to purchase anywhere but at their father's shop; specifying that this imposition should not be laid as an advance upon the original price of these goods, but should be paid as a tax on their arrival in the new farm; for the express purpose of supporting the dignity of the nobleman's family, and for re-imbursing the expenses he pretended to have been at on their account.

This new decree occasioned great uneasiness. The people saw plainly that the steward and their mother-in-law were determined to enslave and ruin them. They again consulted together, and wrote, as before, the most dutiful and persuasive letters to their father—but to no purpose—a deaf ear was turned against all their remonstrances, and their humble requests rejected with contempt.

Finding that this moderate and decent conduct brought them no relief, they had recourse to another expedient; they bound themselves to each other in a solemn engagement,[1] not to deal any more at their father's shop, until this unconstitutional decree should be repealed, which they one and all declared to be a direct violation of the *Great Paper*.

This agreement was so strictly observed, that in a few months the clerks and apprentices in the old gentleman's shop began to raise a terrible outcry. They declared, that their master's trade was declining exceedingly, and that his wife and steward would by their mischievous machinations ruin the whole farm. They sharpened their pens, and attacked the steward, and even the old lady herself, with great severity: insomuch, that it was thought proper to withdraw this attempt also, upon the rights and liberties of the new settlers. One part only of the decree was left still in force, viz. the tax upon *water-gruel*.[2]

Now there were certain men[3] in the old farm, who had obtained an exclusive right of selling *water-gruel*. Vast quantities of this gruel were vended amongst the new settlers, as they were extremely fond of it, and used it universally in their families. They did not, however, trouble themselves much about the tax on *water-gruel;* they were well pleased with the repeal of the other parts of the decree, and fond as they were of this gruel, they considered it as not

[1] Non-importation agreement.   [2] Tea.   [3] The India company.

absolutely necessary to the comfort of life, and determined to give up the use of it in their families, and so avoid the effects of that part of the decree.

The steward found his designs again frustrated: but was not discouraged by the disappointment. He devised another scheme, so artfully contrived, that he thought himself sure of success. He sent for the persons who had the sole right of vending *water-gruel;* and after reminding them of the obligations they were under to the nobleman and his wife for the exclusive privilege they enjoyed, he requested that they would send sundry waggons laden with gruel to the new farm; promising that the accustomed duty which they paid for their exclusive right should be taken off from all the gruel they should so send amongst the new settlers; and that in case their cargoes should come to any damage, the loss should be made good to them out of his master's coffers.

The gruel-merchants readily consented to this proposal; considering that if their cargoes were sold, their profits would be very great; and if they failed, the steward was to pay the damage. On the other hand, the steward hoped that the new settlers would not be able to resist a temptation, thus thrown in their way, of purchasing their favorite gruel, to which they had been so long accustomed; and if they did use it, subject to the tax aforesaid, he would consider this as a voluntary acknowledgment that the nobleman and his wife had a right to lay upon them what impositions they pleased, and as a resignation of the privileges of the *Great Paper.*

But the new settlers were well aware of this decoy. They saw plainly that the gruel was not sent for their accommodation; and that if they suffered any part of it to be sold amongst them, subject to the tax imposed by the new decree, it would be considered as a willing submission to the assumed omnipotence of their mother-in-law, and a precedent for future unlimited impositions. Some, therefore, would not permit the waggons to be unladen at all; but sent them back untouched to the gruel-merchants; and others suffered them to unload, but would not touch the dangerous commodity; so that it lay neglected about the roads and highways till it was quite spoiled. But one of the new settlers, whose name was JACK, either from a keener sense of the injuries intended, or from the necessity of his situation, which was such that he could not send back the gruel, because of a number of mercenaries[1] whom his father had stationed in his house to be a watch over him—he, I say, being almost driven to despair, stove[2] to pieces the casks of gruel which had been sent him, and utterly destroyed the whole cargo.

CHAP. VI.

These violent proceedings were soon known at the old farm. Great was the uproar there. The old nobleman fell into a furious passion, declaring that the new settlers meant to throw off all dependence upon him, and rebel against his authority. His wife also tore the padlocks from her lips, and raved and stormed like a Billingsgate, and the steward lost all patience and moderation—swearing most profanely, *that he would leave no stone unturned, till he had humbled the settlers of the new farm at his feet, and caused their father to tread upon their necks.* Moreover, the gruel-merchants roared and bellowed for the loss of their gruel; and the clerks and apprentices were in the utmost consternation lest the people of the new farm should again agree to have no dealings with their father's shop.

Vengeance was forthwith prepared, especially against *Jack*. With him they determined to begin; hoping that by making a severe example of him, they should so terrify the other families, that they would all submit to the power of the steward and acknowledge the omnipotence of the *great Madam*.

A very large padlock[3] was sent over to be fastened on *Jack's* great gate; the key of which was given to the old nobleman, who was not to suffer it to be opened until *Jack* had paid for the gruel he had spilt, and resigned all claim to the privileges of the *Great Paper*—nor even then, unless he should think fit. Secondly, a decree was made to new model the regulations and economy of *Jack's* family, in such manner that they might in future be more subjected to the

[1] Board of Commissioners.   [2] Destruction of the tea at Boston.
[3] The Boston Port-bill.

will of the steward. And, thirdly, a large gallows was erected before the mansion-house in the old farm, that if any of *Jack's* children should be suspected of misbehavior, they should not be convicted or acquitted by the voice of their brethren, according to the purport of the *Great Paper,* but be tied neck and heels, and sent over to be hanged on this gallows.

On hearing of these severities, the people were highly enraged. They were at a loss how to act, or by what means they should avoid the threatened vengeance. But the old lady and the steward persisted. The great padlock was fastened on *Jack's gate,* and the key given to the nobleman as had been determined on; without waiting to know whether *Jack* would pay for the gruel, or allowing him an opportunity to make any apology or defence.

Poor *Jack* was now in a deplorable condition indeed. The great inlet to his farm was entirely shut up; so that he could neither carry out the produce of his land for sale, nor receive from abroad the necessaries for his family.

But this was not all. The old nobleman, along with the padlock aforesaid, had sent an overseer[1] to hector and domineer over *Jack* and his family, and to endeavour to break his spirits by every possible severity; for which purpose, this overseer was attended by a great number of mercenaries, and armed with more than common authorities.

When the overseer first arrived in *Jack's* family, he was received with great respect, because he was the delegate of their aged father. For, notwithstanding all that had passed, the people of the new farm loved and revered the old nobleman with true filial affection: and attributed his unkindness entirely to the intrigues of the steward.

But this fair weather did not last long. The new overseer took the first opportunity to show that he had no intention of living in harmony and friendship with the family. Some of *Jack's* domestics had put on their Sunday clothes, and waited on the overseer in the great parlor, to pay him their compliments on his arrival;[2] and to request his assistance in reconciling their father to them, and restoring peace

---

[1] General Gage, made Governor of the province.
[2] Address to General Gage.

and cordiality between the old and new farms.   But he, in a most abrupt and rude manner, stopped them short in the midst of their address; called them a parcel of disobedient scoundrels; bid them go about their business; and turning round on his heel, left the room with an air of contempt and disdain.

CHAP. VII.

The people of the new farm seeing the importance of their situation, had appointed a grand committee, consisting of some of the most respectable characters from each family, to manage their affairs in this difficult crisis.   *Jack,* thus oppressed and insulted, requested the advice[1] of the grand committee as to his conduct.   This committee in their answer, sympathized cordially with him in his afflictions.   They exhorted him to bear his suffering with fortitude for a time; assuring him, that they looked upon the insults and punishments inflicted on him with the same indignation as if they had been inflicted on themselves; and promised to stand by and support him to the last.   They recommended it to him to be firm and steady in the cause of liberty and their just rights, and never to acknowledge the *omnipotence* of their mother-in-law, nor submit to the machinations of their enemy the steward.

In the meantime, lest *Jack's* family should suffer for want of necessaries, his great gate being fast locked, contributions were raised for his relief amongst the other families,[2] and handed to him over the garden wall.

The new overseer still persisted in his hostile behavior, taking every opportunity to mortify and insult *Jack* and his family.   Observing that some of the children and domestics held frequent meetings and consultations together, sometimes in the garret, and sometimes in the stable, and understanding that an agreement not to deal with their father's shop, until their grievances should be redressed, was again talked of, he wrote a thundering prohibition,[3] much like a pope's bull, which he caused to be pasted up in every room

[1] Boston consults the congress of the states.
[2] Money raised by the states for the relief of the poor of Boston.
[3] Proclamation at Boston forbidding town meetings.

of the house—in which he declared and protested, that such meetings were treasonable, traitorous, and rebellious, contrary to the dignity of his master, the nobleman, and inconsistent with the duty they owed to his *omnipotent* wife: and threatened that if two of the family should be found whispering together, they should be sent over in chains to the old farm, and hanged upon the great gallows before the mansion-house.

These harsh and unconstitutional proceedings of the overseer, so highly irritated *Jack,* and the other families of the new farm, that . . .

Cetera desunt.

LYING OFFICES

[A LETTER TO THE EDITOR OF THE "NEW JERSEY GAZETTE." JANUARY, 1778]

Mr. Collins,

When necessity first compelled us to take up arms in defence of our country, we thought our only business would be to oppose strength to strength, in the usual course of war: and accordingly, we provided ourselves with guns, bayonets, powder, ball, &c.

But experience shows that we were mistaken. Other weapons of less mortal, but not less dangerous effect, are exercised against us by the enemy, and we are very deficient on our parts. It is now high time that congress should enable us to meet the foe with equal arms. In short, Mr. Collins, we want men of abilities to serve the United States in the capacity of *public liars*.

However strange such an appointment may appear at first view, we find that the experienced commanders of the British army have not thought it unworthy of their attention. It is manifest that our enemies depend much on their superiority in the art of *lying*. In the very commencement of the war, the British minister was at the trouble and expense of sending over a whole shipload of lies in a pamphlet, entitled *An Address to the People of America,* to be dispersed among the people. After this, many other lying pamphlets and papers were discharged from the royal batteries. Lord Howe sent a lie to congress by General Sullivan, requesting a conference for the establishment of peace—knowing, at the same time, he had neither the intention nor the power to make peace. But this was only priming the cannon—his principal aim was to send a thundering lie to Europe, and particularly to France, informing that congress was about to submit, and had actually entered upon a treaty with the British generals for that purpose. And Sir William Howe let off another lie, not long since, by means of the unfortunate John Brown—but that missed its aim.

As soon as the Howes got to New York, they appointed their *liar general,* who played off innumerable lies from the batteries of Rivington and Gaine,[1] to our great annoyance. They have now an able officer of this kind in Philadelphia, who has taken charge of Fort Humphreys[1] and Fort Town.[1] For it cannot be supposed that Messrs. Humphreys and Town are the original authors of those elegant and well-constructed lies which they publish every week.

I have heard of a man in England, some years ago, called a ventriloquist, who had the extraordinary faculty of making his voice seem to come from where he pleased. This man kept a great dog, and for the entertainment of visitors, would throw his voice into the dog's belly; and then wagging the poor beast's jaws with his hands, made him seem to say anything he pleased. Thus it is with Humphreys and Town. The *liar general* is the man with a wonderful voice, and they are only his dogs, whom he causes to utter what he thinks proper. Thus, in a late Evening Post, Mr. Town seems to address the public, in *propria persona,* in a long declamation on congressional tyranny and British clemency—all *lies*—in order to introduce two greater lies sanctioned by the name of Joseph Galloway—whom, to tell the truth, I do suspect to be the very *liar general* himself.

Nothing would be more vain than to attempt to counteract these productions of the British *lying offices* in New York and Philadelphia, with serious answers of truth and reason: like must be opposed to like—and therefore I hope that congress will no longer delay to establish *lying offices*

[1] Printers of newspapers.

on our side of the question, with handsome salaries annexed: and would earnestly recommend this my project to their serious consideration. Let there be an advertisement forthwith published by authority, to the following effect:

"WANTED, for the continental service, a person well qualified for the office of *liar general* to the United States: also three assistants or *petit-liars,* in said office. Those who are willing and able to serve their country in this department, are requested to send in their names to ———— on or before the first day of March next.

"As it is supposed there may be a number of persons well versed in this art amongst the *tories,* free pardon and good encouragement will be given to such as will exert their lying faculties in favor of their country.

"N. B. Specimens of ability will be required of the candidates."

A SENTIMENT

Occasioned by a conversation with Mr. P—— M——, one of the principal men among the Christian Society, called Dunkars, at Ephrata, in the province of Pennsylvania.

The Lord Supreme, from his exalted throne,
Surveys at once earth, heav'n, and worlds unknown;
All things existing must before his eye
Like the plain tracings of a picture lie:
Unutter'd thoughts deep in the heart conceal'd,
In strong expression stand to him reveal'd.
Thousands, and twice ten thousands ev'ry day,
To him or feign'd or real homage pay;
Like clouds of incense rolling to the skies,
In various forms their supplications rise;
Their various forms with him can naught avail,
The secret motives only will prevail;
And the true source of ev'ry offer'd pray'r,
To his all-searching eye must plain appear.

Some place religion on a throne superb,
And deck with jewels her resplendent garb:
Painting and sculpture all their art display,
And lofty tapers dart their lucid ray;

High on the full-ton'd organ's buoyant sound,
The pleasing anthem floats serenely round;
Harmonic strains their thrilling pow'rs combine,
And lift the soul to ecstasy divine.

Deep in Ephrata's gloom *you* fix your seat,
And seek religion in the dark retreat;
In sable weeds you dress the heav'n-born maid,
And place her pensive in the lonely shade:
Recluse, unsocial *you,* your hours employ,
And fearful, banish ev'ry harmless joy.

Each may be right in their peculiar way,
If proper motives should their worship sway;
If but the love divine of God is there,
The spirit genuine of unfeigned pray'r;
'Tis true devotion; and the Lord of love
Such pray'rs and praises kindly will approve.
Whether from golden altars they should rise,
And rapt in sound, roll to the lofty skies,
Or from Ephrata's seat, so meek, so low,
The soft and silent aspirations flow.

Oh! let the Christian bless that glorious day,
When outward forms shall all be done away;
When we in spirit and in truth alone
Shall bend, O God! before thy awful throne;
When thou our purer worship shalt approve,
And make returns of everlasting love.

THE BATTLE OF THE KEGS

N.B. This ballad was occasioned by a real incident. Certain machines, in the form of kegs, charged with gunpowder, were sent down the river to annoy the British shipping then at Philadelphia. The danger of the machines being discovered, the British manned the wharfs and shipping, and discharged their small arms and cannons at everything they saw floating in the river during the ebb tide.

Gallants attend and hear a friend,
   Trill forth harmonious ditty,
Strange things I'll tell which late befel
   In Philadelphia city.

'Twas early day, as poets say,
   Just when the sun was rising,
A soldier stood on a log of wood,
   And saw a thing surprising.

As in amaze he stood to gaze,
   The truth can't be denied, sir,
He spied a score of kegs or more
   Come floating down the tide, sir.

A sailor too in jerkin blue,
   This strange appearance viewing,
First damn'd his eyes, in great surprise,
   Then said some mischief's brewing.

These kegs, I'm told, the rebels hold,
   Pack'd up like pickling herring;
And they're come down t'attack the town,
   In this new way of ferrying.

The soldier flew, the sailor too,
   And scar'd almost to death, sir,
Wore out their shoes, to spread the news,
   And ran till out of breath, sir.

Now up and down throughout the town,
  Most frantic scenes were acted;
And some ran here, and others there,
  Like men almost distracted.

Some fire cried, which some denied,
  But said the earth had quaked;
And girls and boys, with hideous noise,
  Ran thro' the streets half naked.

Sir William he, snug as a flea,
  Lay all this time a snoring,
Nor dream'd of harm as he lay warm,
  In bed with Mrs. L——g.

Now in a fright, he starts upright,
  Awak'd by such a clatter;
He rubs both eyes, and boldly cries,
  For God's sake, what's the matter?

At his bed-side he then espied,
  Sir Erskine at command, sir,
Upon one foot, he had one boot,
  And th' other in his hand, sir.

"Arise, arise," Sir Erskine cries,
  "The rebels—more's the pity,
Without a boat are all afloat,
  And rang'd before the city.

"The motley crew, in vessels new,
  With Satan for their guide, sir,
Pack'd up in bags, or wooden kegs,
  Come driving down the tide, sir.

"Therefore prepare for bloody war,
  These kegs must all be routed,
Or surely we despised shall be,
  And British courage doubted."

The royal band, now ready stand,
    All rang'd in dread array, sir,
With stomach stout to see it out,
    And make a bloody day, sir.

The cannons roar from shore to shore,
    The small arms make a rattle;
Since wars began I'm sure no man
    E'er saw so strange a battle.

The rebel dales, the rebel vales,
    With rebel trees surrounded;
The distant wood, the hills and floods,
    With rebel echoes sounded.

The fish below swam to and fro,
    Attack'd from ev'ry quarter;
Why sure, thought they, the devil's to pay,
    'Mongst folks above the water.

The kegs, 'tis said, tho' strongly made,
    Of rebel staves and hoops, sir,
Could not oppose their powerful foes,
    The conqu'ring British troops, sir.

From morn to night these men of might
    Display'd amazing courage;
And when the sun was fairly down,
    Retir'd to sup their porrage.

An hundred men with each a pen,
    Or more upon my word, sir,
It is most true would be too few,
    Their valor to record, sir.

Such feats did they perform that day,
    Against these wicked kegs, sir,
That years to come, if they get home,
    They'll make their boasts and brags, sir.

SONG VI

O'er the hills far away, at the birth of the morn
I hear the full tone of the sweet sounding horn;
The sportsmen with shoutings all hail the new day
And swift run the hounds o'er the hills far away.

Across the deep valley their course they pursue
And rush thro' the thickets yet silver'd with dew;
Nor hedges nor ditches their speed can delay—
Still sounds the sweet horn o'er hills far away.

JOHN TRUMBULL

John Trumbull, the eldest of the "Yale Poets" and one of the effective satirists of the Revolution, came of a family several times distinguished in the annals of Connecticut. He was born in 1750 in Waterbury, where his father was minister. He was an extreme example of the intellectual precocity common in early New England. The story that at the age of seven he passed with credit the examinations for admission to Yale is well authenticated. Not entering, however, until he was thirteen, he graduated in the class of 1767; and he remained six years longer in New Haven as graduate student and tutor. As he was in advance in his studies and as he had natural ability and a taste for letters, he read widely and enthusiastically in the classics and particularly in English; he is perhaps the first of our American writers to show wide acquaintance with polite literature. He fortunately found other students with similar interests,— Dwight, Humphreys, and later, Barlow. These formed a group, almost a "school," having in common, for the first time in New England, purely literary aims and ambitions,— which soon bore fruit in various ways. For the commencement of 1770, at which he got his master's degree, Trumbull furnished an "Essay on the Use and Advantages of the Fine Arts,"—notable as a protest against the puritan view of those "who finer arts despise, and scoff at verse as heathen lies," and also as perhaps the first piece of American literary criticism. He and his associates advocated a reform in the old rigid curriculum by the introduction of modern studies— English literature and composition. With Dwight he wrote Addisonian essays—"The Meddler" and "The Correspondent"—for the Boston and New Haven papers; and also short poems in the styles then prevailing in London. In 1772-1773, while still a tutor at Yale, he published *The Progress of Dulness* in three parts, satirizing the prevalent errors in education. Part III pleads for the better education of women. In all these writings Trumbull shows liberality and good sense, but little true originality of expression; he is skillful in following the method and style of his English models,—in catching the tone of Pope in verse and Addison in prose.

As he could hardly think of adopting literature as a profession he prepared himself for law, and in 1773 he was admitted to the bar. Going to Boston to read law in the office of John Adams, he found himself in "the centre of American politics." He lamented the commercial loss following the Port Bill in elegiac stanzas,—*An Elegy for the Times,* 1774. During the next year he wrote the first part of his most important work, *M'Fingal.* This is a satire on the loyalists, in imitation of Butler's *Hudibras,* with ingredients also from Macpherson's *Ossian* and Churchill's *Ghost.* The scene is laid in a Massachusetts town shortly after the battle of Lexington; and the story tells of a turbulent town meeting coming to blows over the Revolutionary issue, discussed by a patriot, Honorius (said to have been drawn from John Adams), and the tory M'Fingal. The latter and his constable (Hudibras and Ralpho adapted to New England) are tarred and feathered. In 1782 the poem was completed in four cantos, in the last of which, entitled "The Vision," M'Fingal—like Ossian, a seer—foresees the patriotic triumphs of the Revolution. Like Trumbull's other works, it may be described as new American wine in old English bottles. It shows greatest excellence in its epigrammatic phrasing; some of its couplets have passed for Butler's. It was an effective and frequently reprinted satire during the war; and in its final form was long regarded as a great ornament to American letters.

As one of the "Hartford Wits" Trumbull again did effective service in contributing to *The Anarchiad* (1786-1787), a satire on the chaotic conditions preceding the adoption of the Constitution. He was successful as a lawyer, becoming judge of the highest court of Connecticut. He died in Detroit in 1831.

THE FUTURE GLORY OF AMERICAN LITERATURE

[From "Prospect of the Future Glory of America: being the conclusion of an Oration, delivered at the public commencement of Yale College, September 12, 1770"]

For pleasing Arts behold her matchless charms
The first in letters, as the first in arms.
See bolder genius quit the narrow shore,
And realms of science, yet untraced, explore,
Hiding in brightness of superior day,
The fainting gleam of Europe's setting ray.
Sublime the Muse shall lift her eagle wing;
Of heavenly themes the sacred bards shall sing,
Tell how the blest Redeemer, man to save,
Thro' the deep mansions of the gloomy grave,
Sought the low shades of night, then rising high
Vanquish'd the powers of hell, and soar'd above the sky;
Or paint the scenes of that funereal day,
When earth's last fires shall mark their dreadful way,
In solemn pomp th' eternal Judge descend,
Doom the wide world and give to nature, end;
Or ope heaven's glories to th' astonish'd eye,
And bid their lays with lofty Milton vie;
Or wake from nature's themes the moral song,
And shine with Pope, with Thomson and with Young.
This land her Swift and Addison shall view
The former honors equall'd by the new;
Here shall some Shakespeare charm the rising age,
And hold in magic chains the listening stage;
A second Watts shall string the heavenly lyre,
And other muses other bards inspire.

DWIGHT'S HOMERIC FIRE

[FROM "LINES ADDRESSED TO MESSRS. DWIGHT AND BARLOW, ON THE
PROJECTED PUBLICATION OF THEIR POEMS IN LONDON, DECEMBER,
1775"]

And see, where yon proud Isle[1] her shores extends
The cloud of Critics on your Muse descends!
From every side, with deadly force, shall steer
The fierce Review, the censuring Gazetteer,
Light Magazines, that pointless jests supply,
And quick Gazettes, that coin the current lie.
Each coffee-house shall catch the loud alarms,
The Temple swarm, and Grub-street wake to arms.
As vultures, sailing through the darken'd air,
Whet their keen talons, and their beaks prepare,
O'er warring armies wait th' approaching fray,
And sate their wishes on the future prey.

* * * * * *

Yet heed not these, but join the sons of song,
And scorn the censures of the envious throng;
Prove to the world, in these new-dawning skies,
What genius kindles and what arts arise;
What fav'ring Muses lent their willing aid,
As gay through Pindus' flowery paths you stray'd;
While in your strains the purest morals flow'd,
Rules to the great, and lessons to the good.
All Virtue's friends are yours.   Disclose the lays;
Your country's heroes claim the debt of praise;
Fame shall assent, and future years admire
Barlow's strong flight, and Dwight's Homeric fire.

[1] Great Britain.—See the British Reviewers for the fulfilment
of this prediction.

The English scribblers began their abuse, by asserting that all
the Americans were cowards.   Subsequent events have taught
them a reverent silence on that topic.   They now labor, with
equal wit and eloquence, to prove our universal ignorance and
stupidity.   The present writers in the Quarterly Review have
made it the vehicle of insult and slander upon our genius and
manners.   Whether they will be more successful with the pen,
than with the sword, in prostrating America at their feet, Time,
the ancient arbiter, will determine in due season.—Author's note,
1820.

TOM BRAINLESS AT COLLEGE

[FROM "THE PROGRESS OF DULNESS," PART I. 1772]

Two years thus spent in gathering knowledge,
The lad sets forth t'unlade at college,
While down his sire and priest attend him,
To introduce and recommend him;
Or if detain'd, a letter's sent
Of much apocryphal content,
To set him forth, how dull soever,
As very learn'd and very clever;
A genius of the first emission,
With burning love for erudition;
So studious he'll outwatch the moon
And think the planets set too soon.
He had but little time to fit in;
Examination too must frighten.
Depend upon't he must do well,
He knows much more than he can tell;
Admit him, and in little space
He'll beat his rivals in the race;
His father's incomes are but small,
He comes now, if he comes at all.
    So said, so done, at college now
He enters—well, no matter how;
New scenes awhile his fancy please,
But all must yield to love of ease.
In the same round condemn'd each day,
To study, read, recite and pray;
To make his hours of business double—
He can't endure th' increasing trouble;
And finds at length, as times grow pressing,
All plagues are easier than his lesson.
With sleepy eyes and count'nance heavy,
With much excuse of *non paravi*.[1]
Much absence, *tardes* and *egresses*,
The college-evil on him seizes.

[1] *Non paravi,* I have not prepared for recitation—an excuse commonly given; *tardes* and *egresses* were terms used at college, for coming in late and going out before the conclusion of service.

Then ev'ry book, which ought to please,
Stirs up the seeds of dire disease;
Greek spoils his eyes, the print's so fine,
Grown dim with study, or with wine;
Of Tully's Latin much afraid,
Each page, he calls the doctor's aid;
While geometry, with lines so crooked,
Sprains all his wits to overlook it.
His sickness puts on every name,
Its cause and uses still the same;
'Tis tooth-ache, cholic, gout or stone,
With phases various as the moon;
But though through all the body spread,
Still makes its cap'tal seat, the head.
In all diseases, 'tis expected,
The weakest parts be most infected.

THE QUACKERIES OF LEARNING

[From the Same]

Kind head-ache hail! thou blest disease,
The friend of idleness and ease;
Who mid the still and dreary bound
Where college walls her sons surround,
In spite of fears, in justice' spite,
Assumest o'er laws dispensing right,
Sett'st from his task the blunderer free,
Excused by dulness and by thee.
Thy vot'ries bid a bold defiance
To all the calls and threats of science,
Slight learning human and divine,
And hear no prayers, and fear no fine.
And yet how oft the studious gain,
The dulness of a letter'd brain;
Despising such low things the while,
As English grammar, phrase and style;
Despising ev'ry nicer art,
That aids the tongue, or mends the heart;

Read ancient authors o'er in vain,
Nor taste one beauty they contain;
Humbly on trust accept the sense,
But deal for words at vast expense;
Search well how every term must vary
From Lexicon to Dictionary;
And plodding on in one dull tone,
Gain ancient tongues and lose their own,
Bid every graceful charm defiance,
And woo the skeleton of science.
   Come ye, who finer arts despise,
And scoff at verse as heathen lies;
In all the pride of dulness rage
At Pope, or Milton's deathless page;
Or stung by truth's deep-searching line,
Rave ev'n at rhymes as low as mine;
Say ye, who boast the name of wise,
Wherein substantial learning lies.
Is it, superb in classic lore,
To speak what Homer spoke before,
To write the language Tully wrote,
The style, the cadence and the note?
Is there a charm in sounds of Greek,
No language else can learn to speak;
That cures distemper'd brains at once,
Like Pliny's rhymes for broken bones?
Is there a spirit found in Latin,
That must evap'rate in translating?
And say are sense and genius bound
To any vehicles of sound?
Can knowledge never reach the brains,
Unless convey'd in ancient strains?
While Homer sets before your eyes
Achilles' rage, Ulysses' lies,
Th' amours of Jove in masquerade,
And Mars entrapp'd by Phœbus' aid;
While Virgil sings, in verses grave,
His lovers meeting in a cave,
His ships turn'd nymphs, in pagan fables,
And how the Trojans eat their tables;

While half this learning but displays
The follies of the former days;
And for our linguists, fairly try them,
A tutor'd parrot might defy them.
     Go to the vulgar—'tis decreed,
There you must preach and write or plead;
Broach every curious Latin phrase
From Tully down to Lily's days:
All this your hearers have no share in,
Bate but their laughing and their staring.
Interpreters must pass between,
To let them know a word you mean.
     Yet could you reach that lofty tongue
Which Plato wrote and Homer sung;
Or ape the Latin verse and scanning,
Like Vida, Cowley or Buchanan;
Or bear ten phrase-books in your head;
Yet know, these languages are dead,
And nothing, e'er, by death, was seen
Improved in beauty, strength or mien,
Whether the sexton use his spade,
Or sorcerer wake the parted shade.
Think how would Tully stare or smile
At these wan spectres of his style,
Or Horace in his jovial way
Ask what these babblers mean to say.

THE TOWN-MEETING

[FROM "M'FINGAL," CANTO I.   1775]

When Yankies,[1] skill'd in martial rule,
First put the British troops to school:[2]
Instructed them in warlike trade,
And new manœuvres of parade,

[1] *Yankies,*—a term formerly of derision, but now merely of distinction, given to the people of the four eastern states. [This and the following notes on "M'Fingal" are from Trumbull's "Poetical Works," 1820].

[2] At the battle of Lexington. The reader will easily recollect how often these salutary lessons have been since repeated—from the action of Bunker-Hill to the battle of New Orleans inclusive.

The true war-dance of Yankee reels,
And *manual exercise* of heels;
Made them give up, like saints complete,
The arm of flesh, and trust the feet,
And work, like Christians undissembling,
Salvation out, by fear and trembling;
Taught Percy fashionable races,
And modern modes of Chevy-Chases:[1]
From Boston, in his best array,
Great 'Squire M'Fingal took his way,
And graced with ensigns of renown,
Steer'd homeward to his native town.

His high descent our heralds trace
From Ossian's[2] famed Fingalian race:
For though their name some part may lack,
Old Fingal spelt it with a Mac;
Which great M'Pherson, with submission,
We hope will add the next addition.

His fathers flourish'd in the Highlands
Of Scotia's fog-benighted islands;
Whence gain'd our 'Squire two gifts by right,
Rebellion and the Second-sight.
Of these, the first, in ancient days,
Had gain'd the noblest palm of praise,
'Gainst kings stood forth and many a crown'd head
With terror of its might confounded;
Till rose a king with potent charm
His foes by meekness to disarm,
Whom every Scot and Jacobite
Straight fell in love with at first sight;
Whose gracious speech with aid of pensions,
Hush'd down all murmurs of dissensions,
And with the sound of potent metal
Brought all their buzzing swarms to settle;

[1] Lord Percy commanded the party, that was first opposed to the Americans at Lexington. This allusion to the family renown of Chevy-Chase arose from the precipitate manner of his Lordship's quitting the field of battle, and returning to Boston.

[2] See Fingal, an ancient epic poem, published as the work of Ossian, a Caledonian bard of the third century, by James M'Pherson. The complete name of Ossian, according to the Scottish nomenclature, will be Ossian M'Fingal.

Who rain'd his ministerial manna,
Till loud Sedition sung hosanna;
The grave Lords-Bishops and the Kirk
United in the public work;
Rebellion, from the northern regions,
With Bute and Mansfield swore allegiance;
All hands combin'd to raze, as nuisance,
Of church and state the Constitutions,
Pull down the empire, on whose ruins
They meant to edify their new ones;
Enslave th' American wildernesses,
And rend the provinces in pieces.
With these our 'Squire, among the valiant'st,
Employ'd his time, and tools and talents,
And found this new rebellion pleasing
As his old king-destroying treason.

  Nor less avail'd his optic sleight,
And Scottish gift of second-sight.[1]
No ancient sybil, famed in rhyme,
Saw deeper in the womb of time;
No block in old Dodona's grove
Could ever more orac'lar prove.
Not only saw he all that could be,
But much that never was, nor would be;
Whereby all prophets far outwent he,
Though former days produced a plenty:
For any man with half an eye
What stands before him can espy;
But optics sharp it needs, I ween,
To see what is not to be seen.
As in the days of ancient fame,
Prophets and poets were the same,
And all the praise that poets gain
Is for the tales they forge and feign:
So gain'd our 'Squire his fame by seeing
Such things, as never would have being;

[1] They, who wish to understand the nature, and *modus operandi*, of the Highland vision by second sight, may consult the profound Johnson, in his Tour of the Hebrides.

Whence he for oracles was grown
The very tripod[1] of his town.
Gazettes no sooner rose a lie in,
But straight he fell to prophesying;
Made dreadful slaughter in his course,
O'erthrew provincials, foot and horse,
Brought armies o'er, by sudden pressings,
Of Hanoverians, Swiss and Hessians,
Feasted with blood his Scottish clan,
And hang'd all rebels to a man,
Divided their estates and pelf,
And took a goodly share himself.
All this with spirit energetic,
He did with second-sight prophetic.

Thus stored with intellectual riches,
Skill'd was our 'Squire in making speeches;
Where strength of brains united centers
With strength of lungs surpassing Stentor's.[2]
But as some muskets so contrive it,
As oft to miss the mark they drive at,
And though well aim'd at duck or plover,
Bear wide, and kick their owners over:
So fared our 'Squire, whose reas'ning toil
Would often on himself recoil,
And so much injured more his side,
The stronger arguments he applied;
As old war-elephants, dismay'd,
Trod down the troops they came to aid,
And hurt their own side more in battle,
Than less and ordinary cattle.
Yet at Town-meetings every chief
Pinn'd faith on great M'Fingal's sleeve;
Which when he lifted, all by rote
Raised sympathetic hands to vote.

The Town, our hero's scene of action,
Had long been torn by feuds of faction,

[1] The tripod was a sacred three-legged stool, from which the ancient priests uttered their oracles.
[2] Stentor, the loud-voiced herald in Homer.

And as each party's strength prevails,
It turn'd up different, heads or tails;
With constant rattling, in a trice,
Show'd various sides, as oft as dice.
As that famed weaver, wife t' Ulysses,
By night her day's work pick'd in pieces,
And though she stoutly did bestir her,
Its finishing was ne'er the nearer:
So did this town with ardent zeal
Weave cobwebs for the public weal,
Which, when completed, or before,
A second vote in pieces tore.
They met, made speeches full long-winded,
Resolv'd, protested and rescinded;
Addresses sign'd; then chose committees
To stop all drinking of Bohea teas;[1]
With winds of doctrine veer'd about,
And turn'd all Whig committees out.
Meanwhile our Hero, as their head,
In pomp the Tory faction led,
Still following, as the 'Squire should please,
Successive on, like files of geese.

    And now the town was summon'd, greeting,
To grand parading of Town-meeting;
A show, that strangers might appal,
As Rome's grave senate did the Gaul.
High o'er the rout, on pulpit stairs,[2]
Mid den of thieves in house of prayers,
(That house, which loth a rule to break
Serv'd heaven, but one day in the week,
Open the rest for all supplies
Of news, and politics, and lies;)

[1] One of the subjects of dispute, which brought on the war, was a tax upon tea, on its importation into the colonies. And therefore one of the weapons of opposition was an universal agreement by the people, not to drink any tea, till the tax was taken off. The committees referred to, were called Committees of Correspondence: part of their business was to enforce the execution of the voluntary regulations made by the people in the several towns.

[2] In country towns in New England, the town-meeting is generally held in the church, or meeting-house.

Stood forth the Constable; and bore
His staff, like Merc'ry's wand of yore,
Waved potent round, the peace to keep,
As that laid dead men's souls to sleep.
Above and near th' hermetic staff,
The Moderator's[1] upper half
In grandeur o'er the cushion bow'd,
Like Sol half seen behind a cloud,
Beneath stood voters of all colors,
Whigs, Tories, orators and brawlers;
With every tongue in either faction
Prepared like minute-men[2] for action;
Where truth and falsehood, wrong and right,
Drew all their legions forth to fight.
With equal uproar scarcely rave
Opposing winds in Æolus' cave;
Such dialogues with earnest face
Held never Balaam with his ass.

A REVOLUTIONARY BENCH OF JUSTICE

[FROM THE SAME, CANTO III.]

This said, our 'Squire, yet undismay'd,
Call'd forth the Constable to aid,
And bade him read, in nearer station,
The Riot-act and Proclamation.
He swift, advancing to the ring,
Began, "Our Sovereign Lord, the King"—
When thousand clam'rous tongues he hears,
And clubs and stones assail his ears.
To fly was vain; to fight was idle;
By foes encompass'd in the middle,
His hope, in strategems, he found,
And fell right craftily to ground;

[1] Moderator is the name given to the chairman or speaker of a town-meeting. He is here seated in the pulpit.

[2] Minute-men were that part of the militia of our country, who being drafted, and enrolled by themselves, were prepared to march at a minute's warning wherever the public safety required.

Then crept to seek an hiding place,
'Twas all he could, beneath a brace;
Where soon the conq'ring crew espied him,
And where he lurk'd, they caught and tied him.
　At once with resolution fatal,
Both Whigs and Tories rush'd to battle.
Instead of weapons, either band
Seized on such arms as came to hand.
And as famed Ovid paints th' adventures
Of wrangling Lapithae and Centaurs,
Who at their feast, by Bacchus led,
Threw bottles at each other's head;
And these arms failing in their scuffles,
Attack'd with andirons, tongs and shovels:
So clubs and billets, staves and stones
Met fierce, encountering every sconce,
And cover'd o'er with knobs and pains
Each void receptacle for brains;
Their clamors rend the skies around,
The hills rebellow to the sound;
And many a groan increas'd the din
From batter'd nose and broken shin.
　M'Fingal, rising at the word,
Drew forth his old militia-sword;
Thrice cried "King George," as erst in distress,
Knights of romance invoked a mistress;
And brandishing the blade in air,
Struck terror through th' opposing war.
The Whigs, unsafe within the wind
Of such commotion, shrunk behind.
With whirling steel around address'd,
Fierce through their thickest throng press'd,
(Who roll'd on either side in arch,
Like Red Sea waves in Israel's march)
And like a meteor rushing through,
Struck on their Pole a vengeful blow.
Around, the Whigs, of clubs and stones
Discharged whole volleys, in platoons,
That o'er in whistling fury fly;
But not a foe dares venture nigh.

And now perhaps with glory crown'd
Our 'Squire had fell'd the pole to ground,
Had not some Pow'r, a whig at heart,
Descended down and took their part;[1]
(Whether 'twere Pallas, Mars or Iris,
'Tis scarce worth while to make inquiries)
Who at the nick of time alarming,
Assumed the solemn form of Chairman,
Address'd a Whig, in every scene
The stoutest wrestler on the green,
And pointed where the spade was found,
Late used to set their pole in ground,
And urged, with equal arms and might,
To dare our 'Squire to single fight.
The Whig thus arm'd, untaught to yield,
Advanced tremendous to the field:
Nor did M'Fingal shun the foe,
But stood to brave the desp'rate blow;
While all the party gazed, suspended
To see the deadly combat ended;
And Jove in equal balance weigh'd
The sword against the brandish'd spade,
He weigh'd; but lighter than a dream,
The sword flew up, and kick'd the beam.
Our 'Squire on tiptoe rising fair
Lifts high a noble stroke in air,
Which hung not, but like dreadful engines,
Descended on his foe in vengeance.
But ah! in danger, with dishonor
The sword perfidious fails its owner;
That sword, which oft had stood its ground,
By huge trainbands encircled round;
And on the bench, with blade right loyal,
Had won the day at many a trial,[2]

[1] The learned reader will readily observe the allusions in this scene, to the single combats of Paris and Menelaus in Homer, Æneas and the Turnus in Virgil, and Michael and Satan in Milton.

[2] It was the fashion in New England, at that time, for judges to wear swords on the bench.

Of stones and clubs had braved th' alarms,
Shrunk from these new Vulcanian arms
The spade so temper'd from the sledge,
Nor keen nor solid harm'd its edge,
Now met it, from his arm of might,
Descending with steep force to smite;
The blade snapp'd short—and from his hand,
With rust embrown'd the glittering sand.
Swift turn'd M'Fingal at the view,
And call'd to aid th' attendant crew,
In vain; the Tories all had run,
When scarce the fight was well begun;
Their setting wigs he saw decreas'd
Far in th' horizon tow'rd the west.
Amazed he view'd the shameful sight,
And saw no refuge, but in flight:
But age unwieldy check'd his pace,
Though fear had wing'd his flying race;
For not a trifling prize at stake;
No less than great M'Fingal's back.
With legs and arms he work'd his course,
Like rider that outgoes his horse,
And labor'd hard to get away, as
Old Satan struggling on through chaos;
'Till looking back, he spied in rear
The spade-arm'd chief advanced too near·
Then stopp'd and seized a stone, that lay
An ancient landmark near the way;
Nor shall we as old bards have done,
Affirm it weigh'd an hundred ton;
But such a stone, as at a shift
A modern might suffice to lift,
Since men, to credit their enigmas,
Are dwindled down to dwarfs and pigmies,
And giants exiled to their cronies
To Brobdignags and Patagonias.
But while our Hero turn'd him round,
And tugg'd to raise it from the ground,
The fatal spade discharged a blow
Tremendous on his rear below:

His bent knee fail'd, and void of strength
Stretch'd on the ground his manly length.
Like ancient oak o'erturned, he lay,
Or tower to tempests fall'n a prey,
Or mountain sunk with all his pines,
Or flow'r the plow to dust consigns,
And more things else—but all men know 'em,
If slightly versed in epic poem.
At once the crew, at this dread crisis,
Fall on, and bind him, ere he rises;
And with loud shouts and joyful soul,
Conduct him prisoner to the pole.
When now the mob in lucky hour
Had got their en'mies in their power,
They first proceed, by grave command,
To take the Constable in hand.
Then from the pole's sublimest top
The active crew let down the rope,
At once its other end in haste bind,
And make it fast upon his waistband;
Till like the earth, as stretch'd on tenter,
He hung self-balanced on his centre.
Then upwards, all hands hoisting sail,
They swung him, like a keg of ale,
Till to the pinnacle in height
He vaulted, like balloon or kite.
As Socrates of old at first did
To aid philosophy get hoisted,
And found his thoughts flow strangely clear,
Swung in a basket in mid air:
Our culprit thus, in purer sky,
With like advantage raised his eye,
And looking forth in prospect wide,
His Tory errors clearly spied,
And from his elevated station,
With bawling voice began addressing.
  "Good Gentlemen and friends and kin,
For heaven's sake hear, if not for mine!
I here renounce the Pope, the Turks,
The King, the Devil, and all their works;

And will, set me but once at ease,
Turn Whig or Christian, what you please;
And always mind your rules so justly,
Should I live long as old Methus'lah,
I'll never join in British rage,
Nor help Lord North, nor Gen'ral Gage;
Nor lift my gun in future fights,
Nor take away your Charter-rights;
Nor overcome your new-raised levies,
Destroy your towns, nor burn your navies;
Nor cut your poles down while I've breath,
Though raised more thick than hatchel-teeth:
But leave King George and all his elves
To do their conq'ring work themselves."

This said, they lower'd him down in state,
Spread at all points, like falling cat;
But took a vote first on the question,
That they'd accept this full confession,
And to their fellowship and favor,
Restore him on his good behavior.

Not so our 'Squire submits to rule,
But stood, heroic as a mule.
"You'll find it all in vain," quoth he,
"To play your rebel tricks on me.
All punishments, the world can render,
Serve only to provoke th' offender;
The will gains strength from treatment horrid,
As hides grow harder when they're curried.
No man e'er felt the halter draw,
With good opinion of the law;
Or held in method orthodox
His love of justice, in the stocks;
Or fail'd to lose by sheriff's shears
At once his loyalty and ears.
Have you made Murray[1] look less big,
Or smoked old Williams[1] to a Whig?

[1] Members of the Mandamus Council in Massachusetts. The
operation of smoking Tories was thus performed. The victim
was confined in a close room before a large fire of green wood,
and a cover applied to the top of the chimney.

Did our mobb'd Ol'ver[1] quit his station,
Or heed his vows of resignation?
Has Rivington[2] in dread of stripes,
Ceased lying since you stole his types?
And can you think my faith will alter,
By tarring, whipping or the halter?
I'll stand the worst; for recompense
I trust King George and Providence.
And when with conquest gain'd I come,
Array'd in law and terror home,
Ye'll rue this inauspicious morn,
And curse the day, when ye were born,
In Job's high style of imprecations,
With all his plagues, without his patience."
  Meanwhile beside the pole, the guard
A Bench of Justice had prepared,[3]
Where sitting round in awful sort
The Grand Committee hold their Court;
While all the crew, in silent awe,
Wait from their lips the lore of law.
Few moments with deliberation
They hold the solemn consultation;
When soon in judgment all agree,
And Clerk proclaims the dread decree;
"That 'Squire M'Fingal having grown
The vilest Tory in the town,
And now in full examination
Convicted by his own confession,
Finding no tokens of repentence,
This court proceeds to render sentence:
That first the Mob a slip-knot single
Tie round the neck of said M'Fingal,

[1] Thomas Oliver, Esq., Lieutenant Governor of Massachusetts, He was surrounded at his seat in the country and intimidated by the mob into the signing of his resignation.

[2] Rivington was a Tory printer in New York. Just before the commencement of the war, a party from New Haven attacked his press, and carried off or destroyed the types.

[3] An imitation of legal forms was universally practiced by the mobs in New England, in the trial and condemnation of Tories. This marks a curious trait of national character.

And in due form do tar him next,
And feather, as the law directs;
Then through the town attendant ride him
In cart with Constable beside him,
And having held him up to shame,
Bring to the pole, from whence he came."
    Forthwith the crowd proceed to deck
With halter'd noose M'Fingal's neck,
While he in peril of his soul
Stood tied half-hanging to the pole;
Then lifted high the ponderous jar,
Pour'd o'er his head the smoking tar.
With less profusion once was spread
Oil on the Jewish's monarch's head,
That down his beard and vestments ran,
And cover'd all his outward man.
As when (so Claudian sings) the Gods
And earth-born Giants fell at odds,
And stout Enceladus in malice
Tore mountains up to throw at Pallas;
And while he held them o'er his head,
The river, from their fountains fed,
Pour'd down his back its copious tide,
And wore its channels in his hide:
So from the high-raised urn the torrents
Spread down his side their various currents;
His flowing wig, as next the brim,
First met and drank the sable stream;
Adown his visage stern and grave
Roll'd and adhered the viscid wave;
With arms depending as he stood,
Each cuff capacious holds the flood;
From nose and chin's remotest end,
The tarry icicles descend;
Till all o'erspread, with colors gay,
He glitter'd to the western ray,
Like sleet-bound trees in wintry skies,
Or Lapland idol carved in ice.
And now the feather-bag display'd
Is waved in triumph o'er his head,

And clouds him o'er with feathers missive,
And down, upon the tar, adhesive:
Not Maia's son, with wings for ears,
Such plumage round his visage wears;
Nor Milton's six-wing'd angel gathers
Such superfluity of feathers.
Now all complete appears our 'Squire,
Like Gorgon or Chimæra dire;
Nor more could boast on Plato's plan[1]
To rank among the race of man,
Or prove his claim to human nature,
As a two-legg'd, unfeather'd creature.

Then on the fatal cart, in state
They raised our grand Duumvirate.
And as at Rome a like committee,
Who found an owl within their city,
With solemn rites and grave processions
At every shrine perform'd lustrations;
And lest infection might take place
From such grim fowl with feather'd face,
All Rome attends him through the street
In triumph to his country seat:
With like devotion all the choir
Paraded round our awful 'Squire;
In front the martial music comes
Of horns and fiddles, fifes and drums,
With jingling sound of carriage bells,
And treble creak of rusted wheels.
Behind, the crowd, in lengthen'd row
With proud procession, closed the show.
And at fit periods every throat
Combined in universal shout;
And hail'd great Liberty in chorus,
Or bawl'd "Confusion to the Tories."
Not louder storm the welkin braves
From clamors of conflicting waves;
Less dire in Lybian wilds the noise
When rav'ning lions lift their voice;

[1] Alluding to Plato's famous definition of man, *Animal bipes implume*—a two-legged animal without feathers.

Or triumphs at town-meetings made,
On passing votes to regulate trade.[1]
    Thus having borne them round the town,
Last at the pole they set them down;
And to the tavern take their way
To end in mirth the festal day.

[1] Such votes were frequently passed at town-meetings, with the view to prevent the augmentation of prices, and stop the depreciation of the paper money.

TIMOTHY DWIGHT

Like the great puritans of the seventeenth century, Timothy Dwight was pious, learned, and high-minded; he was, however, more modern and liberal. He was a great theologian, orator, college president, and man of affairs. If he could not become a great poet merely by taking thought, he at least showed a very genuine interest in poetry. He was born in 1752 at Northampton, Massachusetts, the scene of the labors of his grandfather, Jonathan Edwards. He was little less precocious than Trumbull, and quite as ambitious; as a boy, hearing talk of great men, he "formed a settled resolve to equal those whose character and talents he had heard so highly extolled." He graduated at Yale in 1769, and from 1771 to 1779 was tutor in the college. With Trumbull he formed great plans for an American literature. He lengthened the list of the American periodical essayists in "The Meddler" and "The Correspondent," and he began an epic poem. In 1777 and 1778 as a chaplain in the American army he kept up the morale of the soldiers by vigorous sermons and poems; one of the latter, "Columbia," was long preserved in patriotic collections. He then spent five years in Northampton, farming, preaching, and serving in the legislature of Massachusetts. From 1783 to 1795 he was pastor at Greenfield (in the town of Fairfield), Connecticut; and then, until his death in 1817, he was president of Yale College. Here, among other reforms and improvements, he finally introduced the study of English. During summer journeys, in gig and on horseback, through the eastern states, he collected materials, which, with miscellaneous observations and opinions, formed the four volumes of his *Travels in New England and New York* (1821).

Though the *Travels* is his most readable book, Dwight is probably best known as one of the "Yale Poets." He is said to have begun his epic *Conquest of Canaan* at the age of nineteen; his plan to publish it in five books in 1775 (see Trumbull's "Lines," p. 134) was made impossible by the war. Revised and extended to eleven books, and with patriotic references to events and heroes of the war introduced in the similes, it finally appeared at Hartford in 1785, with a dedication to Washington. Like *Paradise Lost* it seeks a Christian subject—in the wars of the Israelites under Joshua. It rivals Homer and Virgil at least in "sustained effort," consisting of nearly ten thousand lines in heroic couplets of remarkably uniform mediocrity—probably in imitation of Pope's *Iliad*. In his preface Dwight calls it "the first of its kind in this country," and excuses its lack of "national interest"; he has at least "thrown in his mite for the advancement of the refined arts on this side of the Atlantic." *The Conquest of Canaan* is the deliberate effort of a young man, ambitious but not poetically gifted, to lay the foundation of an American literature in a great epic poem. Perhaps he himself means to acknowledge the over-boldness of his attempt in quoting on the title-page from Pope:

"Fired, at first sight, with what the Muse imparts
In fearless youth we tempt the height of arts."

In *The Triumph of Infidelity,* published anonymously in 1788, Dwight defends Calvinistic orthodoxy against free-thinking in satirical couplets which suggest Young's *Love of Fame.* In his *Greenfield Hill,* a more interesting poem, published in 1794, his original design, as stated in the preface, was "to imitate, in the several parts, the manner of as many British poets." Though this design was given up, the seven parts in various metres, suggest and echo Spenser, Pope, and Goldsmith; indeed the author himself calls attention to the imitations in notes. The poem in its best parts describes the country and inhabitants of Dwight's parish, and closes in Part VII with a theme very common in Revolutionary poetry—"The Vision, or Prospect of the Future Happiness of America."

GREENFIELD HILL:

A

P   O   E   M,

I N

SEVEN PARTS.

BY TIMOTHY DWIGHT, D.D.

NEW-YORK:—PRINTED BY CHILDS AND SWAINE.

1794.

COLUMBIA

Columbia, Columbia, to glory arise,
The queen of the world, and child of the skies!
Thy genius commands thee; with rapture behold,
While ages on ages thy splendors unfold.
Thy reign is the last, and the noblest of time,
Most fruitful thy soil, most inviting thy clime;
Let the crimes of the east ne'er encrimson thy name,
Be freedom, and science, and virtue, thy fame.

To conquest, and slaughter, let Europe aspire:
Whelm nations in blood, and wrap cities in fire:
Thy heroes the rights of mankind shall defend,
And triumph pursue them, and glory attend.
A world is thy realm: for a world be thy laws,
Enlarg'd as thine empire, and just as thy cause;
On Freedom's broad basis, that empire shall rise,
Extend with the main, and dissolve with the skies.

Fair Science her gates to thy sons shall unbar,
And the east see thy morn hide the beams of her star.
New bards, and new sages, unrival'd shall soar
To fame unextinguish'd when time is no more;
To thee, the last refuge of virtue design'd,
Shall fly from all nations the best of mankind;
Here, grateful to heaven, with transport shall bring
Their incense, more fragrant than odors of spring.

Nor less shall thy fair ones to glory ascend,
And Genius and Beauty in harmony blend;
The graces of form shall awake pure desire,
And the charms of the soul ever cherish the fire;
Their sweetness unmingled, their manners refin'd,
And Virtue's bright image, instamp'd on the mind,
With peace and soft rapture shall teach life to glow,
And light up a smile in the aspect of woe.

Thy fleets to all regions thy pow'r shall display,
The nations admire, and the oceans obey;
Each shore to thy glory its tribute unfold,
And the east and the south yield their spices and gold.

As the day-spring unbounded, thy splendor shall flow,
And earth's little kingdoms before thee shall bow;
While the ensigns of union, in triumph unfurl'd,
Hush the tumult of war, and give peace to the world.
    Thus, as down a lone valley, with cedars o'erspread,
From war's dread confusion I pensively stray'd—
The gloom from the face of fair heav'n retir'd;
The winds ceas'd to murmur; the thunders expir'd;
Perfumes, as of Eden, flow'd sweetly along,
And a voice, as of angels, enchantingly sung:
"Columbia, Columbia, to glory arise,
The queen of the world and the child of the skies."

THE DEATH OF ARAM

[FROM "THE CONQUEST OF CANAAN," BOOK I. 1785]

    And now bright Phosphor wak'd the dawning day,
The tents all whitening in th' expanded ray;
The sun's broad beam the scene of war display'd,
A wide extent, with distant groves o'erspread;
A tall, dark forest gloom'd the northern round,
And eastern hills o'er hills th' horizon bound:
Far south, a plain in vivid green withdrew,
And one unvaried level fill'd the view;
Beyond, Ai's grandeur proudly rose on high,
And azure mountains pierc'd the western sky.
    Around their Leader's tent, th' unnumber'd train
Throng'd from the camp, and gather'd on the plain.
When Zimri slow approach'd; of Asher's race
The first in merit, as the first in place.
Him, not a chief, that dar'd the battling field,
In swiftness equall'd, or in strength excell'd;
Save Joshua's arm, that still unconquer'd shone;
From every rival every prize he won.
    In night's last gloom (so Joshua's will ordain'd)
To find what hopes the cautious foe remain'd,
Or what new strength, allied, increas'd their force,
To Ai's high walls the hero bent his course.
Aram, his friend, unknowing vile dismay,
With willing footsteps shar'd the dangerous way.

In virtue join'd, one soul to both was given;
Each steer'd his path, and led his friend to heaven.

   O'er earth's dim verge as dawn'd the cheerful day,
Near slumbering Ai they cours'd their fearless way;
Unseen, in twining shrubs, a heathen sate,
Mark'd their still path, and boded Aram's fate;
Swift hurl'd, his javelin sought the hero's side,
Pierc'd to the heart, he groan'd, and gasp'd, and died.
The heathen flew, fierce Zimri clave his breast,
But Aram's eyes were clos'd in endless rest.

   Thus, while fond Virtue wish'd in vain to save,
Hale,[1] bright and generous, found a hapless grave.
With genius' living flame his bosom glow'd,
And science charm'd him to her sweet abode:
In worth's fair path his feet adventur'd far;
The pride of peace, the rising grace of war;
In duty firm, in danger calm as even,
To friends unchanging, and sincere to heaven.
How short his course, the prize how early won!
While weeping friendship mourns her favorite gone.
With soul too noble for so base a cause,
Thus André bow'd to war's barbarian laws.
In morn's fair light the opening blossom warm'd,
Its beauty smil'd, its growing fragrance charm'd;
Fierce roar'd th' untimely blast around its head;
The beauty vanish'd and the fragrance fled;
Soon sunk his graces in the wintry tomb,
And sad Columbia wept his hapless doom.

[1] The comparisons of this kind were all written in the early stages of the late war, and annexed to the poem to indulge the Author's own emotions of regard to the persons named in them. As it was impossible to pay this little tribute of respect to all the deserving characters, who have fallen in defence of American liberty, the Author determined to desist, after this first attempt. The lines on Major André are an exception to the above remark, as are those on General Mercer. [Captain Nathan Hale was executed as a spy by the British; Major André similarly by the Americans. In spite of the author's determination to desist the poem contains several other tributes of respect.]

THE SMOOTH DIVINE

[FROM "THE TRIUMPH OF INFIDELITY." 1788]

There smiled the smooth Divine, unused to wound
The sinner's heart, with hell's alarming sound.
No terrors on his gentle tongue attend;
No grating truths the nicest ear offend.
That strange new-birth, that methodistic grace,
Nor in his heart nor sermons found a place.
Plato's fine tales he clumsily retold,
Trite, fireside, moral seesaws, dull as old;
His Christ and Bible plac'd at good remove,
Guilt hell-deserving, and forgiving love.
'Twas best, he said, mankind should cease to sin:
Good fame requir'd it; so did peace within.
Their honors, well he knew, would ne'er be driven;
But hoped they still would please to go to heaven.
Each week he paid his visitation dues;
Coaxed, jested, laughed; rehearsed the private news;
Smoked with each goody, thought her cheese excell'd;
Her pipe he lighted, and her baby held.
Or plac'd in some great town, with lacquer'd shoes,
Trim wig, and trimmer gown, and glistening hose,
He bow'd, talked politics, learned manners mild;
Most meekly questioned, and most smoothly smiled;
At rich men's jests laughed loud, their stories prais'd;
Their wives' new patterns gaz'd, and gaz'd, and gaz'd;
Most daintily on pamper'd turkeys dined;
Nor shrunk with fasting, nor with study pin'd:
Yet from their churches saw his brethren driven,
Who thunder'd truth, and spoke the voice of heaven,
Chill'd trembling guilt, in Satan's headlong path,
Charm'd the feet back, and rous'd the ear of death.
"Let fools," he cried, "starve on, while prudent I
Snug in my nest shall live, and snug shall die."

THE PROSPECT

[FROM "GREENFIELD HILL," PART I. 1794]

From southern isles, on winds of gentlest wing,
Sprinkled with morning dew, and rob'd in green,
Life in her eye, and music in her voice,
Lo Spring returns, and wakes the world to joy!
Forth creep the smiling herbs; expand the flowers;
New-loos'd, and bursting from their icy bonds,
The streams fresh warble, and through every mead
Convey reviving verdure; every bough,
Full-blown and lovely, teems with sweets and songs;
And hills, and plains, and pastures feel the prime.
  As round me here I gaze, what prospects rise?
Etherial! matchless! such as Albion's sons,
Could Albion's isle an equal prospect boast,
In all the harmony of numerous song,
Had tun'd to rapture, and o'er Cooper's hill,
And Windsor's beauteous forest, high uprais'd,
And sent on fame's light wing to every clime.
Far inland, blended groves, and azure hills,
Skirting the broad horizon, lift their pride.
Beyond, a little chasm to view unfolds
Cerulean mountains, verging high on Heaven,
In misty grandeur. Stretch'd in nearer view,
Unnumber'd farms salute the cheerful eye;
Contracted there to little gardens; here outspread
Spacious, with pastures, fields, and meadows rich;
Where the young wheat its glowing green displays,
Or the dark soil bespeaks the recent plough,
Or flocks and herds along the lawn disport.
  Fair is the landscape; but a fairer still
Shall soon enchant the soul—when harvest full
Waves wide its bending wealth. Delightful task!
To trace along the rich, enamell'd ground,
The sweetly varied hues; from India's corn,
Whose black'ning verdure bodes a bounteous crop,
Through lighter grass, and lighter still the flax,
The paler oats, the yellowish barley, wheat
In golden glow, and rye in brighter gold.

These soon the sight shall bless. Now other scenes
The heart dilate, where round, in rural pride
The village spreads its tidy, snug retreats,
That speak the industry of every hand.
   How bless'd the sight of such a numerous train
In such small limits, tasting every good
Of competence, of independence, peace,
And liberty unmingled; every house
On its own ground, and every happy swain
Beholding no superior, but the laws,
And such as virtue, knowledge, useful life,
And zeal, exerted for the public good,
Have rais'd above the throng. For here, in truth,
Not in pretence, man is esteem'd as man.

THE VILLAGE CHURCH AND ACADEMIC SCHOOL

[FROM THE SAME, PART II]

   Beside yon church, that beams a modest ray,
With tidy neatness reputably gay,
When, mild and fair, as Eden's seventh-day light,
In silver silence, shines the Sabbath bright,
In neat attire, the village households come,
And learn the path-way to the eternal home.
Hail solemn ordinance! worthy of the SKIES;
Whence thousand richest blessings daily rise;
Peace, order, cleanliness, and manners sweet,
A sober mind, to rule submission meet,
Enlarging knowledge, life from guilt refin'd,
And love to God, and friendship to mankind.
In the clear splendor of thy vernal morn,
New-quicken'd man to light, and life, is born;
The desert of the mind with virtue blooms;
Its flowers unfold, its fruits exhale perfumes;
Proud guilt dissolves, beneath the searching ray,
And low debasement, trembling, creeps away;
Vice bites the dust; foul Error seeks her den;
And God, descending, dwells anew with men.

Where yonder humbler spire salutes the eye,
Its vane slow turning in the liquid sky,
Where, in light gambols, healthy striplings sport,
Ambitious learning builds her outer court;
A grave preceptor, there, her usher stands,
And rules, without a rod, her little bands.
Some half-grown sprigs of learning grac'd his brow:
Little he knew, though much he wish'd to know,
Inchanted hung o'er Virgil's honey'd lay,
And smil'd, to see desipient Horace play;
Glean'd scraps of Greek; and, curious, trac'd afar,
Through Pope's clear glass, the bright Mæonian star.
Yet oft his students at his wisdom star'd,
For many a student to his side repair'd,
Surpriz'd, they heard him Dilworth's knots untie,
And tell, what lands beyond the Atlantic lie.
    Many his faults; his virtues small, and few;
Some little good he did, or strove to do;
Laborious still, he taught the early mind,
And urg'd to manners meek, and thoughts refin'd;
Truth he impress'd, and every virtue prais'd;
While infant eyes, in wondering silence, gaz'd;
The worth of time would, day by day, unfold,
And tell them, every hour was made of gold.
Brown Industry he lov'd; and oft declar'd
How hardy Sloth, in life's sad evening, far'd.

THE FARMER'S ADVICE TO THE VILLAGERS

[FROM THE SAME, PART VI]

Not long since liv'd a farmer plain,
Intent to gather honest gain,
Laborious, prudent, thrifty, neat,
Of judgment strong, experience great,
In solid homespun clad, and tidy,
And with no coxcomb learning giddy.
Daily, to hear his maxims sound,
Th' approaching neighbors flock'd around;

Daily they saw his counsels prove
The source of union, peace, and love,
The means of prudence, and of wealth,
Of comfort, cheerfulness, and health:
And all, who follow'd his advice,
Appear'd more prosperous, as more wise.

Wearied, at length, with many a call,
The sage resolv'd to summon all:
And gathering, on a pleasant Monday,
A crowd not always seen on Sunday,
Curious to hear, while hard they press'd him,
In friendly terms, he thus address'd 'em.

"My friends, you have my kindest wishes;
Pray think a neighbor not officious,
While thus, to teach you how to live,
My very best advice I give.

"And first, *industrious* be your lives;
Alike employ'd yourselves, and wives:
Your children, join'd in labor gay,
With something useful fill each day.
Those little times of leisure save,
Which most men lose, and all men have;
The half days, when a job is done;
The whole days, when a storm is on.
Few know, without a strict account,
To what these little times amount:
If wasted, while the same your cost,
The sums, you might have earn'd are lost.

"*Learn small things never to despise;*
You little think how fast they rise.
A rich reward the mill obtains,
Tho' but two quarts a bushel gains:
Still rolling on its steady rounds,
The farthings soon are turn'd to pounds.

*   *   *   *   *   *

"*In this New World, life's changing round,*
In three descents, is often found.
The *first,* firm, busy, plodding, poor,
Earns, saves, and daily swells, his store:

By farthings first, and pence, it grows;
In shillings next, and pounds, it flows;
Then spread his widening farms, abroad;
His forests wave, his harvests nod;
Fattening, his numerous cattle play,
And debtors dread his reckoning day.
Ambitious then t' adorn with knowledge
His son, he places him at college;
And sends, in smart attire, and neat,
To travel, thro' each neighboring state;
Builds him a handsome house, or buys,
Sees him a gentleman, and dies.
    "The *second,* born to wealth, and ease,
And taught to think, converse, and please,
Ambitious, with his lady wife,
Aims at a higher walk of life.
Yet, in those wholesome habits train'd,
By which his wealth, and weight, were gain'd,
Bids care in hand with pleasure go,
And blends economy with show.
His houses, fences, garden, dress,
The neat and thrifty man confess.
Improv'd, but with improvement plain,
Intent on office, as on gain,
Exploring, useful sweets to spy,
To public life he turns his eye.
A townsman first; a justice soon;
A member of the house anon;
Perhaps to board, or bench, invited,
He sees the state, and subjects, righted;
And, raptur'd with politic life,
Consigns his children to his wife.
Of household cares amid the round,
For her, too hard the task is found.
At first she struggles, and contends;
Then doubts, desponds, laments, and bends;
Her sons pursue the sad defeat,
And shout their victory complete;
Rejoicing, see their father roam,
And riot, rake, and reign, at home.

Too late he sees, and sees to mourn
His race of every hope forlorn,
Abroad, for comfort, turns his eyes,
Bewails his dire mistakes, and dies.
   "His *heir, train'd only to enjoy,*
Untaught his mind, or hands, t' employ,
Conscious of wealth enough for life,
With business, care, and worth, at strife,
By prudence, conscience, unrestrain'd,
And none, but pleasure's, habits gain'd,
Whirls on the wild career of sense,
Nor danger marks, nor heeds expense.
Soon ended is the giddy round;
And soon the fatal goal is found.
His lands, secur'd for borrow'd gold,
His houses, horses, herds, are sold.
And now, no more for wealth respected,
He sinks, by all his friends neglected;
Friends, who, before, his vices flatter'd,
And liv'd upon the loaves he scatter'd.
Unacted every worthy part,
And pining with a broken heart,
To dirtiest company he flies,
Whores, gambles, turns a sot, and dies.
His children, born to fairer doom,
In rags, pursue him to the tomb.
   "Apprentic'd then to masters stern,
Some real good the orphans learn;
Are bred to toil, and hardy fare,
And grow to usefulness, and care;
And, following their great-grandsire's plan,
Each slow becomes a useful man."

I LOVE THY KINGDOM, LORD

I love thy kingdom, Lord,
The house of thine abode,
The church, our blest Redeemer sav'd
With his own precious blood.

I love thy Church, O God!
Her walls before thee stand,
Dear as the apple of thine eye,
And graven on thy hand.

If e'er to bless thy sons
My voice, or hands, deny,
These hands let useful skill forsake,
This voice in silence die.

If e'er my heart forget
Her welfare, or her woe,
Let every joy this heart forsake,
And every grief o'erflow.

For her my tears shall fall;
For her my prayers ascend;
To her my cares and toils be given,
'Till toils and cares shall end.

Beyond my highest joy
I prize her heavenly ways,
Her sweet communion, solemn vows,
Her hymns of love and praise.

Jesus, thou Friend divine,
Our Saviour and our King,
Thy hand from every snare and foe
Shall great deliverance bring.

Sure as thy truth shall last,
To Zion shall be given
The brightest glories, earth can yield,
And brighter bliss of heaven.

THE REGICIDES IN MASSACHUSETTS

[FROM "TRAVELS IN NEW ENGLAND AND NEW YORK." 1821]

In this town [Hadley, Massachusetts] resided for fifteen or sixteen years the celebrated regicides, Goffe and Whalley. They came hither in the year 1654; and lived in the house of the Rev. Mr. Russell, the Minister. Whalley died in his house. Some years afterwards, the house was pulled down by Mr. Gaylord, the proprietor; and the bones of Whalley were found buried, just without the cellar wall, in a kind of tomb, formed of mason work, and covered with flags of hewn stone.[1] After his decease Goffe quitted Hadley; went into Connecticut, and afterwards, according to tradition, to the neighborhood of New York. Here he is said to have lived some time, and the better to disguise himself, to have carried vegetables at times to market. It is said, that, having been discovered here, he retired secretly to the Colony of Rhode Island, and there lived with a son of Whalley during the remainder of his life.

The following story has been traditionally conveyed down among the inhabitants of Hadley.

In the course of Philip's war, which involved almost all the Indian tribes of New England, and among others those in the neighborhood of this town, the inhabitants thought it proper to observe the 1st of September, 1675, as a day of fasting and prayer. While they were in the church, and employed in their worship, they were surprised by a band of savages. The people instantly betook themselves to their arms, which, according to the custom of the times, they had carried with them to the church; and, rushing out of the house, attacked the invaders. The panic, under which they began the conflict, was however so great, and their number was so disproportioned to that of their enemies, that they fought doubtfully at first, and in a short time began evidently to give way. At this moment, an ancient man with hoary locks, of a most venerable and dignified aspect, and in a dress widely differing from that of the inhabitants, appeared suddenly at their head; and with a firm voice, and an example

---

[1] This fact I had from Mr. Gaylord himself.

of undaunted resolution, reanimated their spirits, led them
again to the conflict, and totally routed the savages.   When
the battle was ended, the stranger disappeared; and no person
knew whence he had come, or whither he had gone.   The relief was so timely, so sudden, so unexpected, and so providen-
tial; the appearance, and the retreat, of him who furnished it,
were so unaccountable; his person was so dignified and commanding, his resolution so superior, and his interference so
decisive; that the inhabitants, without any uncommon exercise of credulity, readily believed him to be an Angel, sent
by Heaven for their preservation.   Nor was this opinion
seriously controverted, until it was discovered, several years
afterward, that Goffe and Whalley had been lodged in the
house of Mr. Russell.   Then it was known, that their de-
liverer was Goffe: Whalley having become superannuated
sometime before the event took place.

HARVARD IN 1796

[From the Same]

The buildings, belonging to the University, are four Colleges, a Chapel, and a house, originally a private dwelling,
now called the College House.   The names of the Colleges
are Massachusetts Hall, Hollis Hall, Stoughton Hall, and
Harvard Hall.   The three first of these contain thirty-two
rooms, each.   Massachusetts Hall has two stories; the other
two, four.   Stoughton Hall is a new, and a neat building.
Harvard Hall contains only public rooms: the library,
chapel, dining-hall, philosophical chamber, a museum, and
a room for philosophical apparatus.   This building is
erected on the site of an ancient College, having the same
name, and burnt in the month of January, 1764, together
with the library, apparatus, &c.   The General Court, being
prevented from sitting in Boston at that time by the small-
pox, held their session in this building.   While it was thus
occupied it took fire, and was consumed.   This was a very
fortunate event for the Institution.   The General Court felt
itself bound, in honor, to restore everything to it, which had
been thus destroyed.   And accordingly furnished a better

building, a better library, and a better philosophical apparatus, than those which had been consumed. . . .

I ought to have mentioned, that the greatest disadvantage,
under which this Seminary labors, is the proximity of Boston. The allurements of this Metropolis have often become
too powerfully seductive to be resisted by the gay, and sometimes even by the grave, youths, who assemble here for their
education. Since the erection of West Boston bridge, the
distance between those towns is reduced from five to little
more than three miles. This fact, as I have been informed
by the Governors of the University, has rendered the evil,
alluded to, still greater. The bustle and splendor of a large
commercial town are necessarily hostile to study. Theatres,
particularly, can hardly fail of fascinating the mind at so
early a period of life. At the same time, the opulence and
liberality of the Capital have often supplied the pecuniary
wants of this Institution, and through the correspondence,
extensively maintained between Boston and Great Britain,
have been derived to it, from that country, many important
benefactions.

JOEL BARLOW

Joel Barlow was born in Redding, Connecticut, in 1754. A boyish inclination to versifying led to his being sent to Yale, where he felt the effect of the poetic revival begun by Trumbull and Dwight. At his graduation in 1778 he read a patriotic poem on *The Prospect of Peace*. He served for three years as chaplain in the American army, taking his duties lightly. After the war he practised law and founded a newspaper in Hartford. With other "Hartford Wits" he contributed to *The Anarchiad* (1786-1787), a satire which formed opinion favorable to the Constitution. Meanwhile he had been working at an ambitious poem, which he published in 1787 as *The Vision of Columbus*. An impressive list of subscribers and a demand for new editions showed the public approval—half patriotic, half literary—of this effort to supply, for the first time, an extended poem on a purely American subject. "It was received," says Barlow's biographer, "with unbounded applause."

Barlow's career, which up to this time paralleled that of the other "Yale Poets," now diverged sharply. From being a Connecticut Yankee he was to become a cosmopolitan. Going abroad in 1788 as agent for an Ohio land company, he spent the next seventeen years in England and France. Associating in London with Dr. Price, Horne Tooke, Tom Paine, and other "friends of liberty," he supported the revolutionary cause in Europe by writing in verse *The Conspiracy of Kings*—a ranting invective against the legitimist *entente* for the suppression of the French Republic—and in prose *Advice to the Privileged Orders in the Several States of Europe* (1792-1795). Proscribed in England for these attacks on "drones of the church, and harpies of the state," he went to France and was made a citizen of the French Republic. At an inn in Chambéry in Savoy, delighted at unexpectedly finding so far from home his favorite New

THE

VISION

OF

COLUMBUS;

A POEM IN NINE BOOKS.

BY JOEL BARLOW, ESQUIRE.

THE SECOND EDITION.

HARTFORD:

Printed by HUDSON and GOODWIN, for the AUTHOR.

M.DCC.LXXXVII.

England dish, he wrote his most readable poem. *The Hasty Pudding,* with its pleasing dedication to Mrs. Washington, is excellent in the mock-heroic class. Barlow did literary work in Paris, was successful in a dangerous mission for the United States Government in Algiers, and accumulated a fortune. When he returned to America in 1805, a Republican in politics and a liberal in religion, though he still asserted his adherence to the "sect of the puritans," he found himself out of sympathy with his orthodox and Federalist friends in New England. Accordingly he took up his residence in Washington, in a comfortable house with a large library. Sent by Madison as minister to France, he sought the Emperor in Poland, was involved in the disastrous retreat from Russia, and died near Cracow, December 24, 1812.

Barlow had two ruling passions—one for poetry, the other for the cause of human freedom—both of which actuated the poem which "proved the one absorbing task and inspiration" of his life. *The Vision of Columbus,* begun just after he left college, was expanded and heightened into *The Columbia,* published (1807) shortly before his death. Begun as a "philosophical poem," it took on various epic features. The preface calls it a "patriotic poem; the subject is national and historical." Columbus is conducted by Hesper to the "Mount of Vision," whence he sees the exploration and settlement of the New World, the growth of the English colonies, the triumphs of the Revolution, the establishing of the national government and the final peaceful federation of the world on American principles. It is thus elevated in conception; but it is uninspired and inflated—presenting indeed in many passages the very type of bombast. It appeared in a large quarto, beautifully printed and bound, with plates from the best artists and engravers, which did credit to its Philadelphia printers. But this pretentious dress only emphasized its pretentious substance; and before it appeared the day of the eighteenth century epic was over.

THE SCIENCE OF LIBERTY

[FROM "ADVICE TO THE PRIVILEGED ORDERS." 1792]

.   .   .   In the United States of America, the science of liberty is universally understood, felt, and practiced, as much by the simple as the wise, the weak as the strong.   Their deep-rooted and inveterate habit of thinking is, that *all men are equal in their rights,* that *it is impossible* to make them *otherwise;* and this being their undisturbed belief, they have no conception how any man in his senses can entertain any other.   This point once settled, everything is settled.   Many operations, which in Europe have been considered as incredible tales or dangerous experiments, are but the infallible consequences of this great principle.   The first of these operations is *the business of election,* which, with that people, is carried on with as much gravity as their daily labor.   There is no jealousy on the occasion, nothing lucrative in office; any man in society may attain to any place in the government, and may exercise its functions.   They believe that there is nothing more difficult in the management of the affairs of a nation, than the affairs of a family; that it only requires more hands.   They believe that it is the juggle of keeping up impositions to blind the eyes of the vulgar, that constitutes the intricacy of state.   Banish the mysticism of inequality, and you banish almost all the evils attendant on human nature.

The people, being habituated to the election of all kinds of officers, the *magnitude* of the office makes no difficulty in the case.   The president of the United States, who has more power while in office than some of the kings of Europe, is chosen with as little commotion as a churchwarden.   There is a public service to be performed, and the people say who shall do it.   The servant feels honored with the confidence reposed in him, and generally expresses his gratitude by a faithful performance.

Another of these operations is making every citizen a soldier, and every soldier a citizen; not only *permitting* every man to arm, but *obliging* him to arm.   This fact, told in Europe, previous to the French revolution, would have gained little credit; or at least it would have been regarded as a mark of an uncivilized people, extremely dangerous to a well-ordered society. Men who build systems on an inversion of nature, are obliged to invert everything that is to make part of that system. It is *because the people are civilized, that they are with safety armed*. It is an effect of their conscious dignity, as citizens enjoying equal rights, that they wish not to invade the rights of others. The danger (where there is any) from armed citizens, is only to the *government,* not to the *society;* and as long as they have nothing to revenge in the government (which they cannot have while it is in their own hands) there are many advantages in their being accustomed to the use of arms, and no possible disadvantage.

Power, habitually in the hands of a whole community, loses all the ordinary associated ideas of power. The exercise of power is a relative term; it supposes an opposition,— something to operate upon. We perceive no exertion of power in the motion of the planetary system, but a very strong one in the movement of a whirlwind; it is because we see obstructions to the latter, but none to the former. Where the government is *not* in the hands of the people, there you find opposition, you perceive two contending interests, and get an idea of the exercise of power; and whether this power be in the hands of the government or of the people, or whether it change from side to side, it is always to be dreaded. But the word *people,* in America, has a different meaning from what it has in Europe. It there means the whole community, and comprehends every human creature; here it means something else, more difficult to define.

Another consequence of the habitual idea of equality, is the *facility of changing the structure of their government,* whenever, and as often as the society shall think there is anything in it to amend. As Mr. Burke has written no "reflections on the revolution" in America, the people there have never yet been told that they have no *right* "to frame a government for themselves"; they have therefore done much in this business, without ever affixing to it the idea of "sacrilege" or "usurpation," or any other term of rant, to be found in that gentleman's vocabulary.

Within a few years the fifteen states have not only framed each its own state constitution, and two successive federal constitutions; but since the settlement of the present federal government in the year 1789, three of the states, Pennsylvania, South Carolina, and Georgia, have totally new modelled their own. And all this is done without the least confusion; the operation being scarcely known beyond the limits of the state where it is performed. Thus they are in the habit of *"choosing their own governors,"* of *"cashiering them for misconduct,"* of *"framing a government for themselves,"* and all those abominable things, the mere naming of which, in Mr. Burke's opinion, has polluted the pulpit in the Old Jewry.[1]

THE HASTY PUDDING

[1796]

Omne tulit punctum qui miscuit utile dulci.
He makes a good breakfast who mixes pudding with molasses.

To Mrs. Washington.

Madam:

. . . Your situation commands the respect and your character the affections of a numerous people. These circumstances impose a duty upon you, which I believe you discharge to your own satisfaction and that of others. The example of your domestic virtues has doubtless a great effect among your countrywomen. I only wish to rank *simplicity of diet* among the virtues. In that case it will certainly be cherished by you, and I should hope more esteemed by others than it is at present.

The Author.

[1] See Dr. Price's Sermon preached in the Old Jewry before the Revolutionary Society, and Mr. Burke's abusive strictures on the above expressions used by the Doctor.

CANTO I.

* * * * * * *

Dear Hasty-Pudding, what unpromis'd joy
Expands my heart to meet thee in Savoy!
Doom'd o'er the world thro' devious paths to roam,
Each clime my country, and each house my home,
My soul is sooth'd, my cares have found an end;
I greet my long lost, unforgotten friend.
For thee thro' Paris, that corrupted town,
How long in vain I wandered up and down,
Where shameless Bacchus, with his drenching hoard,
Cold from his cave usurps the morning board.
London is lost in smoke and steep'd in tea:
No Yankee there can lisp the name of thee;
The uncouth word, a libel on the town,
Would call a proclamation from the crown.
For climes oblique, that fear the sun's full rays,
Chill'd in their fogs, exclude the generous maize,
A grain whose rich luxuriant growth requires
Short gentle showers and bright etherial fires.
But here, though distant from our native shore,
With mutual glee we meet and laugh once more.
The same—I know thee by that yellow face,
That strong complexion of true Indian race,
Which time can never change nor soil impair,
Nor Alpine snows, nor Turkey's morbid air:
For endless years, thro' every mild domain,
Where grows the maize there thou art sure to reign.

But man, more fickle, the bold license claims
In different realms to give thee different names.
Thee the soft nations round the warm Levant
Polenta call, the French of course *Polente;*
Ev'n in thy native regions how I blush
To hear the Pennsylvanians call thee *Mush!*
On Hudson's banks while men of Belgic spawn
Insult and eat thee by the name *Suppawn.*
All spurious appellations, void of truth;
I've better known thee from my earliest youth.

Thy name is *Hasty-Pudding!* thus our sires
Were wont to greet thee fuming from their fires;
And while they argu'd in thy just defence
With logic clear, they thus explain'd the sense:
"In *haste* the boiling cauldron o'er the blaze
Receives and cooks the ready-powder'd maize;
In haste 'tis served; and then in equal haste
With cooling milk we make the sweet repast.
No carving to be done, no knife to grate
The tender ear and wound the stony plate;
But the smooth spoon, just fitted to the lip,
And taught with art the yielding mass to dip,
By frequent journeys to the bowl well stor'd,
Performs the hasty honors of the board."
Such is thy name, significant and clear,
A name, a sound to every Yankee dear,
But most to me, whose heart and palate chaste
Preserve my pure hereditary taste.

There are who strive to stamp with disrepute
The luscious food, because it feeds the brute:
In tropes of high-strain'd wit while gaudy prigs
Compare thy nursling man to pamper'd pigs,
With sovereign scorn I treat the vulgar jest,
Nor fear to share thy bounties with the beast.
What though the generous cow gives me to quaff
The milk nutritious: am I then a calf?
Or can the genius of the noisy swine,
Tho' nurs'd on pudding, thence lay claim to mine?
Sure the sweet song I fashion to thy praise
Runs more melodious than the notes they raise.

My song resounding in its grateful glee
No merit claims; I praise myself in thee.
My father lov'd thee thro' his length of days:
For thee his fields were shaded o'er with maize;
From thee what health, what vigor he possess'd,
Ten sturdy freemen sprung from him attest;
Thy constellation rul'd my natal morn,
And all my bones were made of Indian corn.
Delicious grain, whatever form it take,
To roast or boil, to smother or to bake,

In every dish 'tis welcome still to me,
But most, my Hasty-Pudding, most in thee.
   Let the green succotash with thee contend,
Let beans and corn their sweetest juices blend,
Let butter drench them in its yellow tide,
And a long slice of bacon grace their side:
Not all the plate, how fam'd soe'er it be,
Can please my palate like a bowl of thee.
Some talk of Hoe-cake, fair Virginia's pride;
Rich Johnny-cake this mouth has often tried:
Both please me well, their virtues much the same,
Alike their fabric as allied their fame—
Except in dear New England, where the last
Receives a dash of pumpkin in the paste,
To give it sweetness and improve the taste.
But place them all before me, smoking hot:
The big round dumpling rolling from the pot;
The pudding of the bag, whose quivering breast,
With suet lin'd, leads on the Yankee feast;
The Charlotte brown, within whose crusty sides
A belly soft the pulpy apple hides;
The yellow bread whose face like amber glows,
And all of Indian that the bake-pan knows—
You tempt me not: my fav'rite greets my eyes;
To that lov'd bowl my spoon by instinct flies.

CANTO II.

   To mix the food by vicious rules of art,
To kill the stomach and to sink the heart,
To make mankind, to social virtue sour,
Cram o'er each dish and be what they devour,
For this the kitchen Muse first fram'd her book,
Commanding sweats to stream from every cook;
Children no more their antic gambols tried,
And friends to physic wonder'd why they died.
Not so the Yankee: his abundant feast,
With simples furnish'd and with plainness dress'd,
A numerous offspring gathers round the board,
And cheers alike the servant and the lord,

Whose well-bought hunger prompts the joyous taste;
And health attends them from the short repast.
While the full pail rewards the milk-maid's toil,
The mother sees the morning cauldron boil;
To stir the pudding next demands their care,
To spread the table and the bowls prepare;
To feed the children, as their portions cool,
And comb their heads, and send them off to school.
  Yet may the simplest dish some rules impart,
For nature scorns not all the aids of art.
Ev'n Hasty-Pudding, purest of all food,
May still be bad, indifferent, or good,
As sage experience the short process guides,
Or want of skill or want of care presides.
Whoe'er would form it on the surest plan,
To rear the child and long sustain the man,
To shield the morals while it mends the size
And all the powers of every food supplies,
Attend the lessons that the Muse shall bring,
Suspend your spoons and listen while I sing.
  But since, O man, thy life and health demand
Not food alone but labor from thy hand,
First in the field, beneath the sun's strong rays,
Ask of thy mother earth the needful maize;
She loves the race that courts her yielding soil,
And gives her bounties to the sons of toil.
  When now the ox, obedient to thy call,
Repays the loan that fill'd the winter stall,
Pursue his traces o'er the furrow'd plain,
And plant in measur'd hills the golden grain.
But when the tender germ begins to shoot,
And the green spire declares the sprouting root,
Then guard your nursling from each greedy foe,
Th' insidious worm, the all-devouring crow:
A little ashes sprinkled round the spire,
Soon steep'd in rain, will bid the worm retire;
The feather'd robber with his hungry maw
Swift flies the field before your man of straw,
A frightful image, such as school-boys bring
When met to burn the Pope or hang the King.

Thrice in the season, through each verdant row
Wield the strong plow-share and the faithful hoe—
The faithful hoe a double task that takes,
To till the summer corn and roast the winter cakes.

*   *   *   *   *   *

Now the strong foliage bears the standards high,
And shoots the tall top-gallants to the sky;
The suckling ears their silky fringes bend,
And, pregnant grown, their swelling coats distend;
The loaded stalk, while still the burden grows,
O'erhangs the space that runs between the rows.
High as a hop-field waves the silent grove,
A safe retreat for little thefts of love,
When the pledg'd roasting-ears invite the maid
To meet her swain beneath the new-form'd shade:
His generous hand unloads the cumbrous hill,
And the green spoils her ready basket fill;
Small compensation for the two-fold bliss,
The promis'd wedding and the present kiss.
Slight depredations these: but now the moon
Calls from his hollow tree the sly raccoon;
And while by night he bears his prize away,
The bolder squirrel labors thro' the day;
Both thieves alike, but provident of time—
A virtue rare that almost hides their crime.
Then let them steal the little stores they can,
And fill their grain'ries from the toils of man;
We've one advantage where they take no part—
With all their wiles they ne'er have found the art
To boil the Hasty-Pudding; here we shine
Superior far to tenants of the pine:
This envied boon to man shall still belong
Unshar'd by them in substance or in song.
At last the closing season browns the plain,
And ripe October gathers in the grain;
Deep-loaded carts the spacious corn-house fill,
The sack distended marches to the mill;
The lab'ring mill beneath the burden groans,
And show'rs the future pudding from the stones;

Till the glad house-wife greet the powder'd gold,
And the new crop exterminates the old.

Canto III.

The days grow short; but tho' the falling sun
To the glad swain proclaims the day's work done,
Night's pleasing shades his various task prolong,
And yield new subjects to my various song.
For now, the corn-house fill'd, the harvest home,
Th' invited neighbors to the *Husking* come—
A frolic scene, where work and mirth and play
Unite their charms to chase the hours away.
Where the huge heap lies centr'd in the hall,
The lamp suspended from the cheerful wall,
Brown corn-fed nymphs and strong hard-handed beaux,
Alternate rang'd, extend in circling rows,
Assume their seats, the solid mass attack:
The dry husks rustle, and the corn-cobs crack;
The song, the laugh, alternate notes resound,
And the sweet cider trips in silence round.
The laws of Husking ev'ry wight can tell,
And sure no laws he ever keeps so well:
For each red ear a general kiss he gains,
With each smut ear she smuts the luckless swains;
But when to some sweet maid a prize is cast
Red as her lips and taper as her waist,
She walks the round and culls one favor'd beau,
Who leaps the luscious tribute to bestow.
Various the sport as are the wits and brains
Of well-pleas'd lasses and contending swains,
Till the vast mound of corn is swept away,
And he that gets the last ear wins the day.
  Meanwhile the house-wife urges all her care
The well-earn'd feast to hasten and prepare.
The sifted meal already waits her hand,
The milk is strain'd, the bowls in order stand;
The fire flames high, and, as a pool—that takes
The headlong stream that o'er the mill-dam breaks—
Foams, roars, and rages with incessant toils,
So the vext cauldron rages, roars, and boils.

First with clean salt she seasons well the food;
Then strews the flour, and thickens all the flood;
Long o'er the simmering fire she lets it stand:
To stir it well demands a stronger hand;
The husband takes his turn, and round and round
The ladle flies. At last the toil is crown'd;
When to the board the thronging huskers pour,
And take their seats as at the corn before.

I leave them to their feast. There still belong
More copious matters to my faithful song;
For rules there are, tho' ne'er unfolded yet,
Nice rules and wise, how pudding should be ate.

Some with molasses line the luscious treat,
And mix, like Bards, the useful with the sweet;
A wholesome dish, and well deserving praise;
A great resource in those bleak wintry days
When the chill'd earth lies buried deep in snow,
And raging Boreas dries the shivering cow.

Blest cow, thy praise shall still my notes employ,
Great source of health, the only source of joy!
How oft thy teats these pious hands have prest;
How oft thy bounties prov'd my only feast;
How oft I've fed thee with my fav'rite grain;
And roar'd, like thee, to find thy children slain!
Ye swains who know her various worth to prize,
Ah, house her well from Winter's angry skies,
Potatoes, pumpkins should her sadness cheer,
Corn from your crib, and mashes from your beer;
When Spring returns she'll well acquit your loan,
And nurse at once your infants and her own.

Milk, then, with pudding I should always choose;
To this in future I confine my Muse,
Till she in haste some farther hints unfold,
Well for the young nor useless to the old.
First in your bowl the milk abundant take,
Then drop with care along the silver lake
Your flakes of pudding; these at first will hide
Their little bulk beneath the swelling tide;
But when their growing mass no more can sink,
When the soft island looms above the brink,

Then check your hand: you've got the portions due;
So taught our sires, and what they taught is true.
   There is a choice in spoons. Tho' small appear
The nice distinction, yet to me 'tis clear.
The deep-bowl'd Gallic spoon, contriv'd to scoop
In ample drafts the thin diluted soup,
Performs not well in those substantial things
Whose mass adhesive to the metal clings,
Where the strong labial muscles must embrace
The gentle curve and sweep the hollow space.
With ease to enter and discharge the freight,
A bowl less concave but still more dilate
Becomes the pudding best. The shape, the size,
A secret rests unknown to vulgar eyes:
Experienc'd feeders can alone impart
A rule so much above the lore of art.
These tuneful lips, that thousand spoons have tried,
With just precision could the point decide,
Tho' not in song; the muse but poorly shines
In cones and cubes and geometric lines.
Yet the true form, as near as she can tell,
Is that small section of a goose-egg shell
Which in two equal portions shall divide
The distance from the centre to the side.
   Fear not to slaver; 'tis no deadly sin.
Like the free Frenchman, from your joyous chin
Suspend the ready napkin; or, like me,
Poise with one hand your bowl upon your knee,
Just in the zenith your wise head project—
Your full spoon, rising in a line direct,
Bold as a bucket, heeds no drops that fall;
The wide-mouth'd bowl will surely catch them all.

INVOCATION OF "THE COLUMBIAD"

[FROM "THE COLUMBIAD," BOOK I.]

Almighty Freedom! give my venturous song
The force, the charm that to thy voice belong;
'Tis thine to shape my course, to light my way,
To nerve my country with the patriot lay,
To teach all men where all their interest lies,
How rulers may be just and nations wise:
Strong in thy strength I bend on suppliant knee,
Invoke no miracle, no Muse but thee.

THE COMING OF WAR

[FROM THE SAME, BOOK V.]

Columbus turn'd; when rolling to the shore
Swells o'er the seas an undulating roar;
Slow, dark, portentous, as the meteors sweep
And curtain black the illimitable deep,
High stalks, from surge to surge, a demon Form
That howls thro heaven and breathes a billowing storm.
His head is hung with clouds; his giant hand
Flings a blue flame far flickering to the land;
His blood-stain'd limbs drip carnage as he strides
And taint with gory grume the staggering tides;
Like two red suns his quivering eyeballs glare,
His mouth disgorges all the stores of war,
Pikes, muskets, mortars, guns and globes of fire
And lighted bombs that fusing trails expire.
Percht on his helmet, two twin sisters rode,
The favorite offspring of the murderous god,
Famine and Pestilence; whom whilom bore
His wife, grim Discord on Trinacria's shore:
When first their cyclop sons, from Etna's forge,
Fill'd his foul magazine, his gaping gorge:
Then earth convulsive groan'd, high shriek'd the air,
And hell in gratulation call'd him War.

AMERICAN COLLEGES

[FROM THE SAME, BOOK VIII.]

To nurse the arts and fashion freedom's lore
Young schools of science rise along the shore;
Great without pomp their modest walls expand,
Harvard and Yale and Princeton grace the land,
Penn's student halls his youths with gladness greet,
On James's bank Virginian Muses meet,
Manhattan's mart collegiate domes command,
Bosom'd in groves, see growing Dartmouth stand;
Bright o'er its realm reflecting solar fires,
On yon tall hill Rhode Island's seat expires.
Thousands of humbler name around them rise,
Where homebred freemen seize the solid prize;
Fixt in small spheres, with safer beams to shine,
They reach the useful and refuse the fine,
Found, on its proper base, the social plan,
The broad plain truths, the common sense of man,
His obvious wants, his mutual aids discern,
His rights familiarize, his duties learn,
Feel moral fitness all its force dilate,
Embrace the village and comprise the state.
Each rustic here who turns the furrow'd soil,
The maid, the youth that ply mechanic toil,
In equal rights, in useful arts inured,
Know their just claims, and see their claims secured;
They watch their delegates, each law revise,
Its faults designate and its merits prize,
Obey, but scrutinize; and let the test
Of sage experience prove and fix the best.

AMERICAN SCIENCE

[FROM THE SAME, BOOK VIII.]

And lo, my son, that other sapient band,
The torch of science flaming in their hand!
Through nature's range their searching souls aspire,

Or wake to life the canvas and the lyre.
Fixt in sublimest thought, behold them rise
World after world unfolding to their eyes,
Lead, light, allure them through the total plan,
And give new guidance to the paths of man.
  Yon meteor-mantled hill see Franklin tread,
Heaven's awful thunders rolling o'er his head;
Convolving clouds the billowy skies deform,
And forky flames emblaze the blackening storm.
See the descending streams around him burn,
Glance on his rod and with his finger turn;
He bids conflicting fulminants expire
The guided blast, and holds the imprison'd fire.
No more, when doubling storms the vault o'erspread,
The livid glare shall strike thy race with dread,
Nor towers nor temples, shuddering with the sound,
Sink in the flames and shake the sheeted ground.
His well tried wires, that every tempest wait,
Shall teach mankind to ward the bolts of fate,
With pointed steel o'ertop the trembling spire,
And lead from untouch'd walls the harmless fire;
Fill'd with his fame while distant climes rejoice,
Wherever lightning shines or thunder rears its voice.

AMERICAN POETRY

[FROM THE SAME, BOOK VIII.]

  To equal fame ascends thy tuneful throng,
The boast of genius and the pride of song;
Caught from the cast of every age and clime,
Their lays shall triumph o'er the lapse of time.
  With lynx-eyed glance through nature far to pierce,
With all the powers and every charm of verse,
Each science opening in his ample mind,
His fancy glowing and his taste refined,
See Trumbull lead the train. His skilful hand
Hurls the keen darts of satire round the land.
Pride, knavery, dullness feel his mortal stings,
And listening virtue triumphs while he sings;

Britain's foil'd sons, victorious now no more,
In guilt retiring from the wasted shore,
Strive their curst cruelties to hide in vain;
The world resounds them in his deathless strain.
　On wings of faith to elevate the soul
Beyond the bourn of earth's benighted pole,
For Dwight's high harp the epic Muse sublime
Hails her new empire in the western clime.
Tuned from the tones by seers seraphic sung,
Heaven in his eye and rapture on his tongue,
His voice revives old Canaan's promised land,
The long-fought fields of Jacob's chosen band.
In Hanniel's fate, proud faction finds its doom,
Ai's midnight flames light nations to their tomb,
In visions bright supernal joys are given,
And all the dark futurities of heaven.

A UNION OF THE WORLD

[FROM THE SAME, BOOK X.]

　Eager he look'd: another train of years
Had roll'd unseen and brighten'd still their spheres.
Earth, more resplendent in the floods of day,
Assumed new smiles, and flush'd around him lay:
Green swell the mountains, calm the oceans roll,
Fresh beams of beauty kindle round the pole;
Thro all the range where shores and seas extend,
In tenfold pomp the works of peace ascend.
Robed in the bloom of spring's eternal year,
And ripe with fruits, the same glad fields appear;
O'er hills and vales perennial gardens run,
Cities unwall'd stand sparkling in the sun;
The streams, all freighted from the bounteous plain,
Swell with the load and labor to the main,
Whose stormless waves command a steadier gale
And prop the pinions of a bolder sail;
Sway'd with the weight, each ocean toils,
And joyous nature's full perfection smiles.
　Fill'd with unfolding fate, the vision'd age
Now leads its actors on a broader stage:

When, clothed majestic in the robes of state,
Moved by one voice, in general congress meet
The legates of all empires. Twas the place
Where wretched men first firm'd their wandering pace,
Ere yet, beguiled, the dark delirious hordes
Began to fight for altars and for lords;
Nile washes still the soil, and feels once more
The works of wisdom press his peopled shore.
   In this mid site, this monumental clime,
Rear'd by all realms to brave the wrecks of time
A spacious dome swells up, commodious great,
The last resort, the unchanging scene of state.
On rocks of adamant the walls ascend,
Tall columns heave, and sky-like arches bend;
Bright o'er the golden roofs the glittering spires
Far in the concave meet the solar fires;
Four blazing fronts, with gates unfolding high,
Look with immortal splendor round the sky.
Hither the delegated sires ascend,
And all the cares of every clime attend.
As the blest band, the guardian guides of heaven,
To whom the care of stars and suns is given,
When one great circuit shall have proved their spheres
And time well taught them how to wind their years,
Shall meet in general council, call'd to state
The laws and labors that their charge await,
To learn, to teach, to settle how to hold
Their course more glorious as their lights unfold;
From all the bounds of space (the mandate known)
They wing their passage to the eternal throne;
Each thro his far dim sky illumes the road,
And sails and centres tow'rd the mount of God,
There in mid universe their seats to rear,
Exchange their counsels and their works compare:
So, from all tracts of earth, this gathering throng
In ships and chariots shape their course along,
Reach with unwonted speed the place assign'd,
To hear and give the counsels of mankind.
   South of the sacred mansion, first resort
The assembled sires, and pass the spacious court.

Here in his porch earth's figured Genius stands,
Truth's mighty mirror poizing in his hands.
Graved on the pedestal and chased in gold,
Man's noblest arts their symbol forms unfold:—
His tillage and his trade, with all the store
Of wondrous fabrics and of useful lore;
Labors that fashion to his sovereign sway
Earth's total powers, her soil and air and sea,
Force them to yield their fruits at his known call,
And bear his mandates round the rolling ball;
Beneath the footstool all destructive things,
The mask of priesthood and the mace of kings,
Lie trampled in the dust; for here at last
Fraud, folly, error all their emblems cast.
Each envoy here unloads his wearied hand
Of some old idol from his native land:
One flings a pagod on the mingled heap,
One lays a crescent, one a cross to sleep;
Swords, sceptres, mitres, crowns and globes and stars,
Codes of false fame and stimulants to wars
Sink in the settling mass; since guile began,
These are the agents of the woes of man.

  Now the full concourse, where the arches bend,
Pour through by thousands and the seats ascend.
Far as the centred eye can range around
Or the deep trumpet's solemn voice resound,
Long rows of reverent sires sublime extend,
And cares of worlds on every brow suspend.
High in the front, for soundest wisdom known,
A sire elect in peerless grandeur shone:
He open'd calm the universal cause,
To give each realm its limit and its laws,
Bid the last breath of tired contention cease
And bind all regions in the leagues of peace;
Till one confederate, condependent sway
Spread with the sun and bound the walks of day,
One centred system, one all-ruling soul
Live through the parts and regulate the whole.

  "Here, then," said Hesper, with a blissful smile,
"Behold the fruits of thy long years of toil.

To yon bright borders of Atlantic day
Thy swelling pinions led the trackless way,
And taught mankind such useful deeds to dare,
To trace new seas and happy nations rear;
Till by fraternal hands their sails unfurl'd
Have waved at last in union o'er the world.
Then let thy steadfast soul no more complain
Of dangers braved and griefs endured in vain,
Of courts insidious, envy's poison'd stings,
The loss of empire and the frown of kings,
While these broad views thy better thoughts compose
To spurn the malice of insulting foes,
And all the joys descending ages gain
Repay thy labors and remove thy pain."

PHILIP FRENEAU

Philip Freneau was the first American to show a genuine poetic call and gift. Lyrics like *The Wild Honeysuckle* are traces indicating what in less troubled times he might have accomplished in pure poetry. His most characteristic poems, however, embody the revolutionary spirit and ideas; and he has been properly styled the "Poet of the Revolution." The trait which best interprets his poetry is his passion for human freedom. This he perhaps inherited from his Huguenot ancestry; his grandfather came to America to secure liberty of thought. The French Protestants, however, were less austere and puritanical than those of New England; and the poet, as Professor Pattee believes, "inherited with his French blood a passionate love of beauty." Freneau was born into a home of culture and refinement in New York in 1752. When he entered Princeton in 1768 he had already read much and had written poetry; and he continued to write while in college. He was a classmate of James Madison and Hugh Brackenridge; with the latter he formed a literary friendship recalling the contemporary one of the "Yale Poets," satirized the tories, and composed a commencement poem entitled *The Rising Glory of America*.

After graduation he taught in a school conducted by Brackenridge in Maryland. At the end of three years, during which his movements have not been traced, he appeared in New York in 1775 as a Revolutionary satirist, publishing some eight poetical pamphlets, mainly in the heroic couplet, of which *A Political Litany* and *The Midnight Consultations* are typical. Strangely he now withdrew from the Revolutionary conflict, in which he must have been intensely interested, and spent the next three years in the West Indies. This experience probably developed his imagination, and it furnished material for two remarkable poems, *Santa Cruz* and *The House of Night,* published after his return (in 1778) in Brackenridge's excellent but short-lived *United States Magazine.* In 1780 Freneau was passenger on a ship taken by the British; his six weeks' experience as a captive is described with passionate bitterness in *The British Prison Ship.* For three years, 1781-1784, he was in Philadelphia as editor of *The Freeman's Journal,* writing for this paper some of his best poems—*The Victory of Paul Jones, To the Memory of the Brave Americans,* and *The Wild Honey-suckle.*

Freneau spent much of his life on salt water; from 1784 to 1790 he was active in the coasting trade; and he made use of this experience in poetry. It was he, rather than Scott or Cooper, says his biographer, "who added the domain of the ocean to literature." Collections of his *Poems* were published in 1786 and 1788; these with the edition of 1795 contain his best poetry. From 1790, when he left the sea and married, to 1797, Freneau was mainly engaged in news-paper work. His poems of this time are full of enthusiasm for the revolution in France, which he regarded as a con-tinuation of the great movement begun in America. In 1791 he went to Philadelphia to accept from Jefferson the clerkship for foreign languages in the State Department, and to edit *The National Gazette,* a paper strongly Republican and pro-French, in which he attacked the Federalists in Washington's administration. As he spared Jefferson he was accused of collusion, and of "biting the hand that put bread in his mouth." Careful investigation seems to show that he was guilty of nothing worse than violent partisan feeling. In the popular revulsion against Genet in 1793 he had to give up the *Gazette.* This episode, famous in history, has also some critical importance. To Washington he was "that rascal, Freneau;" in Federalist New England, accord-ing to Timothy Dwight, he was regarded as "a mere incen-diary;" and since literary biography and criticism were long mainly in the hands of New Englanders, he lost accordingly in poetical reputation. As during his life he often subor-dinated poetry to patriotism, so afterward he suffered as a poet for his political sincerity, outspokenness, and courage. He lived on to show in the conflict with England leading to

the War of 1812 that he had not changed his principles;
and he closed his long and chequered career in 1832.

Throughout Freneau wrote verse indefatigably. His
poems have been collected and admirably edited for the
Princeton Historical Association by Professor F. L. Pattee
(1902-1907). Even in the three volumes of this edition
many poems are omitted. Of the hundreds included many
are more interesting to the historian than to the student of
poetry; only a few have genuine poetic merit, and none is
flawless. The best, however,—selected for the following
pages—show that after his period of imitation and apprenticeship, Freneau wrote with originality, often with imagination; that he broke away from the conventionality of the
eighteenth century and even in his couplets employed a diction simple and sincere; that whatever his theme he wrote
from his own ideas and experience; that he treated American nature truthfully and sympathetically. They show that
he was our first authentic poet; that, unaided and under ad-
verse conditions, he introduced a new poetic era; even that,
in some interesting respects, he anticipated the "romantic"
poets—Wordsworth and Coleridge, Bryant and Poe—of the
next generation.

The following poems are reprinted from *The Poems of
Philip Freneau,* edited by Professor F. L. Pattee, with the
permission of the Princeton University Library.

A POLITICAL LITANY

Libera Nos, Domine.—Deliver us, O Lord, not only from British
dependence, but also

From a junto that labor with absolute power,
Whose schemes disappointed have made them look sour,
From the lords of the council, who fight against freedom,
Who still follow on where delusion shall lead them.

From the group at St. James's, who slight our petitions,
And fools that are waiting for further submissions—
From a nation whose manners are rough and severe,
From scoundrels and rascals,—do keep us all clear.

From pirates sent out by command of the king
To murder and plunder, but never to swing.
From Wallace and Greaves, and Vipers and Roses,[1]
Whom, if heaven pleases, we'll give bloody noses.

From the valiant Dunmore, with his crew of banditti,
Who plunder Virginians at Williamsburg city,
From hot-headed Montague, mighty to swear,
The little fat man with his pretty white hair.

From bishops in Britain, who butchers are grown,
From slaves that would die for a smile from the throne,
From assemblies that vote against Congress proceedings,
(Who now see the fruit of their stupid misleadings.)

From Tryon the mighty, who flies from our city,
And swelled with importance disdains the committee:
(But since he is pleased to proclaim us his foes,
What the devil care we where the devil he goes.)

From the caitiff, Lord North, who would bind us in chains,
From a royal king Log, with his tooth-full of brains,
Who dreams, and is certain (when taking a nap)
He has conquered our lands, as they lay on his map.

From a kingdom that bullies, and hectors, and swears,
We send up to heaven our wishes and prayers
That we, disunited, may freemen be still,
And Britain go on—to be damned if she will.

[1] Captains and ships in the British navy, then employed on the American coast.

THE MIDNIGHT CONSULTATIONS;
OR, A TRIP TO BOSTON

* * * * * * *

Twelve was the hour—congenial darkness reigned,
And no bright star a mimic daylight feigned—
First, Gage we saw—a crimson chair of state
Received the honor of his Honor's weight;
This man of straw the regal purple bound,
But dullness, deepest dullness, hovered round.

Next Graves, who wields the trident of the brine,
The tall arch-captain of the embattled line,
All gloomy sat—mumbling of flame and fire,
Balls, cannon, ships, and all their damned attire;
Well pleased to live in never-ending hum,
But empty as the interior of his drum.

Hard by, Burgoyne assumes an ample space,
And seemed to meditate with studious face,
As if again he wished our world to see
Long, dull, dry letters, writ to General Lee—
Huge scrawls of words through endless circuits drawn
Unmeaning as the errand he's upon.—
Is he to conquer—he subdue our land?—
This buckram hero, with his lady's hand?
By Cæsars to be vanquished is a curse,
But by a scribbling fop—by heaven, is worse!

Lord Piercy seemed to snore—but may the Muse
This ill-timed snoring to the peer excuse;
Tired was the long boy of his toilsome day,
Full fifteen miles he fled—a tedious way;
How could he then the dews of Somnus shun,
Perhaps not used to walk—much less to run.

Red-faced as suns, when sinking to repose,
Reclined the infernal captain of the *Rose,*
In fame's proud temple aiming for a niche,
With those who find her at the cannon's breach;
Skilled to direct the cannonading shot,
No Turkish rover half so murdering hot,

Pleased with base vengeance on defenceless towns,
His heart was malice—but his words were, Zounds!
  Howe, vexed to see his starving army's doom,
In prayer, besought the skies for elbow room—
Small was his stock, and theirs, of heavenly grace,
Yet just enough to ask a larger place.—
He cursed the brainless minister that planned
His bootless errand to this hostile land,
But, awed by Gage, his bursting wrath recoiled,
And in his inmost bosom doubly boiled.
  These, chief of all the tyrant-serving train,
Exalted sat—the rest (a pensioned clan),
A sample of the multitude that wait,
Pale sons of famine, at perdition's gate,
North's friends down swarming (so our monarch wills),
Hungry as death, from Caledonian hills;
Whose endless numbers if you bid me tell,
I'll count the atoms of this globe as well,—
Knights, captains, 'squires—a wonder-working band,
Held at small wages 'till they gain the land,
Flocked pensive round—black spleen assailed their hearts,
(The sport of plough-boys, with their arms and arts)
And made them doubt (howe'er for vengeance hot)
Whether they were invincible or not.

*   *   *   *   *   *

  The clock strikes two!—Gage smote upon his breast,
And cried,—"What fate determines, must be best—
But now attend—a counsel I impart
That long has laid the heaviest at my heart—
Three weeks—ye gods!—nay, three long years it seems
Since roast-beef I have touched except in dreams.
In sleep, choice dishes to my view repair,
Waking, I gape and champ the empty air.—
Say, is it just that I, who rule these bands,
Should live on husks, like rakes in foreign lands?–
Come, let us plan some project ere we sleep,
And drink destruction to the rebel sheep.
  "On neighboring isles uncounted cattle stray,
Fat beeves and swine, an ill-defended prey—

These are fit visions for my noonday dish,
These, if my soldiers act as I would wish,
In one short week should glad your maws and mine;
On mutton we will sup—on roast-beef dine."

Shouts of applause re-echoed through the hall,
And what pleased one as surely pleased them all;
Wallace was named to execute the plan,
And thus sheep-stealing pleased them to a man.

Now slumbers stole upon the great man's eye,
His powdered foretop nodded from on high,
His lids just opened to find how matters were,
Dissolve, he said, and so dissolved ye are,
Then downward sunk to slumbers dark and deep,—
Each nerve relaxed—and even his guts asleep.

THE HOUSE OF NIGHT
A Vision

Advertisement.—This peom is founded upon the authority of
Scripture, inasmuch as these sacred books assert, that *the last enemy
that shall be conquered is Death.* For the purpose of poetry he
is here personified, and represented as on his dying bed. The
scene is laid at a solitary palace (the time midnight) which, tho'
before beautiful and joyous, is now become sad and gloomy, as
being the abode and receptacle of Death......The patient finding
his end approaching, composes his epitaph......He dies at last
in the utmost agonies of despair......The circumstances of his
funeral are then recited, and the visionary and fabulous part of
the poem disappears. It concludes with a few reflections on the
impropriety of a too great attachment to the present life, and
incentives to such moral virtues as may assist in conducting us to
a better.

1

Trembling I write my dream, and recollect
A fearful vision at the midnight hour;
So late, Death o'er me spread his sable wings,
Painted with fancies of malignant power!

2

Such was the dream the sage Chaldean saw
Disclos'd to him that felt heav'n's vengeful rod,
Such was the ghost, who through deep silence cried,
Shall mortal man—be juster than his God?

3

Let others draw from smiling skies their theme,
And tell of climes that boast unfading light,
I draw a darker scene, replete with gloom,
I sing the horrors of the House of Night.

4

Stranger, believe the truth experience tells,
Poetic dreams are of a finer cast
Than those which o'er the sober brain diffus'd,
Are but a repetition of some action past.

5

Fancy, I own thy power—when sunk in sleep
Thou play'st thy wild delusive part so well
You lift me into immortality,
Depict new heavens, or draw the scenes of hell.

6

By some sad means, when Reason holds no sway,
Lonely I rov'd at midnight o'er a plain
Where murmuring streams and mingling rivers flow
Far to their springs, or seek the sea again.

7

Sweet vernal May! tho' then thy woods in bloom
Flourish'd, yet nought of this could Fancy see,
No wild pinks bless'd the meads, no green the fields,
And naked seem'd to stand each lifeless tree:

8

Dark was the sky, and not one friendly star
Shone from the zenith or horizon, clear,
Mist sat upon the woods, and darkness rode
In her black chariot, with a wild career.

9

And from the woods the late resounding note
Issued of the loquacious Whip-poor-will,[1]
Hoarse, howling dogs, and nightly roving wolves
Clamor'd from far off cliffs invisible.

10

Rude, from the wide extended Chesapeake
I heard the winds the dashing waves assail,
And saw from far, by picturing fancy form'd,
The black ship travelling through the noisy gale.

11

At last, by chance and guardian fancy led,
I reach'd a noble dome, rais'd fair and high,
And saw the light from upper windows flame,
Presage of mirth and hospitality.

12

And by that light around the dome appear'd
A mournful garden of autumnal hue,
Its lately pleasing flowers all drooping stood
Amidst high weeds that in rank plenty grew.

13

The primrose there, the violet darkly blue,
Daisies and fair narcissus ceas'd to rise,
Gay spotted pinks their charming bloom withdrew,
And polyanthus quench'd its thousand dyes.

14

No pleasant fruit or blossom gaily smil'd,
Nought but unhappy plants or trees were seen,
The yew, the myrtle, and the church-yard elm,
The cypress, with its melancholy green.

---

[1] A bird peculiar to America, of a solitary nature, who never
sings but in the night. Her note resembles the name given to her
by the country people.

15

There cedars dark, the osier, and the pine,
Shorn tamarisks, and weeping willows grew,
The poplar tall, the lotos, and the lime,
And pyracantha did her leaves renew.

16

The poppy there, companion to repose,
Display'd her blossoms that began to fall,
And here the purple amaranthus rose
With mint strong-scented, for the funeral.

17

And here and there with laurel shrubs between
A tombstone lay, inscrib'd with strains of woe,
And stanzas sad, throughout the dismal green,
Lamented for the dead that slept below.

*   *   *   *   *   *

97

"And on that stone engrave this epitaph,
Since death, it seems, must die like mortal men;
Yes—on that stone engrave this epitaph,
Though all hell's furies aim to snatch the pen.

98

"Death in this tomb his weary bones hath laid,
Sick of dominion o'er the human kind—
Behold what devastations he hath made,
Survey the millions by his arm confin'd.

99

"Six thousand years has sovereign sway been mine,
None, but myself, can real glory claim;
Great Regent of the world I reign'd alone,
And princes trembled when my mandate came.

100

"Vast and unmatch'd throughout the world, my fame
Takes place of gods, and asks no mortal date—
No; by myself, and by the heavens, I swear,
Not Alexander's name is half so great.

101

"Nor swords nor darts my prowess could withstand,
All quit their arms and bow'd to my decree,
Even mighty Julius died beneath my hand,
For slaves and Cæsars were the same to me!

102

"Traveller, wouldst thou his noblest trophies seek,
Search in no narrow spot obscure for those;
The sea profound, the surface of all land
Is moulded with the myriads of his foes."

103

Scarce had he spoke, when on the lofty dome
Rush'd from the clouds a hoarse, resounding blast—
Round the four eaves so loud and sad it play'd
As though all music were to breathe its last.

104

Warm was the gale, and such as travellers say
Sport with the winds on Zaara's barren waste;
Black was the sky, a mourning carpet spread,
Its azure blotted, and its stars o'ercast!

105

Lights in the air like burning stars were hurl'd,
Dogs howl'd, heaven mutter'd, and the tempest blew,
The red half-moon peeped from behind a cloud
As if in dread the amazing scene to view.

106

The mournful trees that in the garden stood
Bent to the tempest as it rush'd along,
The elm, the myrtle, and the cypress sad
More melancholy tun'd its bellowing song.

107

No more that elm its noble branches spread,
The yew, the cypress, or the myrtle tree,
Rent from the roots the tempest tore them down,
And all the grove in wild confusion lay.

108

Yet mindful of his dread command, I part
Glad from the magic dome—nor found relief;
Damps from the dead hung heavier round my heart,
While sad remembrance rous'd her stores of grief.

109

O'er a dark field I held my dubious way
Where Jack-a-lanthorn walk'd his lonely round,
Beneath my feet substantial darkness lay,
And screams were heard from the distemper'd ground.

110

Nor look'd I back, till to a far-off wood,
Trembling with fear, my weary feet had sped—
Dark was the night, but at the enchanted dome
I saw the infernal windows flaming red.

*   *   *   *   *   *

132

What is this Death, ye deep read sophists, say?—
Death is no more than one unceasing change;
New forms arise, while other forms decay,
Yet all is Life throughout creation's range.

133

The towering Alps, the haughty Appenine,
The Andes, wrapt in everlasting snow,
The Apalachian and the Ararat,
Sooner or later must to ruin go.

134

Hills sink to plains, and man returns to dust,
The dust supports a reptile or a flower;
Each changeful atom by some other nurs'd
Takes some new form, to perish in an hour.

135

Too nearly join'd to sickness, toils, and pains,
(Perhaps for former crimes imprison'd here)
True to itself the immortal soul remains,
And seeks new mansions in the starry sphere.

136

When Nature bids thee from the world retire,
With joy thy lodging leave, a fated guest;
In Paradise, the land of thy desire,
Existing always, always to be blest.

THE BEAUTIES OF SANTA CRUZ

*   *   *   *   *   *

8

From the vast caverns of old ocean's bed,
Fair Santa Cruz, arising, laves her waist,
The threat'ning waters roar on every side,
For every side by ocean is embrac'd.

9

Sharp, craggy rocks repel the surging brine,
Whose cavern'd sides by restless billows wore,
Resemblance claim to that remoter isle
Where once the winds' proud lord the sceptre bore.

10

Betwixt old Cancer and the midway line,
In happiest climate lies this envied isle,
Trees bloom throughout the year, streams ever flow,
And fragrant Flora wears a lasting smile.

11

Cool, woodland streams from shaded clifts descend,
The dripping rock no want of moisture knows,
Supplied by springs that on the skies depend,
That fountain feeding as the current flows.

12

Such were the isles which happy Flaccus sung,
Where one tree blossoms while another bears,
Where spring forever gay, and ever young,
Walks her gay round through her unwearied years.

13

Such were the climes which youthful Eden saw
Ere crossing fates destroy'd her golden reign—
Reflect upon thy loss, unhappy man,
And seek the vales of Paradise again.

*   *   *   *   *   *

THE HOSPITAL PRISON SHIP

[FROM "THE BRITISH PRISON SHIP."   CANTO III.]

Now tow'rd the *Hunter's* gloomy sides we came,
A slaughter-house, yet hospital in name;
For none came there (to pass through all degrees)
'Till half consum'd, and dying with disease;—
But when too near with laboring oars we plied,
The Mate with curses drove us from the side;
That wretch who, banish'd from the navy crew,
Grown old in blood, did here his trade renew;
His serpent's tongue, when on his charge let loose,
Utter'd reproaches, scandal, and abuse,
Gave all to hell who dar'd his king disown,
And swore mankind were made for George alone:

Ten thousand times, to irritate our woe,
He wish'd us founder'd in the gulf below;
Ten thousand times he brandish'd high his stick,
And swore as often that we were not sick—
And yet so pale!—that we were thought by some
A freight of ghosts from Death's dominions come—
But calm'd at length—for who can always rage,
Or the fierce war of endless passion wage,
He pointed to the stairs that led below
To damps, disease, and varied shapes of woe—
Down to the gloom I took my pensive way,
Along the decks the dying captives lay;
Some struck with madness, some with scurvy pain'd,
But still of putrid fevers most complain'd!
On the hard floors these wasted objects laid,
There toss'd and tumbled in the dismal shade,
There no soft voice their bitter fate bemoan'd,
And Death strode stately, while the victims groan'd;
Of leaky decks I heard them long complain,
Drown'd as they were in deluges of rain,
Denied the comforts of a dying bed,
And not a pillow to support the head—
How could they else but pine, and grieve, and sigh,
Detest a wretched life—and wish to die?

* * * * * *

From Brookland groves a Hessian doctor came,
Not great his skill, nor greater much his fame;
Fair Science never call'd the wretch her son,
And Art disdain'd the stupid man to own;—
Can you admire that Science was so coy,
Or Art refus'd his genius to employ!—
Do men with brutes an equal dullness share,
Or cuts yon grovelling mole the midway air?
In polar worlds can Eden's blossoms blow?
Do trees of God in barren deserts grow?
Are loaded vines to Etna's summit known,
Or swells the peach beneath the torrid zone?—
Yet still he doom'd his genius to the rack,
And, as you may suppose, was own'd a quack.

ON THE MEMORABLE VICTORY

Obtained by the gallant Captain Paul Jones, of the *Good Man Richard,* over the *Seraphis,* etc., under the command of Captain Pearson.

1

O'er the rough main with flowing sheet
The guardian of a numerous fleet,
   Seraphis from the Baltic came;
A ship of less tremendous force
Sail'd by her side the self-same course,
   Countess of Scarb'ro' was her name.

2

And now their native coasts appear,
Britannia's hills their summits rear
   Above the German main;
Fond to suppose their dangers o'er,
They southward coast along the shore,
   Thy waters, gentle Thames, to gain.

3

Full forty guns *Seraphis* bore,
And *Scarb'ro's Countess* twenty-four,
   Mann'd with Old England's boldest tars—
What flag that rides the Gallic seas
Shall dare attack such piles as these,
   Design'd for tumults and for wars!

4

Now from the top-mast's giddy height
A seaman cried—"Four sail in sight
   Approach with favoring gales;"
Pearson, resolv'd to save the fleet,
Stood off to sea these ships to meet,
   And closely brac'd his shivering sails.

5

With him advanc'd the *Countess* bold,
Like a black tar in wars grown old:
    And now these floating piles drew nigh;
But, muse, unfold what chief of fame
In th' other warlike squadron came,
    Whose standards at his masthead fly.

6

'Twas Jones, brave Jones, to battle led
As bold a crew as ever bled
    Upon the sky surrounded main;
The standards of the Western World
Were to the willing winds unfurl'd,
    Denying Britain's tyrant reign.

7

The *Good Man Richard* led the line;
The *Alliance* next: with these combine
    The Gallic ship they *Pallas* call:
The *Vengeance,* arm'd with sword and flame,
These to attack the Britons came—
    But two accomplish'd all.

8

Now Phœbus sought his pearly bed:
But who can tell the scenes of dread,
    The horrors of that fatal night!
Close up these floating castles came;
The *Good Man Richard* bursts in flame;
    Seraphis trembled at the sight.

9

She felt the fury of her ball,
Down, prostrate down, the Britons fall;
    The decks were strew'd with slain:
Jones to the foe his vessel lash'd;
And, while the black artillery flash'd,
    Loud thunders shook the main.

10

Alas! that mortals should employ
Such murdering engines, to destroy
   That frame by heav'n so nicely join'd;
Alas! that e'er the God decreed
That brother should by brother bleed,
   And pour'd such madness in the mind.

11 ·

But thou, brave Jones, no blame shalt bear;
The rights of men demand thy care:
   For these you dare the greedy waves—
No tyrant on destruction bent
Has planned thy conquests—thou art sent
   To humble tyrants and their slaves.

12

See!—dread *Seraphis* flames again—
And art thou, Jones, among the slain,
   And sunk to Neptune's caves below—
He lives—though crowds around him fall,
Still he, unhurt, survives them all;
   Almost alone he fights the foe.

13

And can thy ship these strokes sustain?
Behold thy brave companions slain,
   All clasp'd in ocean's dark embrace.
"Strike, or be sunk!"—the Briton cries—
"Sink, if you can!"—the chief replies,
   Fierce lightnings blazing in his face.

14

Then to the side three guns he drew,
(Almost deserted by his crew)
   And charg'd them deep with woe:
By Pearson's flash he aim'd the balls;
His main-mast totters—down it falls—
   Tremendous was the blow.

15

Pearson as yet disdain'd to yield,
But scarce his secret fears conceal'd,
   And thus was heard to cry—
"With hell, not mortals, I contend;
What art thou—human, or a fiend,
   That dost my force defy?

16

"Return, my lads, the fight renew!"
So call'd bold Pearson to his crew;
   But call'd, alas! in vain;
Some on the decks lay maim'd and dead;
Some to their deep recesses fled,
   And more were buried in the main.

17

Distress'd, forsaken, and alone,
He haul'd his tatter'd standard down,
   And yielded to his fallant foe;
Bold *Pallas* soon the *Countess* took,
Thus both their haughty colors struck,
   Confessing what the brave can do.

18

But, Jones, too dearly didst thou buy
These ships possest so gloriously,
   Too many deaths disgrac'd the fray:
Thy barque that bore the conquering flame,
That the proud Briton overcame,
   Even she forsook thee on thy way;

19

For when the morn began to shine,
Fatal to her, the ocean brine
   Pour'd through each spacious wound;
Quick in the deep she disappear'd,
But Jones to friendly Belgia steer'd,
   With conquest and with glory crown'd.

20

Go on, great man, to daunt the foe,
And bid the haughty Britons know
   They to our Thirteen Stars shall bend;
The Stars that veil'd in dark attire,
Long glimmer'd with a feeble fire,
   But radiant now ascend;

21

Bend to the Stars that flaming rise
In western, not in eastern, skies,
   Fair Freedom's reign restor'd.
So when the Magi, come from far,
Beheld the God-attending Star,
   They trembl'd and ador'd.

TO THE MEMORY OF THE BRAVE AMERICANS

Under General Greene, in South Carolina, who fell in the action of September 8, 1781.

At Eutaw Springs the valiant died;
   Their limbs with dust are covered o'er—
Weep on, ye springs, your tearful tide;
   How many heroes are no more!

If in this wreck of ruin, they
   Can yet be thought to claim a tear,
O smite your gentle breast, and say
   The friends of freedom slumber here!

Thou, who shalt trace this bloody plain,
   If goodness rules thy generous breast,
Sigh for the wasted rural reign;
   Sigh for the shepherds, sunk to rest!

Stranger, their humble graves adorn;
   You too may fall, and ask a tear;
'Tis not the beauty of the morn
   That proves the evening shall be clear.—

They saw their injured country's woe;
    The flaming town, the wasted field;
Then rushed to meet the insulting foe;
    They took the spear—but left the shield.

Led by thy conquering genius, Greene,
    The Britons they compelled to fly;
None distant viewed the fatal plain,
    None grieved, in such a cause to die—

But, like the Parthian, famed of old,
    Who, flying, still their arrows threw,
These routed Britons, full as bold,
    Retreated, and retreating slew.

Now rest in peace, our patriot band;
    Though far from nature's limits thrown,
We trust they find a happier land,
    A brighter sunshine of their own.

THE POLITICAL BALANCE

OR, THE FATES OF BRITAIN AND AMERICA COMPARED.

A TALE

Deciding Fates, in Homer's style, we show,
And bring contending gods once more to view.

As Jove the Olympian (who both I and you know,
Was brother to Neptune, and husband to Juno)
Was lately reviewing his papers of state,
He happened to light on the records of Fate:

In Alphabet order this volume was written—
So he opened at B, for the article Britain—
She struggles so well, said the god, I will see
What the sisters in Pluto's dominions decree.

And first, on the top of a column he read,
"Of a king with a mighty soft place in his head,
Who should join in his temper the ass and the mule,
The third of his name, and by far the worst fool:

"His reign shall be famous for multiplication,
The sire and the king of a whelp generation:
But such is the will and the purpose of fate,
For each child he begets he shall forfeit a State:

"In the course of events, he shall find to his cost
That he cannot regain what he foolishly lost;
Of the nations around he shall be the derision,
And know by experience the rule of division."

So Jupiter read—a god of first rank—
And still had read on—but he came to a blank:
For the Fates had neglected the rest to reveal—
They either forgot it, or chose to conceal:

When a leaf is torn out, or a blot on a page
That pleases our fancy, we fly in a rage—
So, curious to know what the Fates would say next,
No wonder if Jove, disappointed, was vext.

But still as true genius not frequently fails,
He glanced at the Virgin, and thought of the Scales;
And said, "To determine the will of the Fates,
One scale shall weigh Britain, the other the States."

Then turning to Vulcan, his maker of thunder,
Said he, "My dear Vulcan, I pray you look yonder,
Those creatures are tearing each other to pieces,
And, instead of abating, the carnage increases.

"Now, as you are a blacksmith, and lusty stout ham-eater,
You must make me a globe of a shorter diameter;
The world in abridgment, and just as it stands
With all its proportions of waters and lands;

"But its various divisions must be so designed,
That I can unhinge it whene'er I've a mind—
How else shall I know what the portions will weigh,
Or which of the combatants carry the day?"

Old Vulcan complied, (we've no reason to doubt it)
So he put on his apron and straight went about it—
Made centre, and circles as round as a pancake,
And here the Pacific, and there the Atlantic.

An axis he hammered, whose ends were the poles,
(On which the whole body perpetually rolls)
A brazen meridian he added to these,
Where four times repeated were ninety degrees.

I am sure you had laughed to have seen his droll attitude,
When he bent round the surface the circles of latitude,
The zones and the tropics, meridians, equator,
And other fine things that are drawn on salt water.

      *   *   *   *   *   *

At length to discourage all stupid pretensions,
Jove looked at the globe, and approved its dimensions,
And cried in a transport—"Why, what have we here!
Friend Vulcan, it is a most beautiful sphere!

"Now while I am busy in taking apart
This globe that is formed with such exquisite art,
Go, Hermes, to Libra, (you're one of her gallants)
And ask, in my name, for the loan of her balance."

Away posted Hermes, as swift as the gales,
And as swiftly returned with the ponderous scales,
And hung them aloft to a beam in the air,
So equally poised, they had turned with a hair.

Now Jove to Columbia his shoulders applied,
But aiming to lift her, his strength she defied—
Then, turning about to their godships, he says—
"A body so vast is not easy to raise;

"But if you assist me, I still have a notion
Our forces, united, can put her in motion,
And swing her aloft, (though alone I might fail)
And place her, in spite of her bulk, in our scale;

"If six years together the Congress have strove,
And more than divided the empire with Jove;
With a Jove like myself, who am nine times as great,
You can join, like their soldiers, to heave up this weight."

So to it they went, with handspikes and levers,
And upward she sprung, with her mountains and rivers!
Rocks, cities, and islands, deep waters and shallows,
Ships, armies, and forests, high heads and fine fellows:

"Stick to it!" cries Jove, "now heave one and all!
At least we are lifting 'one-eighth of the ball!'
If backward she tumbles—then trouble begins,
And then have a care, my dear boys, of your shins!"

When gods are determined, what project can fail?
So they gave a hard shove, and she mounted the scale;
Suspended aloft, Jove viewed her with awe—
And the gods,[1] for their pay, had a hearty—huzza!

But Neptune bawled out—"Why, Jove, you're a noddy,
Is Britain sufficient to poise that vast body?
'Tis nonsense such castles to build in the air—
As well might an oyster with Britain compare."

"Away to your waters, you blustering bully,"
Said Jove, "or I'll make you repent of your folly;
Is Jupiter, Sir, to be tutored by you?—
Get out of my sight, for I know what to do!"

Then searching about with his fingers for Britain,
Thought he, "This same island I cannot well hit on;
The devil take him who first called her the Great:
If she was—she is vastly diminished of late!"

Like a man that is searching his thigh for a flea,
He peeped and he fumbled, but nothing could see;
At last he exclaimed: "I am surely upon it—
I think I have hold of a Highlander's bonnet."

[1] American soldiers.

But finding his error, he said with a sigh,
"This bonnet is only the island of Skie!"
So away to his namesake the planet he goes,
And borrowed two moons to hang on his nose.

Through these, as through glasses, he saw her quite clear,
And in raptures cried out: "I have found her—she's here!
If this is not Britain, then call me an ass—
She looks like a gem in an ocean of glass.

"But, faith, she's so small I must mind how I shake her;
In a box I'll inclose her, for fear I should break her:
Though a god, I might suffer for being aggressor,
Since scorpions, and vipers, and hornets possess her;

"The white cliffs of Albion I think I descry—
And the hills of Plinlimmon appear rather nigh—
But, Vulcan, inform me what creatures are these,
That smell so of onions, and garlic, and cheese?"

Old Vulcan replied: "Odds splutter a nails!
Why, these are the Welch, and the country is Wales!
When Taffy is vext, no devil is ruder—
Take care how you trouble the offspring of Tudor!

"On the crags of the mountains *hur* living *hur* seeks,
Hur country is planted with garlic and leeks;
So great is *hur* choler, beware how you tease *hur*,
For these are the Britons—unconquered by Cæsar."

"But now, my dear Juno, pray give me my mittens,
(These insects I am going to handle are Britons)
I'll draw up their isle with a finger and thumb,
As a doctor extracts an old tooth from the gum."

Then he raised her aloft—but to shorten our tale,
She looked like a clod in the opposite scale—
Britannia so small, and Columbia so large—
A ship of first rate, and a ferryman's barge!

Cried Pallas to Vulcan, "Why, Jove's in a dream—
Observe how he watches the turn of the beam!
Was ever a mountain outweighed by a grain?
Or what is a drop when compared to the main?"

But Momus alleged—"In my humble opinion,
You should add to Great Britain her foreign dominion,
When this is appended, perhaps she will rise,
And equal her rival in weight and in size."

"Alas! (said the monarch), your project is vain,
But little is left of her foreign domain;
And, scattered about in the liquid expanse,
That little is left to the mercy of France;

"However, we'll lift them and give her fair play"—
And soon in the scale with their mistress they lay;
But the gods were confounded and struck with surprise,
And Vulcan could hardly believe his own eyes!

For (such was the purpose and guidance of fate)
Her foreign dominions diminished her weight—
By which it appeared, to Britain's disaster,
Her foreign possessions were changing their master.

Then, as he replaced them, said Jove with a smile—
"Columbia shall never be ruled by an isle—
But vapors and darkness around her may rise,
And tempests conceal her awhile from our eyes;

"So locusts in Egypt their squadrons display,
And rising, disfigure the face of the day;
So the moon, at her full, has a frequent eclipse,
And the sun in the ocean diurnally dips.

"Then cease your endeavors, ye vermin of Britain—
(And here, in derision, their island he spit on)
'Tis madness to seek what you never can find,
Or to think of uniting what nature disjoined;

"But still you may flutter awhile with your wings,
And spit out your venom and brandish your stings:
Your hearts are as black, and as bitter as gall,
A curse to mankind—and a blot on the Ball."

BARNEY'S INVITATION

Come all ye lads who know no fear,
To wealth and honor with me steer
In the *Hyder Ali* privateer,
   Commanded by brave Barney.

She's new and true, and tight and sound,
Well rigged aloft, and all well found—
Come away and be with laurel crowned,
   Away—and leave your lasses.

Accept our terms without delay,
And make your fortunes while you may,
Such offers are not every day
   In the power of the jolly sailor.

Success and fame attend the brave,
But death the coward and the slave,
Who fears to plow the Atlantic wave,
   To seek the bold invaders.

Come, then, and take a cruising bout,
Our ship sails well, there is no doubt,
She has been tried both in and out,
   And answers expectation.

Let no proud foes whom Europe bore,
Distress our trade, insult our shore—
Teach them to know their reign is o'er,
   Bold Philadelphia sailors!

We'll teach them how to sail so near,
Or to venture on the Delaware,
When we in warlike trim appear
   And cruise without Henlopen.

Who cannot wounds and battle dare
Shall never clasp the blooming fair;
The brave alone their charms should share,
    The brave are their protectors.

With hand and heart united all,
Prepare to conquer or to fall,
Attend, my lads, to honor's call,
    Embark in our *Hyder Ali*.

From an Eastern prince she takes her name,
Who, smit with Freedom's sacred flame,
Usurping Britons brought to shame,
    His country's wrongs avenging;

See, on her stern the waving stars—
Inured to blood, inured to wars,
Come, enter quick, my jolly tars,
    To scourge these warlike Britons.

Here's grog enough—then drink a bout,
I know your hearts are firm and stout;
American blood will never give out,
    And often we have proved it.

Though stormy oceans round us roll,
We'll keep a firm undaunted soul,
Befriended by the cheering bowl,
    Sworn foes to melancholy:

While timorous landsmen lurk on shore,
'Tis ours to go where cannons roar—
On a coasting cruise we'll go once more,
    Despisers of all danger;

And Fortune still, who crowns the brave,
Shall guard us over the gloomy wave;
A fearful heart betrays a knave—
    Success to the *Hyder Ali*.

THE PROGRESS OF BALLOONS

"Perdomita tellus, tumida cesserunt freta,
Inferna nostros regna sensere impetus;
Immune cœlum est, degnus Alcidæ labor,
In alta mundi spatia sublimes feremur."
                                   —*Senec. Herc. Furens.*

Assist me, ye muses, (whose harps are in tune)
To tell of the flight of the gallant balloon!
As high as my subject permit me to soar
To heights unattempted, unthought of before,
Ye grave learned Doctors, whose trade is to sigh,
Who labor to chalk out a road to the sky,
Improve on your plans—or I'll venture to say,
A chymist, of Paris, will show us the way.
The earth on its surface has all been survey'd,
The sea has been travell'd—and deep in the shade
The kingdom of Pluto has heard us at work,
When we dig for his metals wherever they lurk.
But who would have thought that invention could rise
To find out a method to soar to the skies,
And pierce the bright regions, which ages assign'd
To spirits unbodied, and flights of the mind.
Let the gods of Olympus their revels prepare—
By the aid of some pounds of inflammable air
We'll visit them soon—and forsake this dull ball
With coat, shoes and stockings, fat carcase and all!
How France is distinguish'd in Louis's reign!
What cannot her genius and courage attain?
Thro'out the wide world have her arms found the way,
And art to the stars is extending her sway.
At sea let the British their neighbors defy—
The French shall have frigates to traverse the sky,
In this navigation more fortunate prove,
And cruise at their ease in the climates above.
If the English should venture to sea with their fleet,
A host of balloons in a trice shall they meet.
The French from the zenith their wings shall display,
And souse on these sea-dogs and bear them away.

Ye sages, who travel on mighty designs,
To measure meridians and parallel lines—
The task being tedious—take heed, if you please—
Construct a balloon—and you'll do it with ease.
And ye who the heav'n's broad concave survey,
And, aided by glasses, its secrets betray,
Who gaze, the night through, at the wonderful scene,
Yet still are complaining of vapors between,
Ah, seize the conveyance and fearlessly rise
To peep at the lanthorns that light up the skies,
And floating above, on our ocean of air,
Inform us, by letter, what people are there.
In Saturn, advise us if snow ever melts,
And what are the uses of Jupiter's belts;
(Mars being willing) pray send us word, greeting,
If his people are fonder of fighting than eating.
That Venus has horns we've no reason to doubt,
(I forget what they call him who first found it out)
And you'll find, I'm afraid, if you venture too near,
That the spirits of cuckolds inhabit her sphere.
Our folks of good morals it wofully grieves,
That Mercury's people are villains and thieves,
You'll see how it is—but I'll venture to show
For a dozen among them, twelve dozens below.
From long observation one proof may be had
That the men in the moon are incurably mad;
However, compare us, and if they exceed
They must be surprizingly crazy indeed.
    But now, to have done with our planets and moons—
Come, grant me a patent for making balloons—
For I find that the time is approaching—the day
When horses shall fail, and the horsemen decay.
Post riders, at present (call'd Centaurs of old)
Who brave all the seasons, hot weather and cold,
In future shall leave their dull ponies behind
And travel, like ghosts, on the wings of the wind.
The stagemen, whose gallopers scarce have the power
Through the dirt to convey you ten miles in an hour,
When advanc'd to balloons shall so furiously drive
You'll hardly know whether you are dead or alive.

The man who at Boston sets out with the sun,
If the wind should be fair, may be with us at one,
At Gunpowder Ferry drink whiskey at three
And at six be at Edentown, ready for tea.
(The machine shall be order'd, we hardly need say,
To travel in darkness as well as by day)
At Charleston by ten he for sleep shall prepare,
And at twelve the next day be the devil knows where.
When the ladies grow sick of the city in June,
What a jaunt they shall have in the flying balloon!
Whole mornings shall see them at toilets preparing,
And forty miles high be their afternoon's airing.

   Yet more with its fitness for commerce I'm struck;
What loads of tobacco shall fly from Kentuck,
What packs of best beaver—bar-iron and pig,
What budgets of leather from Conocoheague!
If Britain should ever disturb us again,
(As they threaten to do in the next George's reign)
No doubt they will play us a new set of tunes,
And pepper us well from their fighting balloons.
To market the farmers shall shortly repair
With their hogs and potatoes, wholesale, thro' the air,
Skim over the water as light as a feather,
Themselves and their turkeys conversing together.

   Such wonders as these from balloons shall arise—
And the giants of old, that assaulted the skies
With their Ossa on Pelion, shall freely confess
That all they attempted was nothing to this.

LITERARY IMPORTATION

However we wrangled with Britain awhile
We think of her now in a different style,
And many fine things we receive from her isle;
        Among all the rest,
        Some demon possessed
Our dealers in knowledge and sellers of sense
To have a good bishop imported from thence.

The words of Sam Chandler[1] were thought to be vain,
When he argued it so often and proved it so plain
"That Satan must flourish till bishops should reign:"
     Though he went to the wall
     With his project and all,
Another bold Sammy[2] in bishop's array,
Has got something more than his pains for his pay.

It seems we had spirit to humble a throne,
Have genius for science inferior to none,
But hardly encourage a plant of our own:
     If a college be planned,
     'Tis all at a stand
'Till to Europe we send at a shameful expense,
To send us a book-worm to teach us some sense.

Can we never be thought to have learning or grace
Unless it be brought from that horrible place
Where tyranny reigns with her impudent face;
     And popes and pretenders,
     And sly faith-defenders
Have ever been hostile to reason and wit,
Enslaving a world that shall conquer them yet.

'Tis a folly to fret at the picture I draw:
And I say what was said by a Doctor Magraw:
"If they give us their Bishops, they'll give us their law."
     How that will agree
     With such people as we,
Let us leave to the learned to reflect on awhile,
And say what they think in a handsomer style.

[1] Who labored for the establishment of an American Episcopacy, previously to the Revolutionary War.

[2] Bishop Samuel Seabury, of Connecticut.

THE WILD HONEYSUCKLE

Fair flower, that dost so comely grow,
Hid in this silent, dull retreat,
Untouched thy honied blossoms blow,
Unseen thy little branches greet:
    No roving foot shall crush thee here,
    No busy hand provoke a tear.

By Nature's self in white arrayed,
She bade thee shun the vulgar eye,
And planted here the guardian shade,
And sent soft waters murmuring by;
    Thus quietly thy summer goes,
    Thy days declining to repose.

Smit with those charms, that must decay,
I grieve to see your future doom;
They died—nor were those flowers more gay,
The flowers that did in Eden bloom;
    Unpitying frosts, and Autumn's power
    Shall leave no vestige of this flower.

From morning suns and evening dews
At first thy little being came:
If nothing once, you nothing lose,
For when you die you are the same;
    The space between, is but an hour,
    The frail duration of a flower.

THE DEATH SONG OF A CHEROKEE INDIAN

The sun sets in night, and the stars shun the day,
But glory remains when their lights fade away.
Begin, ye tormentors: your threats are in vain
For the son of Alknomock can never complain.

Remember the woods, where in ambush he lay,
And the scalps which he bore from your nation away!
Why do ye delay?—'till I shrink from my pain?
Know the son of Alknomock can never complain.

Remember the arrows he shot from his bow,
Remember your chiefs by his hatchet laid low,
The flame rises high, you exult in my pain?
Know the son of Alknomock will never complain.

I go to the land where my father is gone:
His ghost shall rejoice in the fame of his son,
Death comes like a friend, he relieves me from pain,
And thy son, O Alknomock, has scorned to complain.

THE INDIAN BURYING-GROUND

In spite of all the learned have said,
    I still my old opinion keep;
The posture, that we give the dead,
    Points out the soul's eternal sleep.

Not so the ancients of these lands—
    The Indian, when from life released,
Again is seated with his friends,
    And shares again the joyous feast.[1]

His imaged birds, and painted bowl,
    And venison, for a journey dressed,
Bespeak the nature of the soul,
    Activity, that knows no rest.

His bow, for action ready bent,
    And arrows, with a head of stone,
Can only mean that life is spent,
    And not the old ideas gone.

Thou, stranger, that shalt come this way,
    No fraud upon the dead commit—
Observe the swelling turf, and say
    They do not lie, but here they sit.

[1] The North American Indians bury their dead in a sitting posture; decorating the corpse with wampum, the images of birds, quadrupeds, &c., and (if that of a warrior) with bows, arrows, tomhawks, and other military weapons.

Here still a lofty rock remains,
  On which the curious eye may trace
(Now wasted, half, by wearing rains)
  The fancies of a ruder race.

Here still an aged elm aspires,
  Beneath whose far-projecting shade
(And which the shepherd still admires)
  The children of the forest played!

There oft a restless Indian queen
  (Pale Shebah, with her braided hair)
And many a barbarous form is seen
  To chide the man that lingers there.

By midnight moons, o'er moistening dews;
  In habit for the chase arrayed,
The hunter still the deer pursues,
  The hunter and the deer, a shade!

And long shall timorous fancy see
  The painted chief, and pointed spear,
And Reason's self shall bow the knee
  To shadows and delusions here.

ON THE PROSPECT OF A REVOLUTION IN FRANCE

"Now, at the feast they plan the fall of Troy;
The stern debate Atrides heard with joy."
—*Hom. Odys.*

Borne on the wings of time another year
Sprung from the past, begins its proud career:
From that bright spark which first illumed these lands,
See Europe kindling, as the blaze expands,
Each gloomy tyrant, sworn to chain the mind,
Presumes no more to trample on mankind:
Even potent Louis trembles on his throne,
The generous prince who made our cause his own,

More equal rights his injured subjects claim,
No more a country's strength—that country's shame;
Fame starts astonished at such prizes won,
And rashness wonders how the work was done.

Flushed with new life, and brightening at the view,
Genius, triumphant, moulds the world anew;
To these far climes in swift succession moves
Each art that Reason owns and sense approves.
What though his age is bounded to a span
Time sheds a conscious dignity on man,
Some happier breath his rising passion swells,
Some kinder genius his bold arm impels,
Dull superstition from the world retires,
Disheartened zealots haste to quench their fires;
One equal rule o'er twelve[1] vast States extends,
Europe and Asia join to be our friends,
Our active flag in every clime displayed
Counts stars on colors that shall never fade;
A far-famed chief o'er this vast whole presides
Whose motto Honor is—whom Virtue guides;
His walks forsaken in Virginia's groves,
Applauding thousands bow where'er He moves,
Who laid the basis of this Empire sure
Where public faith should public peace secure.

Still may she rise, exalted in her aims,
And boast to every age her patriot names,
To distant climes extend her gentle sway,
While choice—not force— bids every heart obey:
Ne'er may she fail when Liberty implores,
Nor want true valor to defend her shores,
'Till Europe, humbled, greets our western wave,
And owns an equal—whom she wished a slave.

[1] At this time Rhode Island was not a member of the general
Confederation of the American States.

TO A DOG

OCCASIONED BY PUTTING HIM ON SHORE AT THE ISLAND OF SAPOLA,
FOR THEFT.

Since Nature taught you, Tray, to be a thief,
What blame have you, for working at your trade?
What if you stole a handsome round of beef;
Theft, in your code of laws, no crime was made.

The ten commandments you had never read,
Nor did it ever enter in your head:
But art and Nature, careful to conceal,
Disclos'd not even the Eighth—*Thou shalt not steal.*

Then to the green wood, caitiff, haste away:
There take your chance to live—for Truth must say,
We have no right, for theft, to hang up Tray.

ON THE SLEEP OF PLANTS

When suns are set, and stars in view,
Not only man to slumber yields;
But Nature grants this blessing too,
To yonder plants, in yonder fields.

The Summer heats and lengthening days
(To them the same as toil and care)
Thrice welcome make the evening breeze,
That kindly does their strength repair.

At early dawn each plant survey,
And see, revived by Nature's hand,
With youthful vigor, fresh and gay,
Their blossoms blow, their leaves expand.

Yon' garden plant, with weeds o'er-run,
Not void of thought, perceives its hour,
And, watchful of the parting sun,
Throughout the night conceals her flower.

Like us, the slave of cold and heat,
She too enjoys her little span—
With Reason, only less complete
Than that which makes the boast of man.

Thus, moulded from one common clay,
A varied life adorns the plain;
By Nature subject to decay,
By Nature meant to bloom again!

TO MY BOOK

Seven years are now elaps'd, dear rambling volume,
Since, to all knavish wights a foe,
I sent you forth to vex and gall 'em,
Or drive them to the shades below:
With spirit, still, of Democratic proof,
And still despising Shylock's canker'd hoof:
What doom the fates intend, is hard to say,
Whether to live to some far-distant day,
Or sickening in your prime,
In this bard-baiting clime,
Take pet, make wings, say prayers, and flit away.

"Virtue, order, and religion,
Haste, and seek some other region;
Your plan is laid, to hunt them down,
Destroy the mitre, rend the gown,
And that vile hag, Philosophy, restore"—
Did ever volume plan so much before?

For seven years past, a host of busy foes
Have buzz'd about your nose,
White, black, and grey, by night and day;
Garbling, lying, singing, sighing:
These eastern gales a cloud of insects bring
That fluttering, snivelling, whimpering—on the wing—
And, wafted still as discord's demon guides,
Flock round the flame, that yet shall singe their hides.

Well! let the fates decree whate'er they please:
Whether you're doom'd to drink oblivion's cup,
Or Praise-God Barebones eats you up,
This I can say, you've spread your wings afar,
Hostile to garter, ribbon, crown, and star;
Still on the people's, still on Freedom's side,
With full determin'd aim, to baffle every claim
Of well-born wights, that aim to mount and ride.

THE REPUBLICAN GENIUS OF EUROPE

Emperors and kings! in vain you strive
    Your torments to conceal—
The age is come that shakes your thrones,
Tramples in dust despotic crowns,
    And bids the sceptre fail.

In western worlds the flame began:
    From thence to France it flew—
Through Europe, now, it takes its way,
Beams an insufferable day,
    And lays all tyrants low.

Genius of France! pursue the chase
    Till Reason's laws restore
Man to be Man, in every clime;—
That Being active, great, sublime,
    Debas'd in dust no more.

In dreadful pomp he takes his way
    O'er ruin'd crowns, demolish'd thrones—
        Pale tyrants shrink before his blaze—
Round him terrific lightnings play—
    With eyes of fire, he looks them through,
    Crushes the vile despotic crew,
        And Pride in ruin lays.

TO A CATY-DID [1]

In a branch of willow hid
Sings the evening Caty-did:
From the lofty locust bough
Feeding on a drop of dew,
In her suit of green array'd
Hear her singing in the shade
   Caty-did, Caty-did, Caty-did!

While upon a leaf you tread,
Or repose your little head,
On your sheet of shadows laid,
All the day you nothing said:
Half the night your cheery tongue
Revell'd out its little song,
   Nothing else but Caty-did.

From your lodgings on the leaf
Did you utter joy or grief—?
Did you only mean to say,
I have had my summer's day,
And am passing, soon, away
To the grave of Caty-did:—
   Poor, unhappy Caty-did!

But you would have utter'd more
Had you known of nature's power—
From the world when you retreat,
And a leaf's your winding sheet,
Long before your spirit fled,
Who can tell but nature said,
Live again, my Caty-did!
   Live, and chatter Caty-did.

[1] A well-known insect, when full grown, about two inches in length, and of the exact color of a green leaf. It is of the genus cicada, or grasshopper kind, inhabiting the green foliage of trees and singing such a song as Caty-did in the evening toward autumn.

Tell me, what did Caty do?
Did she mean to trouble you?·
Why was Caty not forbid
To trouble little Caty-did?
Wrong, indeed, at you to fling,
Hurting no one while you sing
   Caty-did! Caty-did! Caty-did!

Why continue to complain?
Caty tells me, she again
Will not give you plague or pain:—
Caty says you may be hid
Caty will not go to bed
While you sing us Caty-did.
   Caty-did! Caty-did! Caty-did!

But, while singing, you forgot
To tell us what did Caty not:
Caty-did not think of cold,
Flocks retiring to the fold,
Winter, with his wrinkles old,
Winter, that yourself foretold
   When you gave us Caty-did.

Stay securely in your nest;
Caty now, will do her best,
All she can, to make you blest;
But, you want no human aid—
Nature, when she form'd you, said,
"Independent you are made,
My dear little Caty-did:
Soon yourself must disappear
With the verdure of the year,"—
And to go, we know not where,
   With your song of Caty-did.

ON A HONEY BEE DRINKING FROM A GLASS OF WINE AND DROWNED THEREIN

Thou, born to sip the lake or spring,
Or quaff the waters of the stream,
Why hither come on vagrant wing?—
Does Bacchus tempting seem—
Did he, for you, this glass prepare?—
Will I admit you to a share?

Did storms harass or foes perplex,
Did wasps or king-birds bring dismay—
Did wars distress, or labors vex,
Or did you miss your way?—
A better seat you could not take
Than on the margin of this lake.

Welcome!—I hail you to my glass:
All welcome, here, you find;
Here, let the cloud of trouble pass,
Here, be all care resigned.—
This fluid never fails to please,
And drown the griefs of men or bees.

What forced you here, we cannot know,
And you will scarcely tell—
But cheery we would have you go
And bid a glad farewell:
On lighter wings we bid you fly,
Your dart will now all foes defy.

Yet take not, oh! too deep a drink,
And in this ocean die;
Here bigger bees than you might sink,
Even bees full six feet high.
Like Pharaoh, then, you would be said
To perish in a sea of red.

Do as you please, your will is mine;
Enjoy it without fear—
And your grave will be this glass of wine,
Your epitaph—a tear—
Go, take you seat in Charon's boat,
We'll tell the hive, you died afloat.

HUGH H. BRACKENRIDGE

Hugh Henry Brackenridge was born in Scotland in 1748, but at the age of five was brought to America by his parents, who settled in York County, Pennsylvania, near the Maryland border. There he was brought up and, by dint of hard work and wide journeyings after books, secured a good elementary education. At fifteen he became teacher in a Maryland school, which he soon left to attend Princeton. Supporting himself at the college by teaching lower classes, he was able to acquire a sound training in the classics and to study theology; in addition, he made the friendship of two promising fellow-students, James Madison and Philip Freneau. Between him and Freneau there grew up especially cordial relations. They wrote together a Commencement poem for the year 1771. Several years later, when Brackenridge became head of a seminary in Maryland, he secured his friend as assistant. In his next venture, editing the *United States Magazine,* he again had the aid of Freneau, who became a principal contributor. During the war Brackenridge served as chaplain in the Revolutionary army. Afterward he studied law, and in 1781 settled in the frontier town of Pittsburgh. There he speedily rose to prominence in his profession and politics, and in time he became the recognised head of the Western bar. After the Whiskey Rebellion of 1794, he was accused of disloyalty to his government, but in a voluminous pamphlet, *Incidents of the Insurrection,* published in Philadelphia in 1795, he thoroughly vindicated his conduct. From 1800 to his death in 1816 he was a justice of the Supreme Court of the state. During the Revolutionary period Brackenridge wrote much patriotic verse and prose, the best example being a drama (written for the students in his seminary), *The Battle of Bunkers-Hill.* He is best known, however, for the prose satire on democracy, *Modern Chivalry,* a kind of "aboriginal classic" of the West, the first part of which appeared in 1792. A second part was published in 1795. In this work, which owes much to Cervantes and something to Butler, the author was not satirizing democracy so much as the abuses of democracy. With the true instincts of a frontiersman and a democrat, he believed in the people, but he believed that they should be shown their shortcomings and have pointed out to them their responsibilities as rulers of themselves.

FROM "THE BATTLE OF BUNKERS-HILL"

Act II.

Scene I. *Boston.*

Enter Gage, Howe *and* Burgoyne.

Burgoyne. How long, brave gen'rals, shall the rebel foe,
In vain arrangements, and mock siege, display
Their haughty insolence?—Shall in this town,
So many thousands, of *Britannia's* troops,
With watch incessant, and sore toil oppress'd,
Remain besieg'd? A vet'ran army pent,
In the enclosure, of so small a space,
By a disorder'd herd, untaught, unofficer'd.
Let not, sweet Heav'n, the envious mouth of fame,
With breath malignant, o'er the Atlantic wave
Bear this to Europe's shores, or tell to France,
Or haughty Spain, of Lexington's retreat.
Who could have thought it, in the womb of time,
That *British* soldiers, in this latter age,
Beat back by peasants, and in flight disgrac'd,
Could tamely brook the base discomfiture;
Nor sallying out, with spirit reassum'd,
Exact due tribute of their victory?
Drive back the foe, to Alleghany hills,
In woody valleys, or on mountain tops,
To mix with wolves and kindred savages.

Gage. This mighty paradox, will soon dissolve.
Hear first, Burgoyne, the valor of these men,

Fir'd with the zeal, of fiercest liberty,
Nor fear of death, so terrible to all,
Can stop their rage. Grey-headed clergymen,
With Holy Bible, and continual prayer,
Bear up their fortitude—and talk of heav'n,
And tell them, that sweet soul, who dies in battle,
Shall walk, with spirits of the just. These words
Add wings to native rage, and hurry them
Impetuous to war. Nor yet in arms
Unpracticed. The day of Lexington
A sad conviction gave our soldiery,
That these Americans, were not that herd,
And rout ungovern'd, which we painted them.

HOWE. Not strange to your maturer thought, Burgoyne,
This matter will appear. A people brave,
Who never yet, of luxury, or soft
Delights, effeminate, and false, have tasted.
But, through hate of chains, and slav'ry, suppos'd,
Forsake their mountain tops, and rush to arms.
Oft have I heard their valor published:
Their perseverance, and untamable,
Fierce mind, when late they fought with us, and drove,
The French encroaching on their settlements,
Back to their frozen lakes. Or when with us
On Cape Breton, they stormed Louisburg.

With us in Canada, they took Quebec;
And at the Havannah, these New England men,
Led on by Putnam, acted gallantly.
I had a brother once, who in that war,
With fame commanded them, and when he fell,
Not unlamented; for these warriors,
So brave themselves, and sensible of merit,
Erected him a costly monument;
And much it grieves me that I draw my sword,
For this late insurrection and revolt,
To chastise them. Would.to Almighty God,
The task unnatural, had been assign'd,

Elsewhere. But since by Heaven, determined,
Let's on, and wipe the day of Lexington.

* * * * * *

Act V.

Scene I. *Bunkers-Hill.*

Warren *with the American Army.*

Warren. To arms, brave countrymen, for see the foe
Comes forth to battle, and would seem to try,
Once more, their fortune in decisive war.
Three thousand, 'gainst seven hundred, rang'd this day,
Shall give the world, an ample specimen,
What strength, and noble confidence, the sound
Of Liberty inspires. That Liberty,
Which, not the thunder of Bellona's voice,
With fleets, and armies, from the *British* shore,
Shall wrest from us. Our noble ancestors,
Out-brav'd the tempests, of the hoary deep,
And on these hills, uncultivate, and wild,
Sought an asylum, from despotic sway;
A short asylum, for that envious power,
With persecution dire, still follows us.
At first, they deem'd our charters forfeited.
Next, our just rights, in government, abridg'd.
Then, thrust in viceroys, and bashaws, to rule,
With lawless sovereignty. Now added force,
Of standing armies, to secure their sway.
Much have we suffer'd from the licens'd rage,
Of brutal soldiery, in each fair town.
Remember March, brave countrymen, that day
When Boston's streets ran blood. Think on that day,
And let the memory, to revenge, stir up,
The temper of your souls. There might we still,
On terms precarious, and disdainful, liv'd,
With daughters ravish'd, and butcher'd sons,
But Heaven forbade the thought. These are the men,
Who in firm phalanx, threaten us with war,
And aim this day, to fix forever down,

The galling chains, which tyranny has forg'd for us,
These count our lands and settlements their own,
And in their intercepted letters, speak,
Of farms, and tenements, secured for friends,
Which, if they gain, brave soldiers, let with blood,
The purchase, be seal'd down.   Let every arm,
This day be active, in fair freedom's cause,
And shower down, from the hill, like Heav'n in wrath,
Full store of lightning, and fierce iron hail,
To blast the adversary.   Let this ground,
Like burning Ætna or Vesuvius top,
Be wrapt in flame—   The word is, LIBERTY,
And Heaven smile on us, in so just a cause.

*   *   *   *   *   *

Scene IV.

WARREN.   *Mortally wounded, falling on his right knee,
covering his breast with his right hand, and supporting himself with his firelock in the left.*

WARREN.   A deadly ball hath limited my life,
And now to God, I offer up my soul.
But O my Countrymen, let not the cause,
The sacred cause of liberty, with me
Faint or expire.   By the last parting breath,
And blood of this your fellow soldier slain,
Be now abjur'd, never to yield the right,
The grand deposit of all-giving Heaven,
To man's free nature, that he rule himself.
With these rude Britons, wage life-scorning war,
Till they admit it, and like hell fall off,
With ebbing billows, from this troubl'd coast,
Where but for them firm concord, and true love,
Should individual, hold their court and reign.
Th' infernal engin'ry of state, resist
To death, that unborn times may be secure,
And while men flourish in the peace you win,
Write each fair name with worthies of the earth.
Weep not your Gen'ral, who is snatch'd this day,
From the embraces of a family,

Five virgin daughters young, and unendow'd,
Now with the foe left lone and fatherless.
Weep not for him who first espous'd the cause
And risking life has met the enemy,
In fatal opposition—But rejoice—
For now I go to mingle with the dead,
Great Brutus, Hampden, Sidney, and the rest,
Of old, or modern memory, who liv'd,
A mound to tyrants, and strong hedge to kings,
Bounding the inundations of their rage,
Against the happiness and peace of man.
I see these heroes where they walk serene,
By crystal currents, on the vale of Heaven,
High in full converse of immortal acts,
Achiev'd for truth and innocence on earth.
Meantime the harmony and thrilling sound
Of mellow lutes, sweet viols, and guitars,
Dwell on the soul and ravish ev'ry nerve.
Anon the murmur of the tight-brac'd drum,
With finely varied fifes to martial airs,
Wind up the spirit to the mighty proof
Of siege and battle, and attempt in arms.
Illustrious group! They beckon me along,
To ray my visage with immortal light,
And bind the amaranth around my brow.
I come, I come, ye first-born of true fame.
Fight on, my Countrymen, be Free, be Free.

CAPTAIN FARRAGO AND TEAGUE

[FROM "MODERN CHIVALRY," CHAPTER I. 1792]

Captain John Farrago was a man about forty-five years of age, of good natural sense and considerable reading; but in some things whimsical, owing perhaps to his greater knowledge of books, than of the world; but in some degree, also, to his having never married, being what we call an old bachelor; a characteristic of which is, usually, singularity and whim. He had the advantage of having had in early life an academic education; but having never applied himself to any of the learned professions, he had lived the greater part of his life near a village of western Pennsylvania, on a small farm, which he cultivated with servants,[1] or hired hands, as he could conveniently supply himself with either. He was himself no idler, for he often held his own plough, or swung his flail, while his hands were embrowned by exposure to the sun, and hardened by the use of the axe. In person he was tall, and what is called raw-boned; his features were strongly marked, and rather coarse but not disagreeable, although his nose somewhat exceeded the usual length. The servant he had at this time was an Irishman, whose name was Teague O'Regan. I shall say nothing at present of the character of this man, because the very name imports what he was.

A strange idea came into the head of the captain about this time, for, by the by, I had forgot to mention that having been a captain of a company of militia, he had gone by the name of captain ever since; for the rule is, once a captain, always a captain; but, as I was observing, the idea had come into his head, to saddle an old horse that he had, and ride about the world a little, with his man Teague at his heels, to see how things were going on here and there, and to observe human nature. For it is a mistake to suppose, that a man cannot learn man by reading him in a corner, as well as on the widest space of transaction. At any rate, it may yield amusement. He accordingly sold off his personal effects, pocketed some cash, and leased out his small farm near the village, retaining only the old saddle-horse, which had been for some time relieved from the ordinary services in the plough or wagon.

TEAGUE AS A CANDIDATE

[FROM THE SAME, CHAPTER III.]

While they were thus discoursing, a bustle had taken place among the crowd. Teague hearing so much about elections, and serving the government, took it into his head,

[1] Redemptioners or those bound for a term, to pay for their passage, were called *servants*.

that he could be a legislator himself. The thing was not displeasing to the people, who seemed to favor his pretensions; owing, in some degree, to there being several of his countrymen among the crowd; but more especially to the fluctuation of the popular mind, and a disposition to what is new and ignoble. For though the weaver was not the most elevated object of choice, yet he was still preferable to this tatterdemalion.

The captain coming up, and finding what was on the carpet, was chagrined at not having been able to give the voters a better idea of the importance of a legislative trust; alarmed also, from an apprehension of the loss of his servant. Under these impressions he resumed his address to the people. Said he, "This is making the matter still worse, gentlemen: this servant of mine is but a bog-trotter, who can scarcely speak the dialect in which your laws ought to be written; but certainly has never read a single treatise on any political subject; for the truth is, he cannot read at all. The young people of the lower class, in Ireland, have seldom the advantage of a good education; especially the descendants of the ancient Irish, who have most of them a great assurance of countenance, but little information or literature. This young man, whose family name is O'Regan, has been my servant for several years; and, except a too great fondness for whiskey, which now and then brings him into scrapes, he has demeaned himself in a manner tolerable enough. But he is totally ignorant of the great principles of legislation; and more especially the particular interests of the government. A free government is a noble acquisition to a people: and this freedom consists in an equal right to make laws, and to have the benefit of the laws when made. Though doubtless, in such a government, the lowest citizen may become chief magistrate; yet it is sufficient to possess the right, not absolutely necessary to exercise it. Or even if you should think proper, now and then, to show your privilege, and exert, in a signal manner, the democratic prerogative, yet is it not descending too low to filch away from me a servant whom I cannot well spare, and for whom I have paid my money? You are surely carrying the matter too far, in thinking to make a senator of this hostler; to take him away from an employment to which he has been bred, and put him to another, to which he has served no apprenticeship: to set those hands, which have lately been employed in currying my horse, to the draughting bills, and preparing business for the house."

The people were tenacious of their choice, and insisted on giving Teague their suffrages; and by the frown upon their brows, seemed to indicate resentment at what had been said; as indirectly charging them with want of judgment; or calling in question their privilege to do what they thought proper. "It is a very strange thing," said one of them, who was a speaker for the rest, "that after having conquered Burgoyne and Cornwallis, and got a government of our own, we cannot put in whom we please. This young man may be your servant, or another man's servant; but if we choose to make him a delegate, what is that to you? He may not be yet skilled in the matter, but there is a good day coming. We will empower him; and it is better to trust a plain man like him, than one of your high-flyers, that will make laws to suit their own purposes."

"I had much rather," said the captain, "you would send the weaver, though I thought that improper, than to invade my household, and thus take from me the person who is employed to curry my horse, and black my boots."

The prolocutor of the people gave him to understand that his objections were useless, for the people had determined on the choice, and Teague they would have, for a representative.

Finding it answered no end to expostulate, he requested to speak a word with Teague by himself. Stepping aside, he said to him, composing his voice, and addressing him in a soft manner: "Teague, you are quite wrong in this matter they have put into your head. Do you know what it is to be a member of a deliberative body? What qualifications are necessary? Do you understand anything of geography? If a question should be put to make a law to dig a canal in some part of the state, can you describe the bearing of the mountains, and the course of the rivers? Or, if commerce is to be pushed to some new quarter, by the force of regulations, are you competent to decide in such a case? There will be questions of law, and astronomy, on the carpet. How you must gape and stare like a fool, when you come to be asked your opinion on these subjects! Are you acquainted with the principles of finance; with the funding public securities; the ways and n.eans of raising the revenue; providing for the discharge of the public debts, and all other things which respect the economy of the government? Even if you had knowledge, have you a facility of speaking? I would suppose you would have too much pride to go to the house just to say, ay or no. This is not the fault of your nature, but of your education; having been accustomed to dig turf in your early years, rather than instructing yourself in the classics, or common school-books.

"When a man becomes a member of a public body, he is like a raccoon, or other beast that climbs up the fork of a tree; the boys pushing at him with pitchforks, or throwing stones, or shooting at him with arrows; the dogs barking in the meantime. One will find fault with your not speaking; another with your speaking, if you speak at all. They will put you in the newspapers, and ridicule you as a perfect beast. There is what they call the *caricatura;* that is, representing you with a dog's head, or a cat's claw. It is the devil to be exposed to the squibs and crackers of the gazette wits and publications. You know no.more about these matters than a goose; and yet you would undertake rashly, without advice, to enter on the office; nay, contrary to advice. For I would not for a hundred guineas, though I have not the half to spare, that the breed of the O'Regans should come to this; bringing on them a worse stain than stealing sheep. You have nothing but your character, Teague, in a new country to depend upon. Let it never be said, that you quitted an honest livelihood, the taking care of my horse, to follow the new-fangled whims of the times, and be a statesman. And, besides, have I not promised to do something clever towards settling you in life hereafter, provided you will serve me faithfully in my travels? Something better than you have thought of may turn up in the course of our rambles."

Teague was moved chiefly with the last part of the address, and consented to relinquish his pretensions.

The captain, glad of this, took him back to the people, and announced his disposition to decline the honor which they had intended him.

Teague acknowledged that he had changed his mind, and was willing to remain in a private station.

The people did not seem well pleased; but as nothing more could be said about the matter, they turned their attention to the weaver, and gave him their suffrages.

ROYALL TYLER

Royall Tyler, born at Boston in 1757, was a member of an influential New England family, was educated at Harvard, and studied law in the office of John Adams. During the Revolution he was aide-de-camp to General Lincoln. In 1787, while serving in the same capacity during Shays's Rebellion, he made his first trip to New York. There he was so greatly attracted to the theatre that within a few weeks he wrote for it a prose comedy, *The Contrast*. This was the first American play to succeed on the stage, and the enthusiastic reception accorded it encouraged the author to produce others, of which the best known was *The Georgia Spec,* written in 1797, and repeatedly performed in Boston. In 1797 he also published *The Algerine Captive,* a fiction masquerading as a book of memoirs. It is less to be commended for its matter, of which the untravelled Tyler knew little at first hand, than for its lively manner and its admirable prose style. After this, Tyler contributed occasionally to periodicals, his work being mostly light verse and entertaining social squibs. But with him, writing was, after all, only an avocation: he was indifferent to literary fame, and published his pieces anonymously. In his legal career, he was successful: he established himself as a lawyer, in time became a judge, and at last reached the position of Chief Justice of the Supreme Court of Vermont. He died at Brattleboro, Vermont, in 1826. Among his contemporaries, Tyler was renowned chiefly as a wit, a versifier, and a jurist; to posterity he is important as the first successful American dramatist.

FROM "THE CONTRAST"

PROLOGUE

Written by a young gentleman of New York, and spoken by
Mr. Wignell.

Exult, each patriot heart!—this night is shown
A piece, which we may fairly call our own;
Where the proud titles of "My Lord! Your Grace!"
To humble *Mr.* and plain *Sir* give place.
Our Author pictures not from foreign climes
The fashions or the follies of the times;
But has confin'd the subject of his work
To the gay scenes—the circles of New York.
On native themes his Muse displays her pow'rs;
If ours the faults, the virtues too are ours.
Why should our thoughts to distant countries roam,
When each refinement may be found at home?
Who travels now to ape the rich or great,
To deck an equipage and roll in state;
To court the graces, or to dance with ease,
Or by hypocrisy to strive to please?
Our free-born ancestors such arts despis'd;
Genuine sincerity alone they priz'd;
Their minds, with honest emulation fir'd;
To solid good—not ornament—aspir'd;
Or, if ambition rous'd a bolder flame,
Stern virtue throve, where indolence was shame.

But modern youths, with imitative sense,
Deem taste in dress the proof of excellence;
And spurn the meanness of your homespun arts,
Since homespun habits would obscure their parts;
Whilst all, which aims at splendor and parade,
Must come from Europe, *and be ready made.*
Strange! we should thus our native worth disclaim,
And check the progress of our rising fame.
Yet *one*, whilst imitation bears the sway,
Aspires to nobler heights, and points the way.

Be rous'd, my friends! his bold example view;
Let your own Bards be proud to copy you!
Should rigid critics reprobate our play,
At least the patriotic heart will say,
"Glorious our fall, since in a noble cause.
The bold *attempt alone* demands applause."
Still may the wisdom of the Comic Muse
Exalt your merits, or your faults accuse.
But think not, 'tis her aim to be severe;—
We all are mortals, and as mortals err.
If candor pleases, we are truly blest;
Vice trembles, when compell'd to stand confess'd.
Let not light Censure on your faults offend,
Which aims not to expose them, but amend.
Thus does our Author to your candor trust;
Conscious, the *free* are generous, as just.

ACT II. Scene I.

*   *   *   *   *   *

LETITIA. By what I can pick out of your flowery description, your brother is no beau.

CHARLOTTE. No, indeed; he makes no pretension to the character. He'd ride, or rather fly, an hundred miles to relieve a distressed object, or to do a gallant act in the service of his country; but should you drop your fan or bouquet in his presence, it is ten to one that some beau at the farther end of the room would have the honor of presenting it to you before he had observed that it fell. I'll tell you one of his antiquated, anti-gallant notions. He said once in my presence, in a room full of company,—would you believe it?—in a large circle of ladies, that the best evidence a gentleman could give a young lady of his respect and affection was to endeavor in a friendly manner to rectify her foibles. I protest I was crimson to the eyes, upon reflecting that I was known as his sister.

LETITIA. Insupportable creature! tell a lady of her faults! if he is so grave, I fear I have no chance of captivating him.

CHARLOTTE. His conversation is like a rich, old-fashioned brocade,—it will stand alone; every sentence is a sentiment. Now may you judge what a time I had with him, in my twelve months' visit to my father. He read me such lectures, out of pure brotherly affection, against the extremes of fashion, dress, flirting, and coquetry, and all the other dear things which he knows I doat upon, that I protest his conversation made me as melancholy as if I had been at church; and heaven knows, though I never prayed to go there but on one occasion, yet I would have exchanged his conversation for a psalm and a sermon. Church is rather melancholy, to be sure; but then I can ogle the beaux, and be regaled with "here endeth the first lesson," but his brotherly *here,* you would think had no end. You captivate him! Why, my dear, he would as soon fall in love with a box of Italian flowers. There is Maria, now, if she were not engaged, she might do something. Oh! how I should like to see that pair of penserosos together, looking as grave as two sailors' wives of a stormy night, with a flow of sentiment meandering through their conversation like purling streams in modern poetry.

LETITIA. Oh! my dear fanciful—

CHARLOTTE. Hush! I hear some person coming through the entry. [*Enter* Servant.

SERVANT. Madam, there's a gentleman below who calls himself Colonel Manly; do you choose to be at home?

CHARLOTTE. Show him in. [*Exit Servant.*] Now for a sober face. [*Enter* Colonel Manly.

MANLY. My dear Charlotte, I am happy that I once more enfold you within the arms of fraternal affection. I know you are going to ask (amiable impatience!) how our parents do,—the venerable pair transmit you their blessings by me. They totter on the verge of a well-spent life, and wish only to see their children settled in the world, to depart in peace.

CHARLOTTE. I am very happy to hear that they are well. [*Coolly.*] Brother, will you give me leave to introduce you to our uncle's ward, one of my most intimate friends?

MANLY [*saluting Letitia.*] I ought to regard your friends as my own.

CHARLOTTE. Come, Letitia, do give us a little dash of your vivacity; my brother is so sentimental and so grave, that I protest he'll give us the vapors.

MANLY. Though sentiment and gravity, I know, are banished the polite world, yet I hoped they might find some countenance in the meeting of such near connections as brother and sister.

CHARLOTTE. Positively, brother, if you go one step further in this strain, you will set me crying, and that, you know, would spoil my eyes; and then I should never get the husband which our good papa and mamma have so kindly wished me—never be established in the world.

MANLY. Forgive me, my sister,—I am no enemy to mirth; I love your sprightliness; and I hope it will one day enliven the hours of some worthy man; but when I mention the respectable authors of my existence,—the cherishers and protectors of my helpless infancy, whose hearts glow with such fondness and attachment that they would willingly lay down their lives for my welfare,—you will excuse me if I am so unfashionable as to speak of them with some degree of respect and reverence.

CHARLOTTE. Well, well, brother; if you won't be gay, we'll not differ; I will be as grave as you wish. [*Affects gravity.*] And so, brother, you have come to the city to exchange some of your commutation notes for a little pleasure?

MANLY. Indeed, you are mistaken; my errand is not of amusement, but business; and as I neither drink nor game, my expenses will be so trivial, I shall have no occasion to sell my notes.

CHARLOTTE. Then you won't have occasion to do a very good thing. Why, here was the Vermont General—he came down some time since, sold all his musty notes at one stroke, and then laid the cash out in trinkets for his dear Fanny. I want a dozen pretty things myself; have you got the notes with you?

MANLY. I shall be ever willing to contribute, as far as it is in my power, to adorn or in any way to please my sister; yet I hope I shall never be obliged for this to sell my notes. I may be romantic, but I preserve them as a sacred deposit.

Their full amount is justly due to me, but as embarrassments, the natural consequences of a long war, disable my country from supporting its credit, I shall wait with patience until it is rich enough to discharge them. If that is not in my day, they shall be transmitted as an honorable certificate to posterity, that I have humbly imitated our illustrious WASHINGTON, in having exposed my health and life in the service of my country, without reaping any other reward than the glory of conquering in so arduous a contest.

CHARLOTTE. Well said heroics. Why, my dear Henry, you have such a lofty way of saying things, that I protest I almost tremble at the thought of introducing you to the polite circles in the city. The belles would think you were a player run mad, with your head filled with old scraps of tragedy; and as to the beaux, they might admire, because they would not understand you. But, however, I must, I believe, introduce you to two or three ladies of my acquaintance.

LETITIA. And that will make him acquainted with thirty or forty beaux.

CHARLOTTE. Oh! brother, you don't know what a fund of happiness you have in store.

MANLY. I fear, sister, I have not refinement sufficient to enjoy it.

CHARLOTTE. Oh! you cannot fail being pleased.

LETITIA. Our ladies are so delicate and dressy.

CHARLOTTE. And our beaux so dressy and delicate.

LETITIA. Our ladies chat and flirt so agreeably.

CHARLOTTE. And our beaux simper and bow so gracefully.

LETITIA. With their hair so trim and neat.

CHARLOTTE. And their faces so soft and sleek.

LETITIA. Their buckles so tonish and bright.

CHARLOTTE. And their hands so slender and white.

LETITIA. I vow, Charlotte, we are quite poetical.

*　　*　　*　　*　　*　　*

ACT III. Scene I.

Dimple's *Room.*

*   *   *   *   *   *

JENNY. So, Mr. Jonathan, I hear you were at the play last night.

JONATHAN. At the play! why, did you think I went to the devil's drawing-room?

JENNY. The devil's drawing-room!

JONATHAN. Yes; why an't cards and dice the devil's device, and the play-house the shop where the devil hangs out the vanities of the world upon the tenter-hooks of temptation? I believe you have not heard how they were acting the old boy one night, and the wicked one came among them sure enough, and went right off in a storm, and carried one quarter of the play-house with him. Oh! no, no, no! you won't catch me at a play-house, I warrant you.

JENNY. Well, Mr. Jonathan, though I don't scruple your veracity, I have some reasons for believing you were there: pray, where were you about six o'clock?

JONATHAN. Why, I went to see one Mr. Morrison, the *hocus pocus* man; they said as how he could eat a case knife.

JENNY. Well, and how did you find the place?

JONATHAN. As I was going about here and there, to and again, to find it, I saw a great crowd of folks going into a long entry that had lanterns over the door; so I asked a man whether that was not the place where they played *hocus pocus?* He was a very civil, kind man, though he did speak like the Hessians; he lifted up his eyes and said, "They play *hocus pocus* tricks enough there, Got knows, mine friend."

JENNY. Well—

JONATHAN. So I went right in, and they showed me away, clean up to the garret, just like meeting-house gallery. And so I saw a power of topping folks, all sitting round in little cabbins, "just like father's corn-cribs"; and then there was such a squeaking with the fiddles, and such a tarnal blaze with the lights, my head was near turned. At last the people that sat near me set up such a hissing—hiss—like so many mad cats; and then they went thump, thump, thump, just like our Peleg threshing wheat, and stamped away, just like the nation; and called out for one Mr. Langolee,—I suppose he helps act the tricks.

JENNY. Well, and what did you do all this time?

JONATHAN. Gor, I—I liked the fun, and so I thumpt away, and hissed as lustily as the best of 'em. One sailor-looking man that sat by me, seeing me stamp, and knowing I was a cute fellow, because I could make a roaring noise, clapped me on the shoulder and said, "You are a d——d hearty cock, smite my timbers!" I told him so I was, but I thought he need not swear so, and make use of such naughty words.

JESSAMY. The savage!—Well, and did you see the man with his tricks?

JONATHAN. Why, I vow, as I was looking out for him, they lifted up a great green cloth and let us look right into the next neighbor's house. Have you a good many houses in New York made so in that 'ere way?

JENNY. Not many; but did you see the family?

JONATHAN. Yes, swamp it; I see'd the family.

JENNY. Well, and how did you like them?

JONATHAN. Why, I vow they were pretty much like other families;—there was a poor, good-natured curse of a husband, and a sad rantipole of a wife.

JENNY. But did you see no other folks?

JONATHAN. Yes. There was one youngster; they called him Mr. Joseph; he talked as sober and as pious as a minister; but, like other ministers that I know, he was a sly tike in his heart for all that. He was going to ask a young woman to spark it with him, and—the Lord have mercy on my soul!—she was another man's wife.

JESSAMY. The Wabash!

JENNY. And did you see any more folks?

JONATHAN. Why, they came on as thick as mustard. For my part, I thought the house was haunted. There was a soldier fellow, who talked about his row de dow, dow, and courted a young woman; but, of all the cute folk I saw, I liked one little fellow—

JENNY. Aye! who was he?

JONATHAN. Why, he had red hair, and a little round plump face like mine, only not altogether so handsome. His name was—Darby;—that was his baptizing name; his other name I forgot. Oh! it was Wig—Wag—Wag-all, Darby Wag-all,—pray, do you know him?—I should like to take a sling with him, or a drap of cider with a pepper-pod in it, to make it warm and comfortable.

JENNY. I can't say I have that pleasure.

JONATHAN. I wish you did; he is a cute fellow. But there was one thing I didn't like in that Mr. Darby; and that was, he was afraid of some of them 'ere shooting irons, such as your troopers wear on training days. Now, I'm a true born Yankee American son of liberty, and I never was afraid of a gun yet in all my life.

JENNY. Well, Mr. Jonathan, you were certainly at the play-house.

JONATHAN. I at the play-house!—Why didn't I see the play, then?

JENNY. Why, the people you saw were players.

JONATHAN. Mercy on my soul! did I see the wicked players?—Mayhap that 'ere Darby that I liked so was the old serpent himself, and had his cloven foot in his pocket. Why, I vow, now I come to think on't, the candles seemed to burn blue, and I am sure where I sat it smelled tarnally of brimstone.

A PLEA FOR FICTION

[PREFACE TO "THE ALGERINE CAPTIVE." 1797]

One of the first observations the author of the following sheets made upon his return to his native country, after an absence of seven years, was the extreme avidity with which books of mere amusement were purchased and perused by all ranks of his countrymen. When he left New England, books of biography, travels, novels, and modern romances, were confined to our seaports; or, if known in the country, were read only in the families of clergymen, physicians, and lawyers: while certain funeral discourses, the last words and dying speeches of Bryan Shaheen, and Levi Ames, and some dreary somebody's Day of Doom, formed the most diverting part of the farmer's library. On his return from captivity, he found a surprising alteration in the public taste. In our inland towns of consequence, social libraries had been instituted, composed of books designed to amuse rather than to instruct; and country booksellers, fostering the new-born taste of the people, had filled the whole land with modern travels, and novels almost as incredible. The diffusion of a taste for any species of writing through all ranks, in so short a time, would appear impracticable to an European. The peasant of Europe must first be taught to read, before he can acquire a taste in letters. In New England, the work is half completed. In no other country are there so many people, who, in proportion to its numbers, can read and write; and, therefore, no sooner was a taste for amusing literature diffused, than all orders of country life, with one accord, forsook the sober sermons and practical pieties of their fathers, for the gay stories and splendid impieties of the traveller and the novelist. The worthy farmer no longer fatigued himself with Bunyan's Pilgrim up the "hill of difficulty," or through the "slough of despond"; but quaffed wine with Brydone in the hermitage of Vesuvius, or sported with Bruce in the fairy-land of Abyssinia; while Dolly the dairy maid, and Jonathan the hired man, threw aside the ballad of the cruel step-mother, over which they had so often wept in concert, and now amused themselves into so agreeable a terror with the haunted houses and hob-goblins of Mrs. Radcliffe, that they were both afraid to sleep alone.

Although a love of literature, however frivolous, may be pleasing to the man of letters, yet there are two things to be deplored in it. The first is, that, while so many books are vended, they are not of our own manufacture. If our wives and daughters will wear gauze and ribbands, it is a pity they are not wrought in our own looms. The second misfortune is, that novels, being the picture of the times, the New England reader is insensibly taught to admire the levity, and often the vices, of the parent country. While the fancy is enchanted, the heart is corrupted. The farmer's daughter, while she pities the misfortune of some modern heroine, is exposed to the attacks of vice, from which her ignorance would have formed her surest shield. If the English novel does not inculcate vice, it at least impresses on the young female mind an erroneous idea of the world in which she is to live. It paints the manners, customs, and habits, of a strange country; excites a fondness for false splendor; and renders the home-spun habits of her own country disgusting.

There are two things wanted, said a friend to the author: that we write our own books of amusement, and that they exhibit our own manners. Why then do you not write the history of your own life? The first part of it, if not highly interesting, would at least display a portrait of New England manners, hitherto unattempted. Your captivity among the Algerines, with some notices of the manners of that ferocious race, so dreaded by commercial powers, and so little known in our country, would at least be interesting; and I see no advantage which the novel writer can have over you, unless your readers should be of the sentiment of the young lady mentioned by Addison in his Spectator, who, as he informs us, borrowed Plutarch's Lives, and, after reading the first volume with infinite delight, supposing it to be a novel, threw aside the others with disgust, because a man of letters had inadvertently told her the work was founded on *fact*.

RELIGIOUS EXERCISES IN A SOUTHERN STATE

[FROM THE SAME, CHAPTER XXIV.]

In one of the states southward of Philadelphia, I was invited on a Sunday to go to church. I will not say which, as I am loth to offend; and our fashionable fellow citizens, of the south arm of the union, may not think divine service any credit to them. My friend apologised for inviting me to so hum-drum an amusement, but assuring me that immediately after service, there was to be a famous match run for a purse of a thousand dollars, besides private bets, between 'Squire L's imported horse Slamerkin and Colonel F's bay mare Jenny Driver. When we arrived at the church, we found a brilliant collection of well-dressed people, anxiously waiting the arrival of the parson—who, it seems, had a small branch of the river M—— to pass; and, we afterwards learned, was detained by the absence of his negro boy, who was to ferry him over. Soon after, our impatience was relieved by the arrival of the parson in his canonicals—a young man not of the most mortified countenance, who, with a switch called a supple jack in his hand, belabored the back and head of the faulty slave all the way from the water to the church door, accompanying every stroke with suitable language. He entered the church, and we followed. He ascended the reading-desk, and, with his face glowing with the exercise of his supple jack, began the service with, "I said I will take heed unto my ways that I sin not with my tongue.—I will keep my tongue as it were with a bridle, when I am before the wicked.—When I mused the fire burned within me, and I spake with my tongue," &c., &c. He preached an animated discourse, of eleven minutes, upon the practical duties of religion, from these words, "Remember the Sabbath day, to keep it holy"; and read the Fourth Commandment in the communion. The whole congregation prayed fervently that their hearts might be inclined to keep this holy law. The blessing was pronounced; and parson and people hastened to the horse race. I found the parson as much respected on the turf as upon the hassock. He was one of the judges of the race; descanted, in the language of the turf, upon the points of the two rival horses; and the sleeve of his cassock was heavily laden with the principal bets. The confidence of his parishioners was not ill founded; for they assured me, upon oath and honor, that he was a gentleman of as much uprightness as his grace the Archbishop of Canterbury. Ay, they would sport him for a sermon or a song against any parson in the union.

ABOARD A SLAVE SHIP

[FROM THE SAME, CHAPTER XXX.]

. . . The day after our arrival at Cacongo, several Portuguese and negro merchants, hardly distinguishable however by their manners, employments, or complexions, came to confer with the captain about the purchase of our cargo of slaves. They contracted to deliver him two hundred and fifty head of slaves in fifteen days' time. To hear these men converse upon the purchase of human beings, with the same indifference, and nearly in the same language, as if they were contracting for so many head of cattle or swine, shocked me exceedingly. But when I suffered my imagination to rove to the habitation of these victims to this infamous cruel commerce, and fancied that I saw the peaceful husbandman dragged from his native farm, the fond husband torn from the embraces of his beloved wife, the mother from her babes, the tender child from the arms of its parent, and all the tender endearing ties of natural and social affection rended by the hand of avaricious violence, my heart sunk within me. I execrated myself for even the involuntary part I bore in this execrable traffic: I thought of my native land, and blushed. When the captain kindly inquired of me how many slaves I thought my privilege in the ship entitled me to transport for my adventure, I rejected my privilege with horror, and declared I would sooner suffer servitude than purchase a slave. This observation was received in the great cabin with repeated bursts of laughter, and excited many a stroke of coarse ridicule. Captain Russell observed, that he would not insist upon my using my privilege if I had so much of the Yankee about me. Here is my clerk, Ned Randolph, will jump at the chance, though the rogue has been rather unlucky in the trade. Out of five-and-twenty negroes he purchased, he never carried but one alive to port, and that poor devil was broken winded; and he was obliged to sell him for half price in Antigua.

Punctual to the day of the delivery, the contractors appeared, and brought with them about one hundred and fifty negroes—men, women, and children. The men were fastened together in pairs by a bar of iron, with a collar to receive the neck at each extremity; a long pole was passed over their shoulder, and between each two was bound by a staple and ring, through which the pole was thrust, and thus twenty, and sometimes, thirty were connected together; while their conductors incessantly applied the scourge to those who loitered, or sought to strangle themselves by lifting their feet from the ground in despair; which sometimes had been successfully attempted. The women and children were bound with cords, and driven forward by the whip. When they arrived at the factory the men were unloosed from the poles, but still chained in pairs, and turned into strong cells built for the purpose. The dumb sorrow of some, the frensy of others, the sobbings and tears of the children, and shrieks of the women, when they were presented to our captain, so affected me, that I was hastening from this scene of barbarity on board the ship, when I was called by the mate, and discovered, to my surprise and horror, that, by my station in the ship, I had a principal and active part of this inhuman transaction imposed upon me. As surgeon, it was my duty to inspect the bodies of the slaves, to see, as the captain expressed himself, that our owners were not shammed off with unsound flesh. In this inspection I was assisted by Randolph the clerk, and two stout sailors. It was transacted with all that unfeeling insolence which wanton barbarity can inflict upon defenceless wretchedness. The man, the affrighted child, the modest matron, and the timid virgin, were alike exposed to this severe scrutiny, equally insulting to humanity and common decency.

I cannot even now reflect on this transaction without shuddering. I have deplored my conduct with tears of anguish; and I pray a merciful God, the common parent of the great family of the universe, who hath made of one flesh and one blood all nations of the earth, that the miseries, the insults, and cruel woundings, I afterwards received when a slave myself, may expiate for the inhumanity I was necessitated to exercise towards these *my brethren of the human race.*

INDEX